From Calcutta
with Love

The World War II Letters
of Richard and Reva Beard

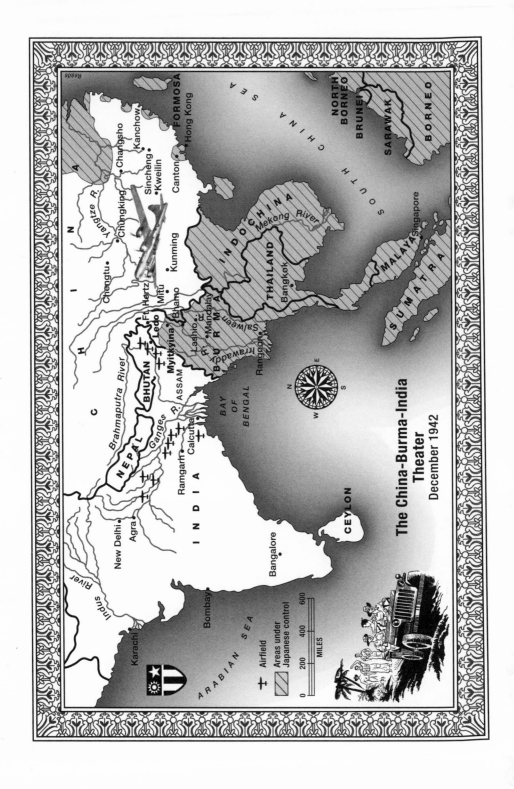

The China-Burma-India
Theater
December 1942

Airfield
Areas under
Japanese control

0   200   400   600
MILES

From Calcutta
with Love

The World War II Letters
of Richard and Reva Beard

*for Carla —
with best wishes,
Elaine Pinkerton*

Edited by Elaine Pinkerton
Foreword by Wendall A. Phillips
Introduction by Otha Spencer

Texas Tech University Press

This book was set in Lapidary 333BT. The paper used in this book meets the minimum requirements of ANSI/NISO Z39.48-1992 (R1997). ∞

Printed in the United States of America

Design by Brandi Price
Maps created by Deborah Reade

Library of Congress Cataloging-in-Publication Data
Beard, Richard, 1909–1997.
     From Calcutta with love : the World War II letters of Richard and Reva Beard / edited by Elaine Pinkerton ; foreword by Wendell A. Phillips ; introduction by Otha Spencer.
          p. cm.
Includes bibliographical references and index.
     ISBN 0-89672-468-9 (cloth : alk. paper)
     1. Beard, Richard, 1909-1997—Correspondence. 2. Beard, Reva, 1914—Correspondence. 3. United States. Army—Officers—Correspondence. 4. World War, 1939-1945—Personal narratives, American. 5. Clinical psychologists—United States—Correspondence. 6. Housewives—United States—Correspondence. 7. World War, 1939–1945—South Asia. 8. World war, 1939-1945—Asia, Southeastern. I. Beard, Reva, 1914– II. Pinkerton, Elaine. III. Title.
     D811.5 .B28 2002
     940.54'8173'0922--dc21

                                        2001004254

     01 02 03 04 05 06 07 08 09 / 9 8 7 6 5 4 3 2 1

Texas Tech University Press
Box 41037
Lubbock, Texas 79409-1037 USA

1-800-832-4042
ttup@ttu.edu
www.ttup.ttu.edu

Contents

Foreword

Sometimes the most painful aspect of life is when one's contributions are forgotten.

Such may be the case with service by Americans in the China-Burma-India (CBI) theater of World War II. *From Calcutta with Love* is an extraordinary collection of letters, the first ever published with an American's perspective of "the forgotten theater." In being remembered, those of us who served in CBI are being honored, an homage long overdue.

Lieutenant Richard Beard and I served in the same theater in World War II; however, we were worlds apart in many ways. He was an officer serving in Calcutta, India, as a neuropsychiatrist in the 142nd General Hospital; his position dealt with the mental health of service men and women. I was a radio operator—an enlisted man—flying the "Hump" in cargo aircraft delivering war materiel and personnel from India to Burma and all parts of China, and was stationed at an Army Air Force base at Chengkung, China. We flew unarmed in C-46 and C-47 cargo planes into combat areas with necessary supplies to sustain the soldiers.

Lieutenant Beard's letters breathe life into the experience of China-Burma-India. Richard was one of us. We were men fighting and working together, living on hope, to protect all we had left behind. We were men who longed to be home in the arms of the women we loved.

From Calcutta with Love comprises letters written from India and Ohio between Richard and his wife Reva. These letters are about love and yearning for home. For Richard, writing to Reva was a lifeline. He poured his heart out through the tip of a pen. Richard Leonard Beard, clinical psychologist and Second Lieutenant in the 12th Bomber Group, was a graceful and voluminous writer with a flare for description—a communicator. His letters inform, entertain, and reveal honest feelings about the war and his role in it.

Through her letters, Reva constantly reassured Richard of her love and devotion. She confided to Richard that life seemed to stand still without him. Like other war wives throughout the United States, Reva talked with her friends of nothing but missing her husband and the latest war news. Like hundreds of others, she lived for the daily mail. She wrote to Richard that his letters would be "a privilege for anyone to read." Although she offered to send them to the Findlay, Ohio, newspaper for publication, Richard apparently never consented to such a plan.

The importance of mail call during World War II cannot be imagined in this age of e-mail and cell phones. Like Richard Beard, we all wrote letters home. Letter writing meant a connection to the past and an opportunity to imagine a postwar future. Penning the daily letter home was a cherished interval in a hectic day. For soldiers in every theater, the mailman's arrival or the bugle call heralding the distribution of mail was the highlight of the day.

In the far-flung areas of Burma and China, however, it was common to get a bundle of letters at a time, sometimes a week's worth at one time. Even if one's duties permitted writing home often, outgoing mail might not find transportation on a timely basis. It did not generally have a high priority.

Service men and women (yes, there were many nurses and a few Red Cross volunteers in the CBI, too) longed for news from home. So many were just teenagers when they were called on to serve their country; they became men and women very quickly.

Most of us did not keep our wartime letters over the years. They were lost, overlooked, accidentally discarded. Richard Beard was a college professor from the time the war ended until his death in 1997, and in pursuit of his academic goals, he and Reva moved several times. From home to home, the thin onionskin pages of their correspondence—carefully filed and kept in cabinets—moved with them. Within the pages of his World War II letters, Richard mentioned the suggestion of friends that he should write a book about his India experience. At some level, perhaps he knew that his letters were not meant for oblivion. Decades passed, however, and it was only after Richard Beard died that his letters and those of his wife Reva were discovered by their daughter Elaine. This remarkable correspondence comes to light at an important moment in history, a time when those who remember World War II firsthand are still here to enjoy them.

In *From Calcutta with Love,* there is the intimacy of an eighteen-month private conversation, and yet the letters are universal in their message of how we survived the loneliness and separation of overseas duty.

Perhaps the first emotional pitfall soldiers had to face during World War II was breaking the biblical commandment, "Thou shalt not kill." Furthermore, they experienced the disconcerting realization that—like cogs in a machine—they were expendable. In the CBI theater, as in other wartime arenas, personal letters helped relieve the pain of these realizations. Connecting us to our loved ones at home, letters softened the loneliness. For those who found war unbearable, Lieutenant Beard's services as a clinical psychologist offered ways of coping with war-related neuroses and breakdowns.

The reader senses that letters to and from Reva kept Richard Beard in balance. Surrounded as he was by the illnesses

and neuroses of the 142nd General Hospital's neuropsychiatric ward, Richard Beard maintained his own sanity through
corresponding. Ultimately, *From Calcutta with Love* is a personal
memoir of World War II never found in public histories.

> Wendall A. Phillips
> National Chaplain,
> Past National Commander
> China-Burma-India Veterans Association

Note: Phillips has traveled the country coast-to-coast, covering over thirty thousand miles yearly, on behalf of those left behind in the China-Burma-India theater of World War II.

Introduction

The men and women who served in World War II, regardless of their role, were heroes, providing material for the written, published, and accepted history of the conflict. Without those heroes fighting face-to-face with the enemy, there could have been no victory. In the China-Burma-India theater (CBI), the enemy was not always the Japanese. Soldiers fought loneliness, confusion, mountains, disease, weather, and, often, inept leadership.

However, there were other heroes. Families and friends "back home" did not carry guns or fly planes, but they served as valiantly and as proudly. They were the unrecognized participants in the war: They fought broken families, shortages, ration books, loneliness, and the ever-present dread of the chaplain's visit. They lived daily with the constant mantra, "A war's on/use it up/wear it out/make it do/or do without." Their heroism is recorded only in personal memory, memoirs, and letters.

Service in war is never completely forgotten. To remember, to talk, and to write about it is a lifetime odyssey. Tom Brokaw, in *The Greatest Generation Speaks,* paid tribute to the personal memories of war's participants. Likewise, the letters of Richard and Reva Beard, published in *From Calcutta with Love,* gave World War II history another and more personal voice.

Lieutenant Beard was stationed in the CBI, on the staff of the 142nd General Hospital, Calcutta, India. Professionally,

Lieutenant Beard was dedicated to his duty and his patients. Personally, Beard was a disgruntled man, critical of the army, lonesome for his wife of six years, certain that his talents were not being used well and tired of incompetents, inappropriate assignments, and patients who feigned illness.

Like most soldiers going to a foreign country, Sergeant Richard Beard went through extreme cultural shock when he arrived in India. Although he was amazed and surprised at the beauty of the country, animals, plants, and scenery, he could not immediately accept its squalor, poverty, backwardness, strange cultural practices, monsoons, and primitive railroad system. Beard was, indeed, "a stranger in a strange world."

The personal frustration, which Lieutenant Beard wrote about in his letters, made him a typical soldier in World War II. Almost everything to him, in military slang, was SNAFU, military street talk for "Situation Normal, All Fouled Up." I was an Army Air Forces pilot in the CBI, stationed less than a hundred miles from Lieutenant Beard, and I felt the same frustration. Hardly a day passed when we did not pray, "Lord, if we win this war, it will be because you sent us a navy and the marines."

A few perks kept the normal officer or enlisted man going from day to day; these were things that made life bearable. The first, and most important, was regular mail to and from home. Mail was the soul and fabric of morale, anxiously awaited and always a priority in handling and transport. Flight crews flying over the Hump were instructed that, in case of trouble over the Himalayas, mail was to be jettisoned only as a last resort. Regular mail, to and from his wife Reva (his nickname for his wife was "Ritter"), kept Lieutenant Beard reasonably happy and efficient in his job.

What will quickly strike the reader is Richard Beard's beautiful writing and delicate expressions of affection for his "lovely Ritter." He "saw her face in everything beautiful" and constantly expressed his "desire to be in her arms." His poetic choice of words reached the level of Robert Browning's "The best is yet to be" as he dreamed, six thousand miles away, of their life together after the war.

Professionally, Lieutenant Beard, through clear eloquence, expressed genuine concern for his disturbed patients and the torment they felt. Richard Beard was a man of intense feelings, whether anger, loneliness, or love; the reader will share these feelings through Beard's writing that penetrates the soul.

Richard vented his anger and frustration in his letters. This was a way military personnel soothed their pent-up feelings. The army understood this and rarely censored a letter because of caustic comments about military life. Censors knew that a complaining soldier was usually a happier soldier.

Another carrot that kept hope alive was the "point system," whereby a soldier could work toward a specific number of points composed of time overseas, number of missions, and so forth, to "rotate" home. Many of Lieutenant Beard's letters stress the point system and his estimated date for going home. The normal rotation time for ground forces was two years. However, in 1945, after Germany was defeated, the service time was lowered, dependent on a suitable replacement. Soldiers kept close account of their time in service or whatever counted as points.

In the air force, crews normally flew 650 hours, but the system had to be changed because crews were flying missions too frequently, often to the point of exhaustion and at greater risk of accident. Some were flying 165 hours a month. The rotation number was increased to 750 hours with a minimum time of one year, which averaged about 65 hours per month. Crews complained bitterly, but accidents went down and crews were not as tired.

Rumor was a great sustaining factor in soldier morale. Rumor was always "authentic information" someone had learned from a secret source. Rumor was what a soldier wished would happen, usually concerning new assignments, pay raises, end of the war, and so forth. Of course, in fairness to most soldiers, the great morale sustainer was patriotism and their dedication to winning the war. Despite their frustration, the concept that "we're all in it together," made life bearable.

Elaine Pinkerton, daughter of Richard and Reva Beard, has included an accurate and interesting history of the CBI theater, through the eyes of the army ground forces of which her father was a part. Yet, histories are different, depending on who writes them. The army has its history, the air force has its history, and each participating country has its history of war—they are all different. The British have written their history, the Chinese will give their side, and the Japanese have written their history. Each will be different, each will have a bias, but all will contribute to a total history of the Great War in Asia.

––––––––

The CBI theater was one of the most complex and frustrating of any theater of World War II. Often called the forgotten war, it was a holding action until the war in Europe had been won. The CBI was a combined military effort of the United States, British Commonwealth, China, Burma, India, Canada, and Australia, with both air and ground forces.

Major General Orlando Ward, Chief of Military History, Department of the Army, in 1952, wrote

> The history of the China-Burma-India theater will be an eye opener and a lesson to those, who, in the future, have to deal with allies in far distant lands about whom so much should be known and so little is. (Romanus and Sunderland, 1953, p. ix)

Major General Ward wrote again in 1953, "There is one thing more difficult than fighting a war with Allies—this is to fight a war without them" (Romanus and Sunderland, 1956, p. vii). Major General Richard W. Stephens, Chief of Military History, Department of Army, in 1958, added,

> The history of China, Burma and India, . . . in World War II, ended as it began. As in 1942, so in 1945, the Americans in China were still attempting to improve the Chinese Army so that China might be an effective partner in the United Nations war against Japan. (Romanus and Sunderland, 1959, p. vii)

In these comments from the army's top historians, we see (1) lack of preparation, (2) lack of cooperation between allies with the same goal, and (3) ultimate failure. Even though the war was won, for example, the Communists took China in 1949.

It is understandable that historian Boyd Sinclair recorded his history of the CBI as an acronym: **C**onfusion **B**eyond **I**magination. The war in the CBI was directed by personalities with their own agendas, their own skills, and their own stubborn quest for military power. Wars are not always decided on the battlefields or in the air. Leaders of the various countries involved have their own wills, desires, egos, ambitions, and downright "cussedness" that influence their actions.

One of the most influential figures in the CBI was Madame Chiang Kai-shek, the demanding third wife of Generalissimo Chiang Kai-shek, China's military and political leader. Madame Chiang spoke perfect English, was a graduate of Wellesley College, knew the American mind, and was ready to lay down anyone's life for her beloved China. Madame Chiang wanted to preserve the charm of the old

China she loved and knew that only the Americans could finance and successfully fight the war, with modern weapons, against the Japanese.

Generalissimo Chiang, often called the Methodist Buddha, was less interested in fighting the Japanese than the Chinese Communists. Chiang had broken from the Communist Party in 1925 at the death of Sun Yat-sen and became leader of the Nationalist party. He knew that if the Communists captured him, he would be executed. He sorely tried the patience of the western allies by refusing to commit his armies to battle against the Japanese. Chiang's philosophy was an old Taoist principle: "Through not doing, all things are done." However, Chiang was the strength and spirit of China and, according to U. S. Ambassador Clarence E. Gauss, "Without his leadership, unity in China would vanish and there would be no resistance to Japan" (Department of State, 1942, p. 604).

General Tu Yu-ming, Chinese commander in Burma, explained why his army would not fight: "The Fifth Army is our best . . . it is the only one that has any field guns, and I cannot afford to risk those guns. If I lose them, the Fifth Army will no longer be our best" (Craven and Cate, 1958, p. 118).

Another headstrong leader in the CBI was Lieutenant General Joseph Stilwell, called "Vinegar Joe," one of America's all-time great field commanders and a military genius who believed that war was won on the ground. Stilwell was placed in charge of all Chinese ground forces, and this rankled the Generalissimo. Stilwell had been in China since 1911, spoke fluent countryside Chinese, and got along with no one except his troops. Eventually, Chiang forced President Roosevelt to remove Stilwell from China. Stilwell wrote in his diary, "Get me out of this odorous sewer . . . and I'll never more shovel manure" (Fisher, 1944, p. 66).

In 1937, Texas-born Claire Lee Chennault, after retirement from the Army Air Forces, had been hired by Madame Chiang to come to China, train pilots, and build a Chinese

Air Force. However, too often, the Chinese pilots killed themselves rather than the enemy, and China did not have enough planes to build an air defense. The Chinese concept of "saving face" prevented students from "washing out" in flight training; all were graduated but few could fly. Madame Chiang's solution, of course, was the United States.

President Franklin D. Roosevelt, through his family, had a background of more than a century in Chinese affairs and was partial to China and its leaders. Henry Luce, founder of *Time, Fortune,* and *Life* magazines, was born in China of missionary parents, taught by Chinese tutors, was a great supporter of China, and used his influence to help China. Madame Chiang could get almost anything she wanted from the president and U. S. Congress, and the one thing she most wanted was American planes and pilots.

For example, in 1940, with permission of President Roosevelt, Claire Chennault was allowed to return to the United States and recruit pilots, mechanics, and aircraft support personnel from the three services to develop a flying team called the American Volunteer Group (AVG). The AVG was a mercenary group paid by China to fight the Japanese. The British gave Chennault one hundred outmoded lend-lease Curtiss P-40Bs in exchange for the United States's promise to the British to replace them with better fighters later.

In 1941, the AVG personnel left San Francisco, California, in unmarked Dutch ships for the trip to Burma, and the P-40s were shipped in crates. The P-40s were assembled and crews trained in Burma until they were ready to fight in China. The P-40s were painted with sharks' teeth and red eyes that seemed to spook the Japanese pilots. The Chinese called them *"Fei-Hu"* (Flying Tigers). Chennault taught an unorthodox type of "hit-and-run" tactic whereby the AVG pilots flew out of the sun, hit the Japanese, and ran for cover. There was no World War I "Red Baron" type of jousting in the sky. Some pilots, enamored of World War I air combat, thought this was cowardly. They wanted to stay and fight.

Pearl Harbor was bombed on December 7, 1941, and the United States declared war against Japan on December 8. The AVG Tigers were then free for combat and on December 20, the Tigers met the first Japanese bombers. Ten Mitsubishi "Sallys" headed lazily toward Kunming. Seventeen Tigers looked down, made a pass and shot down four bombers, and hit the remaining six who turned back trailing smoke. From that point on, the Japanese lost control of the skies over China.

Too often, the Flying Tigers were the symbol of the CBI. Few people realize that they only fought six months, from December 20, 1941 to July 4, 1942. With their tiger shark planes, they created an icon recognized throughout the world. They raised the morale of the Allies at a time when it seemed that Japan could not be stopped. Since World War II, when I tell people I flew the Hump, they ask "Flying Tigers?" and seem disappointed when I say, "No, I flew a transport."

There was little allied cooperation because each of the countries had different objectives. Britain wanted China to have just enough supplies to stay in the war but not enough to become a power that would threaten Burma or India. The British did not want the Ledo Road built because it might allow the Chinese into India. The British did not fight in China and did not want the Chinese to fight in Burma. Winston Churchill's goal was to protect India, Britain's "jewel of the Orient." Mohandas Gandhi was demanding Indian independence as a price for India's fighting against Japan, and this had the British in a royal twit.

At one time, it was feared that Chiang Kai-shek might make peace with Japan in exchange for Japan's fighting the Communists. This would seriously undermine the main U.S. interest in China as a base for bombing the Japanese mainland. The United States kept the Hump in operation so that China could stay in the war.[1]

Finally, the war was won, but not from bases in the CBI. General Curtis "Iron Pants" LeMay brought his B-29s into

India. Lieutenant Beard mentioned the B-29s roaring over Calcutta on takeoff. Ideologically, they were to be based in India, north of Calcutta, fly to Chengtu, China, refuel, bomb the Japanese mainland and return to Chengtu, refuel and return to India. Considering crew rest and refueling at Chengtu, that was a seven-day mission. The B-29 missions from India were a miserable failure. No one could comprehend the great distances in the CBI, the impossible supply problem, towering mountains, and terrible weather. Only when General LeMay moved the B-29s to the Mariannas and the *Enola Gay* bombed Hiroshima, did the war end successfully for the Allies.

It is tragic that there was so much allied conflict in the administration of the Sino-Japanese war and small wonder that the CBI was called **C**onfusion **B**eyond **I**magination. This kept the psychiatric wards of army hospitals full of patients for clinical psychologists like Richard Beard to treat. The Medical Department recorded that 18.7 percent of all patients evacuated to the United States during 1942–45 were sent home for neuropsychiatric disorders.

With his dedicated contributions to medical care and his personal tour of discontent, Lieutenant Richard Beard served well in the Medical Department of the Army Service Forces. During World War II, the U.S. Army was divided into three major commands: the Army Ground Forces (AGF), the Army Air Forces (AAF), and the Army Service Forces (ASF). In addition, like the higher levels of CBI administration, the ASF, under the command of General Brehon B. Somervell, struggled constantly from its inception in 1942 until its termination in 1946 to build a common unity of purpose and organization.

It is difficult to believe the complexity of the ASF. It was responsible for food, clothing, munitions, transportation, handling pay and allowances, building military bases, port systems, administrating the medical service, organization and management of entertainment, the post exchange system, and redeployment and demobilization. At a hearing of the House Committee on Appropriations, the chairman of the committee remarked to General Somervell, "It would seem that you are kept pretty busy." The general replied, "There are a great many duties, sir" (Millett, 1954, p. 3). Charley Murphy, a *Life* magazine reporter, called General Somervell "dynamite in a Tiffany box, all lace and velvet and courtliness outside, fury and purposefulness within" (as cited in Millett, 1954, p. 7).

With its staggering complexity, worldwide responsibilities, and lack of departmental compatibility, the ASF, through its Medical Service, made some very positive and lasting contributions to the army and to the world. The list includes research in the use of Atabrine as a malarial suppressive; field testing of penicillin and sulfonamide compounds in the treatment of wounds; development of DDT which proved effective in the control of louse-borne typhus, one of the scourges of armies for centuries. The army's program of immunizing every soldier against typhoid, paratyphoid, smallpox, and tetanus, kept these diseases to an almost insignificant level.

New methods for the treatment of venereal diseases reduced the average number of daily absences from duty from 45 per 100,000 soldiers in World War I to 13 in 100,000 in World War II. With the stigma removed, soldiers reported to army doctors for treatment rather than using dangerous self-treatment or going to local native doctors with questionable methods.

At one time, it was reported that Claire Chennault, in China, set up his own brothel, with medically inspected women. General Stilwell found out about it and almost ordered Chennault out of China. This incident is not found in any official history.

The army made a serious attempt to "scare the pants off" military personnel so they would keep their pants on and avoid the dangers of native sex and stay out of opium dens in China. Guided tours were available to anyone who would go and I remember the horrors of visiting an opium den in Shanghai, led by a medical officer and a military policeman. Lieutenant Beard, toward the end of his tour in Calcutta wrote a long report on his professional visit to a Calcutta brothel, led by a medical Officer of the Day and the sergeant of the guard. He was shocked beyond comprehension at what he saw. The document cannot be quoted fully in this introduction for reasons of space and propriety. But some excerpts, even omitting the worst description, let readers know that war in a foreign undeveloped country can be more horrible than guns and bombs.

UNDER THE VILLAGE PALMS
or Why Not? It's Been Going on a Long Time
by Richard Beard, 1945

We drove into the darkened village about 10:00 o'clock at night . . . [the] blackened shop had an open kerosene lamp . . . revealing skirted shapes, sitting quietly on benches or sleeping boards. A musty odor saturated the air, drenching our spirits . . . The Twentieth century was moving into a community sagging under the dreadful burden of a thousand years of unchanging superstition, poverty and human degradation. . . . the ground was black; worn shiny and hard. Vermin, rodents, sweat, excrement, filth, waste . . . figures silently melted into the shadows . . . the group surgeon . . . examined five of the women . . . all five had running sores caused by uncleanness . . . gonorrhea was present in each case and two had incipient syphilis . . .

Military restrictions do not cure, nor even prevent infection. The ideological myth of continence is promoted by the army . . . [which] often resulted in an occasional disease, tersely written in orders "for cause," and teminating in Privacy for the NCO . . . Two British sergeants were seated on the edge of a huge bed, . . . one of them fanned a sleeping child. . . .

The Madame faced the OD, "American officer very rich . . . With you, not a rupee, not two annas, for notheeng. Just love, you and me?" Her arms slipped around his neck and she raised her legs. . . . the OD extricated himself . . . muttering a threat to me, "One word of this and . . . " I followed closely behind his retreating hulk. . . only to find the bedeviled woman had leaped on me . . . In panic, I tripped, shook her loose and ran . . . to the jeep and walked out into the night for a breath of fresh air.

Neuropsychiatric disorders were a major problem, to which the diagnosis, treatment, and disposal were jobs assigned to clinical psychologists such as Richard Beard. The medical teams later determined that much of the loss of manpower for these disorders could be decreased by an emphasis on prevention. Combat fatigue, poor leadership, and the feeling that war was unnecessary were normal causes of psychiatric disorders. Reducing the cause of stress often allowed soldiers to return to limited service in areas where they felt the army made better use of their skills.

At no time during World War II was the Surgeon General's need for medical personnel fully met or the problem of efficient use of personnel ever solved satisfactorily. Yet, a comparison of World War I and World War II showed great progress. In World War I, per thousand cases, there were 715 admissions for disease and 9.1 deaths from disease, 4.4 deaths from wounds and 1.4 deaths from injuries; in World War II there were 573.2 admissions and 0.6 deaths from disease and 1.1 deaths from wounds and 2.3 deaths from injuries per thousand patients.

There was a war, and men and women were sent overseas; and men and women were forced to stay at home. Both suffered torments in different forms, but kept their love strong, their loneliness less bitter, and their burdens lighter by letters such as Elaine Pinkerton has published in her tribute to Richard and Reva, her father and mother, in *From Calcutta with Love*.

Otha Spencer*

*World War II U.S. Air Force pilot and author of *Flying the Hump: Memories of an Air War*

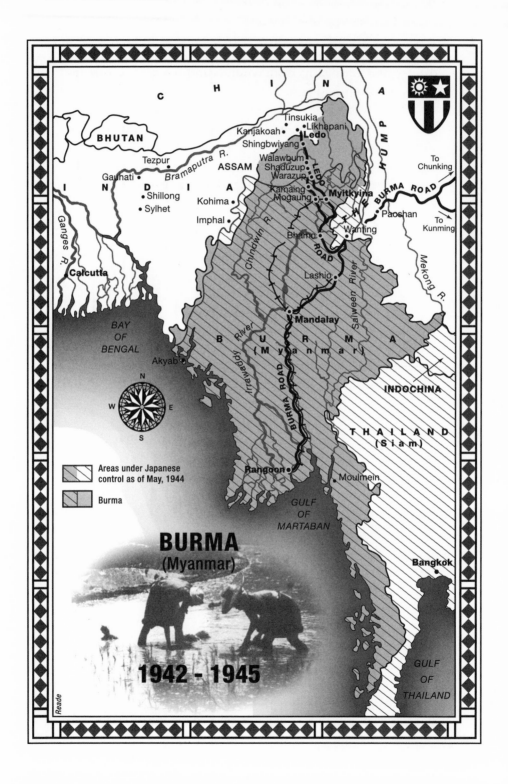

BURMA
(Myanmar)

1942 - 1945

Acknowledgments

To Homer C. Cooper, World War II China-Burma-India veteran, whose GI perspective helped me better understand the CBI theater.

To the CBI veterans who shared their time and opened their memory banks both through letters and during the 1999 CBI reunion.

To my editor at Texas Tech University Press, Jacqueline McLean, whose wisdom and guidance were incredibly helpful at every stage of this book's development.

To Lea Williams, for the commitment, insight, and many hour of editing that helped make this book a reality.

To Lesley North, Rebecca Bloom, and Erica P. Cooper, eagle-eyed editors and wordsmiths; to Grant Kalivoda, computer ace.

To my writing friends—Peggy vanHulsteyn, Jann Arrington Wolcott, Julie Weston, Kathie Carlson, Layne Vickers Smith, Claudia Jessup, Danica Tutush, Ann Hosfeld, Sharon Spence, Lynnette Baughman, Doug MacKinnon, Andrew Carroll, and David Maurer. Many others supported me with cheer and excellent suggestions as the project developed. I am indebted to Andrew Carroll, Mollie Dickinson, Marianne Cramer, June Dickinson, Martha Davis, and Miriam Landor for their help and enthusiasm.

To St. John's College Library Guild, which played a crucial role in launching this book, and to the helpful personnel at New Mexico State Library, who supplied me with research materials from interlibrary loan. To members of the Santa Fe

Ding Hao Basha #132, from whom I learned so much about CBI.

For Bob, my mother Reva and all the family, and above all for the wonderful men and women who served in the CBI theater during World War II.

A Letter from the Editor

Dear Reader:

During World War II, my parents were half a world apart. While my father Richard was stationed in India, my mother Reva waited at home in Ohio. Married for six years and deeply in love, my parents wrote to one another daily. Fifty years later, the wartime letters of Richard and Reva came into my possession.

My aim in *From Calcutta with Love* is to celebrate the love and idealism embodied in this wonderful letter legacy. Stationed in the China-Burma-India (CBI) theater of the war, my father Richard spent two years overseas in India. He served as a clinical psychologist at the 142nd hospital in Calcutta. Although he played a supporting rather than a lead role in World War II, he was always my greatest hero. This book serves as my tribute to him.

Thirty-three years old and a Ph.D. graduate in clinical psychology, my father was drafted immediately after completion of his dissertation and course work at Ohio State University. Weary of school, Richard opted not to go into officer's training. It was not until after he had spent several months at bases in Pennsylvania and North Carolina and was shipped out to India that he would receive a lieutenant's commission.

After the war, Richard had a long and distinguished career as a college professor and was a leader in the counseling field. He was loved by hundreds of grateful students.

During the fifty years I was blessed by having him as my father, I considered myself his favorite student. He would

1

have been immensely pleased to know that his letters not only help me but now inform readers about life for an Army psychologist on the fringes of World War II. Reading the letters taught me that through remembrance of those we cherish, love endures forever.

Ironically, at the time my brother Johnny sent me the World War II correspondence, Richard developed Alzheimer's disease. Disheartened, unable to move beyond paralyzing despair at my father's condition, I postponed the task of reading the letters. For many years, I imagined that, before my father died, I would go through the letters with him. When we both had the time, he could neither talk nor understand.

With Richard gone, there seemed nothing else to do but open the dusty cardboard box of letters. I well remember that snowy January day. I needed closure and felt that this painful act would provide an acknowledgment of his death. It would be my final good-bye. To my amazement, the task I had dreaded turned into my favorite pastime. Once I started reading the letters, I was captivated.

Richard describes an endless train trek from Bombay to Calcutta, sweeping monsoons, stars over Bengal, gold-burnished afternoons, bugs, squalor, and India's paradoxical, exotic beauty. He complains to Reva about the apparent senselessness of the Army's decisions and maneuvers. The letters depict daily events in the 142nd hospital in Calcutta, his psychological counseling, eccentrics, characters, poker games, and nightly movies. Humorously and sometimes angrily, Richard expresses his frustration at being stuck in India when all he wants is to return to "home, wife and love."

Despite the fascination of India, the snake charmers, the temples, the rice paddies, the chaotic streets, and an endless kaleidoscope of the exotic, my father wanted only to return to the wife he fondly nicknamed "Ritter." His days and nights began and ended with thoughts of Reva. His letters reflect his longing for the day he could be in her arms once again.

Reva writes of life in Findlay—teaching a shy student named Robert how to read, bridge games and outings with other female schoolteachers, life within an extended family, and trips to the post office for Richard's letters and presents. She agrees to the plan of adopting a child, thus affirming her devotion to their life together. Reva's letters reinforce her love for and devotion to Richard that, in turn, emphasize their future after the war ends.

I read through long winter nights, eavesdropping on the vibrant, idealistic Richard and Reva before they became my parents. I laughed, cried, and marveled at the wit and beauty of my father's prose. I sensed that Richard was writing not just for Reva but for posterity. The beauty of the letters made me both sad—because my father was gone forever—and happy, because he chose me as his child. Ultimately, the letters healed me.

Another reason for writing this book is idiosyncratic: a fascination with India has possessed me since early childhood. From age five, the magical year that Richard and Reva adopted Johnny and me, I grew up with thoughts of India. Although my father didn't talk much about India, I imagined what it was like. I spun my own tales based on the ivory figurines, brass elephants, fine wool embroidery, marble, semi-precious stones, silks, and shawls that he had brought home. Reading the letters fleshed out those early visions.

In his last months, Richard reminded me of Don Quixote, transforming the lowly into something noble and grand. He never truly accepted his diminished circumstances. He railed against them, sometimes cleverly, sometimes desperately.

Before his illness, Richard was a man of words and letters. All his life, he loved expounding, explaining, and debating. As we made our way around the Alzheimer's floor during our last time together, he could say only a few words at a time. It didn't matter: his beaming expression bespoke his happiness. After "presenting" me to the front desk nurses, he "introduced" me to the kitchen staff. At the small office, the nurses smiled and nodded at him, as wordless in their communication as he in his. I recalled the times he introduced me as his daughter to his professional colleagues and his students. Small matter that we were not at the University of Virginia any longer. Touched by his re-enactment of an earlier time, I resisted tears and played the game with him.

By the time Richard was relegated to the third floor of a section euphemistically named the Health Center, his days and nights were reversed. In the daytime, he slept. At night, he paced the halls. He alone knew where his solitary midnight meandering took him, and he couldn't tell. It broke my heart to think of the loneliness of his pacing. It has been said that Alzheimer's victims fear the dark: perhaps the endless walks lessened his terror.

I remembered a walk that I took with him in the verdant August of 1965. I was about to receive my master's degree in English from the University of Virginia. College professor and graduating daughter, we both wore caps and gowns. The ceremony began and along with other professors and graduates, we proceeded from Cabell Hall to the Rotunda. The "grounds," as Thomas Jefferson preferred to call the campus of his "academic village," had never looked more beautiful.

The halls of the nursing home were worlds away from the University of Virginia campus, and now Richard was leaving me behind. Over and over again, I tried to determine what went wrong. Why should my father, who served his country faithfully albeit sardonically, during World War II, and who had lived productively, with flair and brilliance, have to suffer such a harsh ending? In vain, I wondered why he had become a mere mockery of himself. It was as though he had already died.

It was in Richard's weekly letters to me that the Alzheimer's slowly became apparent. After receiving my master's degree, I married and moved from Virginia to New Mexico. In thirty years, during which I raised two sons, divorced, taught school, and wrote, Richard and I wrote long, detailed letters to one another at the end of every week. This communication kept us very close. Much as he had written from Calcutta, Richard expressed his philosophy, his take on current events, fine-tuned descriptions of the world around him. We read and discussed the same books. He followed my teaching and writing career closely.

In the mid-1990s, his letters grew shorter. Malapropisms and odd word choices marred Richard's normally lucid prose. He changed thoughts in midsentence. Over time, a smaller percentage of the letters were written by him and more by my mother. He would type a paragraph and then Reva would hand-write the rest of the letter. Then, in 1994, words began to fail him altogether. Now, the letters were completely written by Reva. They contained, among other items, heartrending descriptions of what was happening to my father. After fifty years, Richard's chronicles died, leaving a vacuum in my life that nothing could replace.

My parents moved to a retirement community that looked more like a country club than a nursing home. Perched on a hill overlooking scenic Charlottesville, Virginia, the grounds and building left Richard befuddled. His home office would not fit in the new quarters, so his three-thousand-volume library shrank to five hundred books. His files of names, addresses, and letters accumulated during a lifetime of teaching were sacrificed. Miraculously, the WW II letters survived. Without his books and letters, Richard was more disoriented than ever. Walking the halls in a mental fog, he sometimes got lost between his apartment and the mailroom. When he finally wound down, it was more often than not in a room that belonged to someone else. During my spring visit that year, staying with my mother in her apartment, I could hardly sleep at night thinking about my father upstairs in what his world had become. It was heartbreaking to watch, agonizing to contemplate.

Although this stage continued for less than a year, it seemed eternal. Frequently calling and writing my mother, I tried to help from a distance. Reva visited Richard three times a day in the health center. Her health was quite frail, and I feared that caretaking was wearing her out. Finally, I prayed for my father's release from his tedious, confined, and apparently senseless existence. In a few days, he died of a stroke. The loss of him was a terrible blow: I plummeted. Even in his Alzheimer's-altered state, I wanted him back.

A year after my father's death, my mother sent me a tribute printed in the spring issue of the University of Virginia's Alumni News. The author, one of my father's former students, was deeply affected by the obituary of Dr. Richard Leonard Beard.

> It might sound a bit trite but Dr. Beard had a fatherly presence in my personal and academic growth . . . at the beginning of my doctoral program, Dr. Beard pulled me aside for a chat. He suggested that I might want to give up my casual dress and adopt a more professional, polished appearance. It was the gentle way he offered this guidance that had the most positive effect as I went enthusiastically about doing as he suggested. . . . As much as any other part of my years at Virginia, I can still see him strolling through the education department at Ruffner Hall, small in stature but a giant in character, warmth and leadership. It is sad when we wait too long to recognize those who have affected us the most. After leaving Virginia, I never spoke to Dr. Beard again. Yet, like many of his students who benefitted from his presence, I will miss him.

The irony of life, its bittersweet experiences, never ceases to amaze me. I am deeply sad about having lost a wonderful father, but I am happy to have had him in my life. I miss my father more than I ever imagined I would, but I rejoice in his wonderful letters. It is my hope that they will stand as a memorial not only to his unique way of serving in World War II but also to the remarkable man he was.

After my father's death, he came to me in a dream. The scene was a forest, in the daytime. Driving a huge military vehicle, a "Humvee," Richard maneuvered uphill on an undulating dirt road. I sat next to him in the passenger seat. Towering ponderosa pines bordered the road's dark earth. Suddenly, Richard wearied of driving. We halted and disembarked. No words were spoken, but I knew then that for him it was the end of the road. I was to continue.

Richard smiled as he gestured me on my way. The Humvee was out of gas. I was to make the journey on alone and on foot. He exuded confidence in my ability to hike on without his company. I was lonely and daunted, not knowing how I could meet the challenge.

I know now that the forest road represented not only our mutual, intertwined travels through life but also the Ledo-Burma Road and my father's World War II experience. Most importantly, the dream indicated the direction my writing should take.

From Calcutta with Love, in fact, has been my life's work since that dream occurred. Indeed, the book is a chronicle of roads and journeys. During World War II, the huge challenge of the CBI theater, the Ledo-Burma supply line, and a 1,700-mile tortuous dirt road through hills and jungle represented China's last overland link to India. The Japanese forces had seized Burma. The reopening of this route was an American goal throughout the CBI campaign.

Although Richard was somewhat removed from battle, as I read and savored his letters, I learned more about the CBI theater with its monsoons, insects, disease, and isolation. Just as Alzheimer's had stolen my father's reason, the war environment could rob men of their will to live, driving them to madness.

Ultimately, the letters of Richard and Reva helped counter grim memories of my father's Alzheimer's. Although the disease conquered him in the end, what a glorious love and life he had lived. Reading his "letter memoir" brought back the father I had known and cherished for fifty years.

This is not my book; it is Richard's. I am merely the scribe through which *From Calcutta with Love* came to light. In literary collaboration with my late father, I explored the CBI theater of that most disastrous human endeavor, World War II. I was able to remember and present my father as he would have wished.

Richard's letters bring to life a forgotten theater of World War II, third in importance after the European and Pacific theaters. Reva's responses convey the plight of the wives and sweethearts left at home. Together, their letters tell a love story and present a slice of history. Ultimately, the letters of Richard and Reva give World War II history yet another voice.

Please be aware that space limitations did not allow me to include all the letters. Richard and Reva mention receiving epistles that are not in the published collection. I trust that these omissions will not distract.

When I think of my parents' love and letters, I am reminded of the following stanza from John Donne's *A Valediction Forbidding Mourning:*

> If they be two, they are two so
> As stiff twin compasses are two
> Thy soul, the fixt foot, makes no show
> To move, but doth, if the other do.

Reading these epistles entertained, informed, and healed me after the loss of my father. I learned that through remembrance, love never dies. It is my deepest hope that the World War II correspondence of Richard and Reva will enrich your life as it has mine.

Elaine Pinkerton
Santa Fe, New Mexico

The China-Burma-India Theater
and My Father Richard

In his pivotal work *The Greatest Generation,* Tom Brokaw reminds us of how profoundly World War II shaped the twentieth century. As I researched the Second World War, I was overwhelmed with its magnitude. Merely pondering World War II data—over sixty countries involved, over fifty-seven million people dead—conveys its catastrophic impact.

Yet another statistic motivated me to publish this book of my father's letters and my mother's responses: veterans of World War II are dying in great numbers. Estimates range from 232 to 1,000 per day. When the last veteran goes, so will the only remaining firsthand memories of the twentieth century's defining event. Most of the books and memorabilia documenting personal experiences during World War II are from fronts other than the CBI theater. This fact and the positive influence my adoptive father had on my life give his CBI impressions a special importance. Long overdue, the time has come for greater recognition of CBI, the forgotten theater, veterans, and their stories.

Psychologist Lieutenant Beard served far from military maneuvers, but his role was vital for the mental health of soldiers that ended up in Calcutta's 142nd General Hospital. On an individual basis and in group sessions, my father counseled the shattered, the depressed, the sick at heart, and the emotionally unstable.

Before his overseas assignment, he spent the spring of 1944 at Selfridge Field in Michigan and Seymour Johnson Field in North Carolina. Letters written from this period reflect his amusement and frequent annoyance at the Army's training methods. The early letters contained expressions of love that grew, as time passed, into an elaborate tapestry. The letters helped my father transcend the despair that consumed many around him. Richard's written correspondence warded off the uncertainty, the strangeness, and discomfort of his India sojourn.

When the United States Army became aware that my father—Sergeant Richard L. Beard (1909-1997) of the 12th Bomb Group—had a Ph.D. in clinical psychology, they commissioned him as a Second Lieutenant and assigned him to psychological diagnosis and counseling duties with the 142nd General Hospital in Calcutta, India. He was soon promoted to First Lieutenant.

Then as now, military life and warfare exacerbated the stresses brought to the army from civilian life. Men who had adapted "normally" to problems in their earlier lives were introduced to new psychological and emotional stresses. My father's task was to determine the nature of disorders that varied considerably from one soldier to the next. The neuropsychiatric ward's challenge was to devise appropriate treatments for each ailment.

The initial adjustment all newly inducted World War II soldiers faced was giving up the relative freedom of civilian life. Each soldier was required by law to take an oath surrendering civil rights. He entered into an all-male society that greatly restricted one's freedom to come and go, speak one's mind, make decisions, and choose one's associates.

Basic training put the new inductees into a 24-hour forced living-and-working association with persons from all over the country—a virtual melting pot of different educational levels, work experiences, religions, and attitudes. If one was to be successful by military standards, he had to surrender many previous beliefs and behavior patterns that had worked in civilian life.

Attitudinal and behavioral parochialism was the enemy of the new conformity demanded by the army. Wearing the uniform was the visible symbol that those who had been different were now alike. A soldier had to learn to shout, upon command, his eight-digit Army Serial Number instead of his name. In robotic style, he learned how to perform his duties "by the numbers." "Thou shall not kill" was the first standard that had to be eliminated. Instead, the new soldier was taught "kill or be killed." He learned to kill other human beings (defined by his government as the "enemy") or to perform a supporting role (delivering supplies, weapons and ammunition, transportation, information, medical, etc.) for those who did the killing.

Induction into the United States Army forced the soldier into a caste system. Officers were "gentlemen by Act of Congress" and had to be saluted and addressed as "Sir." Their partners were "ladies," whereas enlisted men (privates, corporals, sergeants) were simply "men" whose partners were merely "wives." Where possible, officers and enlisted men wore different uniforms, had different privileges, lived in separate quarters, ate in separate messes, and socialized in different clubs. Overseas, officers censored the letters written to loved ones and friends. Officers issued orders, often without explaining their reasons, and enlisted men executed those orders, presumably without questioning.

When an enlisted man, such as Lieutenant Beard, my father, was commissioned as an officer, he had to give up his old buddies and assume a new identity, including a new Army Serial Number. These conventions were strictly enforced in the United States and in noncombat areas overseas. In combat areas, these strictures were modified or bypassed.

11

This undemocratic regimen was intended to train different kinds of people to become interchangeable parts, so that when a man went down, his replacement could step in and carry the load without extensive further training.

I would like to set forth the flavor and personalities of the CBI theater and let the reader judge personally the world that my father entered at the beginning of this correspondence.

Soon after the Japanese attack on Pearl Harbor, December 7, 1941, the CBI theater's principal mission became clear: keep China in the war. At that time, Japan had fifty-one infantry divisions, twenty-one of which had been fighting China since 1937. Thirteen Japanese divisions were in Manchuria holding the front against the Soviet Union. Of the remaining divisions, eleven (accompanied by seven hundred aircraft) were assigned to operations in Southeast Asia and the Southwest Pacific. With astonishing rapidity, they overran the Philippines, the Netherland Indies (now Indonesia), Thailand, Indochina, the Malay Peninsula, Guam, Midway, and Wake Island, and soon were on the eastern border of Burma (now Myanmar).

It became obvious to Allied leaders that if China were to surrender, many of those twenty-one Japanese divisions in China could be reassigned to join in the conquest of Australia, Burma, and India, and perhaps even threaten the Middle East. Possibly, those Japanese divisions could be used against U.S. troops in the Pacific.

Keeping China in the war was imperative. However, providing China with the necessary arms, supplies, and training posed immense difficulties. Prime among those problems was Japanese control of most of the coastal regions of Asia, including such major port cities as Tientsin, Shanghai, Canton, Hong Kong, Haiphong, Saigon, and Singapore. Moreover, soon after the Burma campaign began, the Japanese captured Moulmein and Rangoon (now Yangon), and the old Burma Road, the back-door supply route to China. Calcutta, although in Allied hands, was not available as an active port because of the threat of Japanese submarines.

Because of the enemy's rapid successes, the routes available to supply China with arms and supplies required the establishment of the longest supply line in military history. Ships leaving the United States from both eastern and western coasts had to take routes that avoided German bombers and submarines and Japanese submarines to Karachi or Bombay on the western coast of India; transfer their cargoes and men to the very inefficient Indian trains across to Calcutta; and use trains, river boats, or truck convoys to Air Transport Command bases in Assam. From these bases, cargo was flown over the Hump (Himalayan Mountains) to Kunming, China, and then distributed from there to the Allied fighting units in China.

Graft, theft, and inefficiency impeded deliveries at every step of the way. Indeed, U.S. Army railroad battalions had to take over the Indian rail system to make the process function at all. That did not solve the multitude of problems on the China end of this long route. War between China and Japan was nothing new: the Sino-Japanese war had been raging years before World War II began. Japan controlled China's coastline, and her conquest of Burma closed the only land route to China.

Looming over the CBI theater was the acerbic, larger-than-life General Joseph Stilwell—better known as "Vinegar Joe" or "Uncle Joe." When Mandalay, Burma, fell in May of 1942, Stilwell had to get twenty-four Americans from Mandalay to Myitkynia. His hopes of going by railroad were dashed, literally, when two engines collided. Stilwell, who had fought as a ground soldier in World War I and still wore his helmet from that era, refused to be rescued. He gathered together twenty-six Americans, thirteen Brits, and various civilians, Indian cooks, and mechanics—113 stragglers in all, and he and his band walked out of some of the worst country in the world. Their trek lasted nearly twenty days.

They crossed rivers deemed impassible, fought dengue and dysentery, suffered from leeches and malaria, skirted the monsoon season, and often ran out of food. Thanks only to the fierce discipline of Vinegar Joe, the stragglers all made it out alive.

Stilwell's dislike of the Chinese Generalissimo Chiang Kai-shek was thinly veiled. In his private diary, Stilwell recorded impressions of the general, including the epithets *peanut, dope,* and *stink in the nostrils.* In October of 1944, Stilwell's lack of diplomacy brought about the removal of his command. That was two months after my father arrived in India.

While Stilwell was the hero of ground forces, General Claire Lee Chennault was the hero of the air. His courageous airborne fleet, the famous Flying Tigers, flew the notorious Hump of the Himalayas. Although "the Tigers" is the casual name for this group, they were formerly the American Volunteer Group (AVG). These pilots were organized and trained by Chennault at Toungoo, Burma, and fought in China. The planes that flew the Hump day after day were those of the Air Transport Command (ATC), Combat Cargo, and Troop Carrier Squadrons. Often at the cost of their lives, these war heroes freighted military cargo from Assam airfields on the India side, over the Hump, to China. The first group to fly the Hump, the Tigers disbanded July 4, 1942.

Other luminaries in the forgotten theater of World War II include Merrill's Marauders, [1] whose mission was to clear the enemy from the Ledo Road being built across Burma; Field Marshall William Slim and his Fourteenth Army (which included British, Indian, and Nepalese soldiers); Field Marshall Archibald Wavell, first British commander in the CBI theater; Lord Louis Mountbatten, head of the Southeast Asia command; and British Brigadier General Orde Wingate and his fighting Chindits, comprising British, Nigerian, Chinese, Gurkha, and indigenous Burmese soldiers.

14

Any portrait of the CBI theater features the Ledo Road. Ultimately stretching one thousand miles across Burma into China, it was the longest overland supply line in the world. With Japan's closure of another possible supply route, the Burma Road, work began on the Ledo Road, also referred to as the Stilwell Road.[2]

The Ledo Road slashed a jagged scar through jungles and mountains that extended from Ledo in Assam to Kunming in China. India was an important staging ground for the U.S. Army Air Force and the Ledo Road, connecting India to China, provided a new lifeline across northern Burma.

Shortly after starting the Ledo Road in 1942, the British declared it "mission impossible" and quit their efforts. Vinegar Joe Stilwell believed in the road and continued fighting for it. Stilwell met with the future viceroy of India, General Archibald Wavell. On December 14, 1942, as an outcome of this meeting, the Ledo Road became an American project.

Despite Stilwell's optimistic determination, the road remained somewhat of a mission impossible. Edward Fischer, in his account of the CBI theater titled *The Chancy War,* wrote,

> The engineers (who built the road) endured untold hardships. Wet all the time, they slept in waterlogged tents, bamboo lean-tos, and jungle hammocks. The soggy jungle was infested with long purple leeches inflicting bites that festered. Tractors tumbled over steep banks when rain-saturated shelves collapsed. Slides and bottomless mud buried bulldozers (p. 30).

Merrill's Marauders were perhaps the best known of service troops engaged in the road-building project. In addition to malaria and hellish monsoons, they had to worry about cobras, tigers, and rogue elephants. As the road progressed, virgin jungle and former tea plantations were transformed into bivouac areas. In addition to environmental obstacles, the project was fraught with human complications. Workers on the Ledo Road spoke seventy-five different languages and dialects, forcing supervisors to communicate orders in sign language. Because the workers comprised numerous religions and sects, dozens of different kinds of rations had to be provided. The caste system necessitated strict segregation of various groups. The saying of the day was, "The Ledo Road can't be built. Too much mud, too much rain, too much malaria." Yet, this last hope of getting supplies from India to China by a land route was a must: it *had* to be built. The engineer companies supplemented by native labor not only built the impossible road but built a dual pipeline along the road to furnish gasoline and oil to the China effort.

The unique challenges of the CBI theater resulted in many different kinds of stress. In order to put my father's wartime contribution into perspective vis-à-vis the CBI theater, I reviewed some of the major risks and frustrations that U.S. soldiers faced in specific operations in CBI. Depending on the individual, these stresses could result in psychological problems that required the attention of Lieutenant Richard L. Beard.

Vastness and Complexities of the CBI

The total land area of China, Burma, and India (which in the 1940s included today's Pakistan and Bangladesh) was more than one and one-half times the total land area of the United States, and much greater than the land areas in either the island areas of the Pacific or the U.S. military sectors in Europe. Whereas millions of American soldiers served in Europe and millions more in the Pacific, only 350,000 served in the CBI theater.

China-Burma-India was a lonely theater, particularly for those who served in India's Assam Province, in northern Burma, and especially in the numerous detachments scattered across those parts of China controlled by the Allies. Many detachments, such as radio, weather, intelligence, or pipeline specialists, comprised only four to six men. Furthermore, the many subcultures of CBI, involving differences in language, local beliefs, and behavior patterns, led to enormous complications when American soldiers attempted to communicate and work with local people. For example, good interpreters were scarce; most of the Chinese who understood and spoke English were from North China, and therefore had difficulties with the quite different languages spoken in those parts where most of the seventy thousand Americans who were stationed in China served. Avoiding illness in a theater where all water had to be boiled and most vegetables and fruits had to be cooked before eating became frustrating. What's more, most American medical officers had little training relevant for many of the diseases encountered in CBI. Diseases cost more Allied deaths in CBI than the bullets and bombs of the enemy.

Flights over the Hump

Flying supplies and arms from Assam Province air bases over the Himalayan Mountains to Kunming, China, was considered as dangerous as flying combat missions over Germany. Hundreds of planes, their crews, and cargoes were lost to the formidable peaks. Dangers included icing of the plane's wings, fog, sleet, and hail. Fierce downdrafts caused planes to lose as much as a mile of altitude per minute, and updrafts resulted in equally swift gains in altitude. The heavy monsoon rains from May to late October caused tremendous visibility problems.

Air Transport Command (ATC) of the U.S. Army Air Force, Combat Cargo, and troop carrier units were the major freight and people haulers in C-46 and C-47 aircraft. Some bomber units converted B-24s to C-87 cargo and

C-109 tankers for Hump flying. C-109 tankers were referred to as "C-109 BOOM" because so many of them blew up.

The workhorse C-47 transports (a military version of the DC-3) were very dependable, but could deliver only two and one-half tons per trip. In the frequent bad weather, they could barely clear the high mountain passes. C-46 transports, which could carry four tons, would go down if either of the two engines quit. The Himalayan route was called "The Aluminum Trail" because in clear weather, the glint from crashes could be seen from the air all along the way. Delivery costs were high: It cost a ton of gasoline to deliver one ton of supplies and two gallons of gas to deliver one gallon to China. Fortunately, the capture of Myitkyina in July 1944 and the destruction of the Japanese air force in Burma made a lower route possible, greatly reducing the loss of planes, crews, and cargoes.

Merrill's Marauders and the Mars Task Force

Best known of the Allied armies and air units to serve in CBI were Merrill's Marauders and their successors in the Mars Task Force. Of legendary dimensions was the campaign of the Marauders, through the jungles and swamps of Northern Burma, to drive out the Japanese. The Marauders were used in far more battles than allowed by the limits of human endurance, and their forces were virtually depleted by mite typhus, malaria, and amoebic dysentery. A man could be relieved of duty only if he had a fever over 101 degrees for three or more consecutive days. Despite these conditions, the Marauders and their American-trained and equipped Chinese comrades—after an incredibly fierce battle of seventy-eight days—captured the town of Myitkyina in July 1944, whose airfield was of strategic importance.

Myitkyina was the major stronghold, railhead, and port (Irrawaddy River) of the Japanese. Less than one-half of the original force of Marauders reached Myitkyina. Once there, illness and wounds took huge tolls. The Marauders were succeeded by the Mars Task Force, who captured the remaining territory held in Northern Burma by the Japanese. The Flying Tigers, Hell's Angels Squadron, helped try to win the battle of Rangoon, but were not successful. When the British forces, assisted greatly by American supply air drops, drove the Japanese out of Rangoon, the enemy was forced to abandon Burma and retreat into Thailand, thus clearing the way for a land route, the Ledo Road to China.

The Ledo Road

The old Burma Road was the original "back door" to China. It began with the port at Rangoon, used rail to Lashio, then depended on trucks and animals for the trek through high mountain passes and steep gorges to Kunming in China. When the Japanese captured Rangoon in 1942 and then overran the rest of Burma, being stopped only at Imphal and Kohima in eastern India, the Burma Road was lost as a supply route to China.

A major reason for the Merrill's Marauders' campaign to recapture northern Burma was to make possible the construction of a 478-mile land route from Ledo, Assam Province, India, to connect near Wanting in northeastern Burma with the upper part of the old Burma Road. As stated earlier, building a road across that mountainous terrain was declared mission impossible by most military experts, but nonetheless, the project was tackled. Army engineering battalions began to follow the Marauders; construction at times carried on within hearing range of battle fire.

The road builders faced enormous obstacles. The thick tangle of jungle vines, towering trees, and steep, slippery terrain often made accurate surveying impossible. Mountains, steep gorges, and torrential streams had to be conquered. The annual rainfall in Burma averaged 150 inches and as much as 14 inches a day during the monsoon, but an unfortunate 175 inches fell in 1944. An average of thirteen huge culverts per mile was necessary to dispose of the runoff in one long portion of the road. The construction battalions were plagued by diseases, mud, and leeches.

Despite all of the problems, they completed the impossible, and in January 1945, Army truck battalions of 150 two-and-one-half-ton trucks in each of two convoys began to haul arms and supplies from Ledo to Kunming. Even the fastest convoys took thirteen days to accomplish the 1,089-mile journey from Ledo to Kunming, an average of about eighty-five miles in each long day of driving.

In 1945, the Ledo Road at last opened. By August 15 of that year, the Japanese surrendered. The last American troops, which included Lieutenant Richard L. Beard, were sent home in late spring of 1946.

Part One

1944: Leaving Home

China-Burma-India veterans often remark that this theater of World War II was lowest on the United States government's list of priorities: the last to receive supplies and soldiers, and after the war ended, given the fewest medals for valor. Not that CBI soldiers lacked for valor. The circumstances under which they fought and worked were among the most daunting of the war.[1]

History books verify these impressions. In *Stilwell's Mission to China* (1953) we read,

> When General Stilwell landed in India, he stepped upon a stage whose dimensions were gigantic. The area of China, Burma and India was about equal to that of the United States, but its population of nearly 900,000,000 was almost seven times that of Stilwell's nation. The human scene in China, Burma, and India was as complex as the geographic.[2]

Reports of the CBI arena invariably feature descriptions of the incredible dangers and discomforts of this particular war zone: the many subcultures and language differences, the world's highest mountains, relentless monsoons, scorching heat, intense cold, forbidding jungles, hordes of insects, disabling and killing diseases about which U.S. Army physicians knew little, and veteran Japanese forces. Just hacking a half-mile path through the Burmese jungle entanglement could take a platoon of soldiers a full day; those who served in Burma referred to it as "the green hell."

Richard Leonard Beard, Ph.D., neither fought his way through the jungles of Burma nor flew over the Himalayan Hump. His World War II responsibilities would lie with the shattered emotions and psyches of soldiers who had broken down under the strain of the Far Eastern wartime environment. He also battled with loneliness for his wife Reva and his own strong reactions to the teeming humanity of India.

Although Richard loved his country and served willingly in World War II, he felt that he would have better served the country teaching in an academic classroom rather than working with mental cases in an army hospital.

In writing to Reva, Richard often "travels" home to an imagined future. On September 19, he asks her to continue saving cartoons for him and to stack up *Life* and *Time* magazines in reverse order so that he will be able to read past news from time missed. He envisions a getaway trip with Reva after his return, spending several weeks in a cabin on Lake Michigan with no task more strenuous than reading. The frustration and occasional melancholy that pervade the letters of 1945 and 1946 are not present in 1944. The earliest letters are basically lighthearted in tone. Offsetting the complaints about food, army procedures, and the universal lack of privacy was Richard's tendency to see humor in nearly every situation. Quips, jokes, and dry wit abound. Transcending Richard's impatience at being in India for eighteen months was his passion for beautiful "Ritter," as he liked to call her, his bride at home in Findlay, Ohio. Expressions of ardor weave deliriously through the letters. If anything could be called an overriding theme of this correspondence, it is the love and devotion of a husband and wife.

India's ancient culture, glorious skies, and dramatic weather and wildlife fascinated the young psychologist. In cataloging bird life, he expresses astonishment at the size of these creatures. Richard's appreciation for the glory of nature interrupts his narrative of a tedious, interminable train ride across India—losing freight, waiting three hours for a ferry, sleeping on the floor, gathering more men as they lumber on, being "jammed in unmercifully." Reading lush descriptive passages in the midst of travel accounts, one senses that Richard was writing not only to encourage Reva but as a form of self-therapy.

The letters not only give insight into the character and personality of Richard, but also treat the reader to a kind of

Innocents Abroad travelogue. Before his assignment to serve in India, Richard had never been outside his native land. His accounts of the subcontinent contain intense feelings of enchanted discovery, a vivid sense of place, and often brilliant nuances of description. The pages of "1944: Leaving Home," introduce themes that will run throughout the correspondence. In addition to seeing constant assurances of love, often sweetened with a bouquet of roses,[3] we read descriptions of the Army and astonishment at its mode of operation, of India street scenes, and of Richard's fellow soldiers. He laments the passage of time and the months that have apparently flown by. On the upside, his spirit is lightened by the camaraderie he feels for other GIs. This feeling will continue to sustain him, although the circle of friends grows more selective, no matter how discouraged he becomes with his situation.

Reva's letters comprise integral threads in this World War II tapestry of letters. Many of her accounts are about teaching elementary school in Findlay, Ohio. In a letter dated October 25, Reva happily describes a classroom breakthrough. Robert, a shy student afraid to speak in class, has finally learned, through her private tutoring, to read. Like many wartime wives across America, she wearied of living with her parents and being "entertained" by relatives. She wrote to Richard about the obstacles encountered in the quest to adopt a child, something they had agreed upon before the war took Richard to India.

To put the 1944 letters within the context of CBI, we must look at a few key personalities and events. War in Asia preceded World War II by nearly a decade, during which the Japanese had been seizing major cities in large portions of China. It was during this conflict that the Chinese built a 681-mile road to Burma. The CBI theater, which three years later would be split into the China and Burma-India theaters, was established in December 1941.

Commander of the theater General Joseph Stilwell played a dual role as chief of staff to Generalissimo Chiang Kai-shek and part of Admiral Lord Louis Mountbatten's Southeast Asia command. Simply put, his goal was to back China in the war by transporting munitions and other supplies from India to China, an integral part of the effort to weaken Japan's efforts in the Pacific theater. Keeping China in the war meant tying up two million Japanese troops who otherwise could have been used against American forces in the Pacific.

The New York Times of May 21, 1944 announces the success of Merrill's Marauders near Myitkyina and a "Chinese smash across the Salween River." "If successful," writes reporter Sidney Shalett, "the Chinese drive may be the keystone to gains of almost unlimited strategic significance in North Burma and China" (p. 6B) Shalett adds,

> The strategy seemed sound; it showed that the allies were keeping their eye on the ball. For if the supply route into China can be opened up with reasonable quickness, before the Japanese do too much damage in South Central China, the effects of the Japanese gains can be reduced and eventually nullified (p. 6B).

Shalett pays tribute to the incredible advances through dense Burmese jungle by Merrill's Marauders and stresses the goal of linking the old Burma Road with the new Ledo Road. When this is accomplished, speculates the reporter, "The way will be open for the beginning of what first may be a trickle of supplies and then a mighty flood of munitions, which has been promised to China."

Such were the broad brush strokes of the CBI at the beginning of Richard's service in the war. His earliest letters describe the Army routine for Reva and are written with a thoroughness that will characterize the entire correspondence.

Richard mentions the weather, names and often descriptions of the men with whom he interacts, and his impressions of how he fits into the picture. During March and April of 1944, Richard and his peers express frustration at the army's inefficiency. They can only guess that they will be sent to the CBI theater. The uncertainty continues until the end of June.

The letters with the heading "At Sea" were written from late June through early September. Censorship prohibited revealing details of possible use to the enemy, so Richard could not mention either location or date of writing. Painting vivid word pictures, he takes Reva with him on the trip. Life aboard ship includes hours spent observing the roiling ocean, talking with his close friend Kenny Bayless, losing at poker. As he will do throughout the letters, Richard depicts his poker buddies in brief character sketches. He describes for Reva the beard and mustache he has decided to grow. Photographs of a clean-shaven Richard during his tour in India show that he grew tired of whiskers.

The "At Sea" letters are filled with flashbacks to the domestic life Richard and Reva shared in Ohio during his days as a graduate student. He fondly recalls the times snowstorms confined them to the home and cocooning in an overcrowded library. Perhaps reminded by poker games with the fellows, he longs for a return to evening cribbage games with Reva.

The young psychologist's observances of anniversaries and holidays play an important part in sustaining his ties to home. Like soldiers who serve in any war, he was faced with the possibility that he might not return home. He faces that reality and holds on tightly to his intense dreams of a future with his wife and a family.

Throughout the autumn months, Richard describes overflowing plumbing in his apartment, the burning ghats (bathing areas on the banks of rivers or ponds), and an insect invasion on Armistice Day (during which he is writing by candlelight, as no one refueled the generator). Because he has not yet been recognized as a clinical psychologist, his work is mainly of the paper-shuffling variety.

As Christmas approaches, he and his fellow GIs console themselves with packages from home and nightly poker games interrupted by power outages. His December 15 letter professes his intense love and assures Reva that he will always be with her in mind and spirit.

Richard and Reva were married July 3, 1937, in Cincinnati, Ohio, at the home of their friend Reverend Kidder.

March 9, 1944

My Dearest,

I love you! I love you! It does bear repeating, doesn't it? I have never grown tired of hearing it, and how I wish I could hear it from you tonight. I am trying awfully hard to be brave, Dearest. So don't worry about me—just take care of yourself.

Your mother and I watched the train until it pulled out. I hope you found a good seat. It looked to me as if there was at least one nice coach on the train.

We headed directly home the same way we went this morning. Your mother thought we should eat in Marion, so we decided on a nice looking restaurant in the center of town. It turned out to be a clean, pleasant place with the meals not only well cooked but attractively served in small portions.

We then made our next stop in Upper Sandusky, where your mother picked up some cups and saucers she wanted at one of those china places.

I decided to stop in Carey and see Evelyn. Of course I wanted to see her, but I also thought she might be good for my morale. Max is in Italy now, and moving closer to the front, although he hasn't been in combat yet. He is in the Infantry and is in charge of headquarters as I understand it. Evelyn was thin when I saw her in the spring but she is thinner now and doesn't look well, possibly because she was always on the buxom order.

I'll be at your folks' Saturday and Sunday night if you should call.

> Lots and lots of love,
> My Dearest,
> Goodnight sweetheart,
> Reva

> Seymour Johnson Field
> March 13, 1944

To my dearest Reva:

Today is Monday—Monday eve to be exact and I am in the noisy day-room of the 711th Training Group. (We are

29

here for several days as attached men.) I recall now that in yesterday's letter (the last to you—I wired Friday— telephoned Saturday) I neglected to say much about what has happened thus far: Here it is:

Friday night: Up at 6:00; very chilly but the stove is next to my bed—top bunk; movies and orientation talk in morning; chaplain and CO in afternoon. Things are leisurely here—about 6 hrs. out of the day.

Sunday: Loafed—met a Robinson from Bellaire who is a cousin of Alice Robinson of Ohio State—talked a lot.

Monday: Haircut—it took all morning—25 barbers— several hundred men. Pitched tents and rolled pack and stood retreat in afternoon.

So, honey, I still don't know very much about the prospects. One thing I do know—this is the finest group of fellows I've been tossed with or among yet. It may be because I am so popular that I feel that way. It is funny, but I never became very popular at Selfridge—but here, though most of the boys carry more rank than I, I find myself turning down invitations constantly—further, the boys recognize me as an authority on almost any subject I talk upon. Few or none of them know that I am a doctor—maybe that's the reason. Enough of the persiflage!

No letters from you yet. I know that one must be on the Field, but apparently they haven't routed them through yet. Here's holding my breath, dearest!

It has been a lovely day—clear—springlike! To our springs to come together, sweetest girl—and keep your head up.

> Love and kisses and caresses,
> Dick

March 13, 1944

My Dearest,

I feel slighted today—your folks got a letter and I didn't. My turn will probably come tomorrow, but the mail certainly seems slow to me. Your Dad and Clete brought the studio couch tonight and he told me about your letter.

I went to the Employment Office today. That position is a Civil Service appointment.

He has already recommended someone for it but took my name, address, qualifications etc. in case she isn't approved. He said he just sent her application in Saturday. I decided not to do any further looking until I know more about your situation. I got an application for substituting from Ray's office girl, filled it in to-night and will take it up. I understand there is little substituting in the city, so I didn't see Kinley. If I could get something, that would make a good fill-in for the present.

I talked with the fellow that used to work at the L&W⁴ when Jack did and works at the Employment Bureau now. He got turned down at the Induction Center in Toledo for flat feet.

Isn't that something! If one were to use that for their basis of judgment, you should never have been inducted.

I am wondering how much you are confined to camp and what Goldsboro is like. But then, I suppose you will have told me all that and things are probably too uncertain for me to come down anyway.

Goodnight my sweetheart. I'll conclude this tomorrow.

XXXXX

March 14, 1944

My Dearest,

I wrote this afternoon but will write this brief note before bed so Daddy can mail it in the morning.

I think I'll go over to your folks and stay all night Saturday night as I had planned. That will give me a change and a chance to say hello to them. Use your judgment about calling but if you have any news, call because it apparently takes a long time for the mail to get through since I haven't gotten a letter yet.

Now that my folks have a phone (2994MX) if some other night is more convenient, that will be just as well. I called your

31

mother several times this evening and got "busy" from the operator.

Our gasoline has been cut to two gallons for a coupon. It is really getting tight.

In the bank today, Lee Erchalitz showed me a letter from his brother Norbert, who has been flying over Germany. Paul Dreisbach is in England. He says the most he has to do now is swap yarns and try to keep warm.

I have an appointment for next Monday to get the spring fixed. I have to leave the car for two days. They find out what it needs, then telephone Toledo for the part.

The time certainly passes slowly. It seems like ages since you left. If only the war could end tomorrow!

Goodnight, my Dear. I'll be dreaming of you.

Love and kisses,

Reva

March 15, 1944

Dearest,

I finally received a letter from you this afternoon. I was about to telegraph asking for a return telegram. We didn't realize until after the train pulled out of the Columbus Station that we might have seen you from the side windows in the station.

I may drive around to tell your folks about my letter this eve. I tried to telephone your mother this afternoon but she must be gone. It is raining now. If it doesn't stop, I may just telephone this eve.

I am feeling blue, probably no more so than you are. Is that team out, and is the only possibility just plain overseas units? If you do have to go, it would be some consolation if I thought you were just going for a few months.

Every day I hear of things that burn me up, but the hardest thing to understand is how some fail at the Induction Center with less "wrong" with them than you, and you pass every test that comes along.

*How are you feeling? You didn't tell me anything about your-
self, only mentioned not having a big appetite. Why can't the army
let me look after your welfare? Why can't we draw a lucky number?*

*Daddy says Mr. Amundson would like me to help them out at
the store for the rest of the week at 50 cents per hour. It seems it
could be steady if I want it. In the first place, I doubt if I want
that kind of work steadily and secondly, but most important, I
don't want to tie myself down as long as there is still a possibility
of my going with you. You might write me your views on the subject. However, I guess I'll work the rest of the week at least. That
will help occupy my mind.*

*The newsman just announced that the Russians are 25 miles
from the Rumanian border. We have news on here the first thing
in the morning and the last thing at night and three or four times
between.*

*I am enclosing your GI prescription for glasses. I found it in
my case and thought you might want it. I am going to send Miriam a card and give her your address yet this eve.*

*What are your barracks like? I don't hear the rain on the roof
here, Dearest.*

> *Lots and lots of love,*
> *Goodnight, my Dearest,*
> *Reva*

March 23, 1944

My Dearest,

*I have been alone this evening. The folks are just opening the
door downstairs now. I was afraid it might be a bad evening so decided to clean out a few drawers and do similar tasks to keep myself
busy. There is still plenty of rearranging that should be done. I
should do something about our pictures too, some of them are getting in bad shape.*

*I came across a picture of you in Toledo, seated in the little
chair in the corner in front of the two bookcases meeting in the
corner. We didn't realize then that we would think of those as the
"good old days."*

Dearest, don't you have any idea or even any rumors as to what they are going to do with you? How many classification men does a squadron usually have?

The first of April, the new postage rates go into effect. Aren't they hitting the wrong people?

The columnists in tonight's Blade *were concerned over our foreign policy.* [The *Toledo Blade* was one of Ohio's leading newspapers.] *A cartoon showed Churchill and Stalin each with a basket of good apples and FDR with one apple that had fallen to the ground and an empty basket.*

I listen to each newscast in hopes that it will bring some startling news in our favor and hope it will end soon, but really feeling pessimistic. May the optimists be right!

I love you! I love you!
Goodnight, Dearest,
Reva

March 25, 1944

My Dearest,

My role seems to be one of waiting and hoping these days. I am afraid that you may have left Seymour Johnson by now. But to avoid any possible misunderstanding, I telegraphed you that I would be at home all day.

Mother is downtown and it is rainy and gloomy outside. I wanted to be near the telephone so here I stick.

I hope I can get over some of the feeling of bitterness over your treatment in the army so far. I realize that others have fared worse and so on, but I can't help pitying ourselves.

I talked with Gladys this aft. and she says Johnnie leaves Monday morning. He is worked up today over losing his dog last evening. He was driving out N. Main and it jumped out of the car without his being aware of it.

Gladys has a suggested job for me. Some insurance company wants a woman to make biweekly collections for them and it seems there is some selling with it. Reported salary about $40 a week with car expenses paid. I told her I wasn't considering anything right now. But if I do have to stay here, it might be something to fill the gap until I can teach.

It would probably be quite a bit of wear and tear on the car though.

I sort of hoped you'd carry a Bible. It doesn't do much good to have faith in humanity. I don't mean to be pessimistic. Of course if you go you are coming back and soon.

I'm afraid I'm not writing the kind of letters one is supposed to write service men. It may also be that I so much want to have the feeling that I'll be with you soon. You just can't get away from this little leech.

I just looked out the window, my Dear, and what was rain a few moments ago is now snow. It is melting almost as soon as it hits the ground though.

I am sorry your food has been so poor. How is the PX? It is 6:30 so I suppose I'd better go down and find something to eat. Mother will have a fit if I haven't eaten when she comes home.

I just got around to reading the article you sent about Thurber. I think there is something to his quotation "Millions for agriculture—not one cent for Literature." Mrs. Martha Smith was found dead yesterday from a heart attack. She was 67.

Your folks said they sent you a registered letter the first of the week, so it sounds as if you might have gotten reimbursed. I am taking it for granted that you will let me know if you need any money.

> Please look out for yourself, My Dearest.
> I hope I get to hear your voice tonight.
> Loads of Love and Affection, Sweetheart,
> Reva

P.S. Later Saturday night. I just talked with you which did wonders for my spirits. I'm looking forward to seeing you soon, My Dear.

Greensboro, N.C.
April 24, 1944

Dearest Ritter:

It is Monday morning—and raining—and ugly rumors about the kind of work we are to do here go flapping around.

You should have heard this guy—Cpls., Sgts., S/Sgts., T/Sgts., F/Sgts., and M/Sgts.—roar at the non-coms for their inefficiency Saturday night. The poor fellows were used to Basic Training recruits who take anything without murmuring.

As I wrote the food is good here, but the mess hall is poorly set up and there is no schedule for the various barracks. Consequently, as many as a hundred men or more may be in line, trying to get in.

It is now 9:00 a.m. and we have just had our first fiasco. To everybody but the Sgt. in charge, it was obvious that it was raining, but we marched to the muddy drill field anyway.

Then a veritable deluge came down and the men herded for the barracks, regardless of what the snotty little ass had said.

So now we are to have a lecture on military courtesy—which is an incredibly naive thing to discuss with those who have been in the Army for a year or longer.

I want to tell you about some of the poker hands which I received in the play Saturday on the train and yesterday on the bunk. Saturday I held 4 - 7's, 4 - 5's, and 4 - aces at various times in 7 card stud. In the case of the aces (one was the joker) the boys betting against me had full houses and straights and flushes. It was wonderful! Then Sunday, during a hot period, I caught 4 - 7's again. This time, honey, it was for money!

(Time passes)

This afternoon was marked by intermittent rain, during which we hurried to the gym and listened to an incredible lecture (from an educational viewpoint) on carbines and pistols.

I played some poker today and dropped $2.00. Keep your fingers crossed, dear!

Tonight the sky has cleared and the sun is shining burnished copper across my blankets. I intend to write a letter or two and then to bed.

Love, dearest,
Dick

P.S. Three big peach halves tonight—as I was at the close of the mess line! Good eating.

April 24, 1944

My Dearest,

I'm not sure that I told you how much that telegram did for me. I just worried a little about not hearing from you Saturday morning.

Junior Burns from Benton Ridge, who flew in the transports from Romulus, crashed on the way back from India and I guess is missing.

John Maxwell, according to Gladys, is in Camp Branding, Florida, taking his basic training and writing complaining letters home. He says every muscle aches and even muscles he didn't know he had.

With the odd jobs I had to do, I didn't even get around to unpacking today and then I guess I was tired. I got to bed late and then got up as soon as I awakened to call your folks to see if they had received a telegram, and they had.

I am anxious to hear about the setup there and hope it is better.

As always I miss you, and I am whispering—I love you! I love you!

Goodnight, my Dearest,
Reva

Greensboro, N.C.
April 29, 1944

Dearest:

I'm so sorry that I have nothing to tell you—but we just don't learn anything. We are assured by the non-coms that we are surely going over— but we don't learn anything else about it.

I am writing this at noon of a clear, cold day. Tomorrow, incidentally, is a regular day of duty here—and for the first time since I've been in the Army, I'll have worked straight through. One wouldn't mind it in the least if there were reasons for it, but this repetition of subjects heard several weeks ago approaches the absurd. However, the absurd is normal here, I guess.

Last night I played no poker but wrote various letters. Poor English but you know what I mean. The boys have been yelling for me but I am determined—you come first, naturally.

We were told that we will get paid and that makes many of the "broke" boys happy.

For several days the poker games will rage, until, as one Lt. said yesterday, 5 or 6 fellows are millionaires and the rest paupers.

I'm looking forward to our telephone conversation tonight. I hope the examination proceeded smoothly at Maumee. In that respect, do what you consider wisest.

Love to you, dearest,
Dick

April 30, 1944

My Dearest,

I hope you are feeling better tonight. I don't understand why they give you those shots so close together. For goodness sake, don't let them give you any more soon.

I certainly am glad to know that there is a good possibility of your getting home. But if you would have gotten a furlough anyway it is too bad that we couldn't spend it having fun.

I am wondering if your suntans will be warm enough.

Tonight I drove around by the Kageys. Gladys along with Mrs. Bishop and Leita King are going to Cleveland tomorrow to stay for a couple of days. Phyllis and I were there and kidded her about leaving Ralph in our care.

I read a six-page letter from Johnnie written to Ralph. He has a tale of woe. He is in the infantry in a camp located in a swamp, living in a hut with a Russian Jew, a Bohemian and a Frenchman from Cleveland and helps the hillbillies read and write their letters and march, march, march. Phyllis thinks she may go down there for awhile.

I think Marilyn had a nice birthday party. I was only up there about half the time. The children were good, but 25 of them in an apartment is too many.

I am getting your suntans in shape to wear if you need them when you get home.

> *Lots and Lots of Love,*
> *My Sweetheart,*
> *Reva*

May 1, 1944

My Dearest,

I received a nice lot of mail from you today. Five letters!

You spoke of the "overage" rumor. What is considered "overage"?

I'll have to get the list of birthdays from your mother. I know the month of everyone's but not the date.

I went downtown this afternoon and had an interview with Kinley about teaching. He was very pleasant and sent his regards to you. He thought it ridiculous, a Ph.D. and a corporal. He said that was quite in keeping with the army, though. He had a year's experience in the last war and his son with a B.S. from Miami in Business Administration is a Buck Private in Artillery, in the army

11 months and has been on the Anzio Beach Head for some time. He is quite bitter about it.

If I got the job, I would get $1180 in the scale, but he said they will probably pay $150 or maybe $200 above the scale.

He gave me an application form to fill in and return. I may fill it in and hold it until I talk with you.

I saw your Mother and Bonnie in the infant's store. I bought Margie a gift, a fancy bottle container.

I am not looking forward to anything else, but I am looking forward to seeing you soon. It is now past twelve o'clock.

> *So, Goodnight, My Dearest,*
> *Love and Kisses,*
> *Reva*

May 13, 1944

My Dearest,

Just a note to tell you how much I'm thinking of you and how much I hated to see you leave.

On Tuesday, I shall be remembering that evening 14 years ago. In spite of all our trials, it has been a wonderful 14 years. And I have hopes that some day soon we shall be able to settle down to living quietly in our own way.

I have just been directing Miriam in wrapping our Mother's Day gifts. She has kept me busy talking with her since you left. But now I'm tired, my Sweetheart, and though I've been lying on the davenport I think I'd better get into PJs soon. How I wish you were here. I'll dream of you, my Dearest.

> *Goodnight, my Darling,*
> *Reva*

May 21, 1944

My Dearest,

It was nice hearing your voice this morning. I waited all week for that. You sounded tired, though. I hope you got to go back to sleep.

I told you this morning that everyone is OK. Daddy isn't exactly ill but he has a boil on the back of his neck, which is causing him quite a lot of trouble. Right now he is taking the sulfa drug which the doctor gave him to get the poison out of his system.

Miriam says that a lot of people seem to be waiting until after the war to adopt children. Do you think we should write to that agency I contacted to let them know we will be interested?

The type of bombing reported over Europe today really sounds like the invasion ought to be near. Shirer was very critical of our foreign policy and repeated, not only should it be planned with reference to the conquered countries but that it's a job for statesmen and not the military. He has been very critical the last couple of weeks which, if I remember correctly, is unusual in him.

Take care of yourself, My Darling. I love you so.

Goodnight Sweetheart,
Reva

May 25, 1944

My Dearest,

You will probably receive this the 29th. How I wish I could come along with it. The peonies, though not as far along as six years ago, will be out by the 29th. Six years have gone along very fast, but still, when one thinks of the changes in the world and in ourselves too, it has been quite a long time. I have relived that day many times—getting the church ready (it was beautiful), getting dressed, having our pictures taken in the yard, waiting for the Kidwells and Miriam, dashing to the church, the ceremony (soon over), Hazel's rice, the reception, and then being able to wear the little gold band always. The thrill still comes back with a little tingle as I relive it. Life can be cruel, but it can be good, too. And

I'm trying to focus my eyes on the good things of the past and the good things I hope are to come.

Dearest, may we be together the May 29ths to come. This year together in spirit. Darling, hold me tight. I love you so.

Your Devoted Wife,

Reva

June 6, 1944 (2nd letter)

My Dearest,

I wrote three letters yesterday. Tonight, it is cool and I am writing at the desk instead of in bed. The gas grate is on and I've been listening to the news. One doesn't get much satisfaction from listening since the reports are about the same but I thought possibly another front would be opening up.

I didn't do much today but went to the P.O. and stopped at the cleaners to get my winter coat. Flags lined the street and looked pretty.

I believe father's day is not far off. I'll have to get them something the next time I go downtown. My father can use a belt, but yours will be a problem.

It is 12:45, so I guess it is my bedtime. I don't get up until 10 or after. I wish you could put in those hours too, my Dear.

If this could only end—and you could kiss me goodnight, and there weren't a war.

Much love my Sweetheart,

Reva

June 19, 1944

My Dearest,

I am in the station writing on my knee. It started raining as we pulled in and consequently is cooler. It has stopped but looks like it will rain more.

The taxi stopped for me to go to the express office, waited, then drove me around to the front of the station and delivered my bag to the checking office. I had 3/4ths of an hour so walked uptown and ate a small breakfast and then it was train time.

A Red Cap took my bag up but there was an awful jam at the train. However, it was air-conditioned and I didn't mind too much having to sit on my bag part of the way. The train was a little late. I have eaten and have 2 1/2 hour to wait. They are going to see if they can get me a Pullman.

I don't mind a wait going your direction but going away from you, they make me want to turn around and fly to you. Just as if I don't want to do that all the time. When the war is over, I keep saying to myself, we'll have lots of fun—and it has to be over soon. We'll make up this lost time.

I hope you aren't too tired, and I'm wishing you the best of luck in everything you do.

You know I wish it but my saying so may help.

Lots and lots of Love and Kisses,

> *Reva*

> *June 23, 1944*

My Dearest,

No mail came a.m. then this afternoon two letters one written Tuesday night and your letter of Wednesday just before leaving. I was prepared for it, but still my heart went to my toes when I read it. Of course I'm going to miss you terribly but I do realize that the most important thing is your safe return to me. So, my Dearest, please take good care of yourself.

You said that you were sending four envelopes Wednesday, so I should get some mail tomorrow and possibly your address.

The war seems to be progressing nicely and one commentator predicted the war would be over with Germany in October. It still seems slow to me.

It was too bad Rhea was pulled out of your group. Do you think Barbara will be going to see him now? One never knows whether things happen for the best or not.

I wrote to the Family and Children's Bureau in Columbus and asked them to consider our application, if not now under these circumstances, then at the end of the war.

For the summer and maybe for the winter, I have given up taking any school work. I think I'll look for a temporary job and then hope a school turns up before fall. It would be wonderful if the war could be over before then. I suppose that is day dreaming. But Darling, I'll be doing a lot of dreaming—dreaming of you, your nearness, your arms about me.

I know you love me but your letters and assurances of love are such a comfort. If I can't have your presence, they are the best substitute.

I'm staying pretty close to the home for a couple of days in hope you may get a chance to call.

Good luck, My Darling, you have my love and devotion, Dearest One,

> *Reva*

June 24, 1944

My Darling,

Your other three envelopes came today, one containing Wednesday morning's letter, strange that the one written at 4:30 should arrive yesterday. I thought perhaps you might get an opportunity to call. I worked at Gamble's from 3:30 to 9:30 but gave your mother their telephone number so she would know where to locate me. I'll stay around tomorrow—just in case. Do you realize this is the first move you've made since you've been in the army that I haven't pretty definitely known where you were going!

How are those headaches and backaches? Could it be migraines? I wish I could persuade the army that you need me to look after you.

There are a lot of letters I should write but am procrastinating. Other letters are a task. Yours make me feel like I'm having a little talk with you each evening. Come home to me soon and cap it with a goodnight embrace and kiss.

I wrote to the Family and Children's Bureau last night and asked them if they wouldn't consider our application seriously now to please do immediately after the war.

I see by today's paper that the government marshal had nylon hose to sell in Greensboro. The sale started at 10 a.m. and women got in line starting at 7 a.m. They were allowed three pair and were sold out in a hour. I would have been willing to stand in line if I'd been there. Probably a lot of army wives did.

It disgusts me though when I hear people complaining about such minor things and these income tax gripers really pain me. All I want is my husband home! When you get home, honey, I'll probably be so satisfied, I'll sit around and get fat!

Darling, I love you so very much.

> *Sweet dreams and Goodnight,*
> *Devotedly,*
> *Reva*

June 28, 1944

Dearest One:

I have tried several times to get through on the telephone but only the strong survive in the crest of the literally hundreds involved at the 20 booths and since I did talk with you once, I don't feel right about preventing some thin fellow his one chance to make a last phone call. Keep your faith in me strong, dearest, for I am putting my all in you. Please carry on with your plans for adopting a child. I have written to the folks about it. If you decide in favor of a baby (Mama!) instead of teaching next year I shall be more pleased than to know that you added a few dollars to the bank account.

> All my love, my life,
> Dick

June 29, 1944

To My Dearest Husband,

All my good wishes and deepest devotion on July 3rd. I wish I could send you something more tangible but since I can't, please accept all my love!

Darling, the vanity case came this morning. It is lovely and just what I wanted. And the note with it was just as lovely.

I shall give the watch to Daddy, although if he wants it, I suppose he'll want to buy it.

I received a letter from the Children's Bureau in Columbus and as I suspected, they want both the father and mother in the home for a little while at least before the father enters military service. They said they would keep us on the active list and to let them know when we return to Columbus. So I doubt they will do us much good if we don't return to Columbus.

I think I'll contact the Chicago agencies.

Darling, the main purpose of this letter is to tell you I shall be thinking of you even more than usual July 3rd and of course hoping we shall be together on future July 3rds.

> *Most Devotedly and Many Kisses*
> *on our Seventh Anniversary,*
> *Reva*

At Sea

Dearest Ritter:

Kenny Bayless and I hung over the rail this morning talking about home and our experiences while watching the soap suds boil past the ship. Just to our left, and off the middle section of the ship, the incoming swell met the rush of the wave raised by the prow, and the sun made iridescent a shaft of rainbow. (I just read that last sentence to Kenny and he half raised, shook a hand in the air, and shouted in a strained French accent, "Magnifique! Splendide! Viva La France!")

Kenny is a graduate of Bucknell and had planned to teach, but was drafted before he had a chance to get started in the profession. I told him about our proposed house and how after the war, no one could pry me away from HOME. I have had more travel than I ever contemplated and henceforth I intend to leave it to restless souls.

Last night's poker proved again that I hold poorer cards than anyone else, that is consistently poorer, in the game. I lost $7.00 after a hard struggle. It irks me so darn much, though, to hit like wildfire for one night and then fight desperately for a week of losing before I can ever hope to win. Too, I think I have my fill of poker, but there isn't anything else to do.

>Ah, my darling, for the love of
>you—goodnight,
>Dick

At Sea

Dearest:

There is no lack of life about me. At my feet is a blackjack game. Several fellows are chatting just below me to the left. Down the aisle a few feet, Si Bland is leading an impromptu blank-face act with a dozen clowns. Bayless and Berengarten are trying to read. In the meantime, fellows try to get through the crowded aisles. Fun!

I am still in splendid health—the products of my trip thus far are coming along famously. I refer to my mustache and beard—both of which you would love to see. The mustache is heavy and very black. The beard is iron gray and all my enemies insist that my ruddy features are rapidly becoming very dashing indeed. Distinguished, I think the word is!

I am worried, dearest, for I did not give you sufficient warning of the time that would elapse between my leaving the U.S. and when you next hear from me. I only hope that your faith and trust remains strong and clear—For I am sure that all will turn out well.

>For this moment,
>>All my love,
>>and all moments,
>>Dick

At Sea

Dearest:

May I write a little love note, my sweet? In my lexicon, one word stands out above all other: LONGING—for you.

Day after day, week after week that longing grows—and it will continue to grow, my dear, throughout the months to come.

Our years together now take on added significance since I must live in memory.

Especially am I fond of recalling our Saturday morning breakfasts. Then, do you remember how many rides we have had together? The intimacy of those experiences is even more poignant now that I am traveling alone and there are so many restrictions on what I can tell you.

Do you recollect the two or three days at 2109 when snow and ice storms confined us to the house and there was no school? Returning to bed, listening to the radio, lunch, warmth, and quiet reading in that over-crowded library of mine? (and yours.)

And our evening cribbage and poker? It was fun, honey, and I want it to happen again soon—very soon.

> All my love,
> Darling,
> All my love,
> Dick

At Sea

Dearest Ritter:

I am constantly wondering how you are ever going to make any sense out of these letters, for they are marked in no way (not allowed) and I question whether I could sort them chronologically myself. If you have any leisure, it might please you to try it, though.

This is going to be something of a gripe letter. You recall how nicely you used to serve as a release for me? Do you mind?

Take the case of Silas Bland. Since I have known him he has always been in debt to me. Now he drapes his lazy whiskered self on his bunk all day long and expects me, as a buyer, to get him toothpaste, candy, ink etc. and pay for them myself—hoping that he will make good. He has a partial pay coming today, so on the strength of that he borrowed $5.00 and lost it all in poker last night. Now he is broke again. As a human specimen I have never met a more personable, spoiled hypocrite in my life.

Our poker (and I have been playing very poorly recently) has degenerated socially.

Herion cries all the time, whether he wins or not. At poker, he is the most disagreeable man I have ever met. Cleveland is truculent most of the time. Old bald-headed Watts (the lawyer) and I have struck up a strange friendship. I think he is impressed by my lack of screaming and throwing of cards when I lose. Rex Lauck proved unusually merciless last night. Sgt. Bob Comfort is a nice kid who is called the "Kid" because he is so youthful. Si Bland dramatized every hand he lost with gestures and facial grimaces worthy of The Passion Play.

Last night the waves dashed against the side of the hull and the ship pitched and tossed briskly. We had creamed chicken for dinner. I smoked heavily during the poker game and resultant ship rocking almost upset my stomach. I tossed until 4:00 a.m. then drifted off into a troubled sleep. Incidentally, you usually figure in my dreams quite prominently. That shows how well my subconscious is at work.

This letter is perhaps more confusing than usual. I have been interrupted at least 20 times, including time out for our second meal. Our candy is rationed now, four cartons to a buyer and today 64 men tried to buy 96 bars at 3 for 10 cents from me. Some fun!

So, darling, may I say a tender goodnight,
Love, Dick

August 1, 1944

My Darling,

We chose what turned out to be a very warm day to go to Toledo. I was very warm and perspiring all day—to my amazement the big stores there aren't air-conditioned.

I got a purplish wine shade. I thought a red would be too bright. This is really a pretty color but I'm afraid you won't approve of the style. I couldn't find a pattern that I liked in a fitted coat to use my fur to an advantage. So I got a tuxedo on the strength that you will like it when you see it. The fur will be down the front you know. I hesitated, knowing you don't care so much for them but if it is really made to fit me maybe you will change your mind.

I visited "The Child and Family Agency" 1035 Superior St. Toledo. They feel that they have to supply Toledo people first but said that their number is increasing so that they may be able to go outside of the city. I had a nice interview and they gave me an application blank to fill in which requires both our signatures. The first part is data concerning our religion, finances and references. I have copied the last two paragraphs which I think necessitates your signature. I suggest you sign it and send it to the agency, providing you agree. Of course they would probably like a letter from you too. I will sign the application and return it to the agency.

Most of their children come from the Crittenton home. So naturally most of them are young babies. (You have them 1 year before adoption is completed.)

I saw Helen Patton on the street and drove out to Leona's and saw her and Gertie.

They invited me down for the weekend following this coming one. I really hate to get out and go but they were so insistent I couldn't graciously say no. They'll probably be good for me though—I hope I get a letter in the meantime so I can enjoy it. I'm watching for the mail man these days.

These days certainly will make me appreciate days of common ordinary living.

> *Goodnight My Darling*
> *and Loads of Love and Kisses,*
> *Reva*

At Sea

My Darling:

Perhaps the happiest hour of the day—of course it is the happiest hour—is that which I spend with you—as I scrawl words and lines across the white paper in the dim light of the hold.

Almost a month it has been now—and there is more to go. How I hope against hope that you are recalling stories of how long it takes convoys to make the trip you must guess we are making. How you must watch the postman's retreating footsteps each day—gnawing doubt and an endless fear charging you a forfeit of peace of mind and comfort.

We are in a storm area and the huge gray steel ship lunges, twists, totters, pauses, grinds over rocky precipices of water, shakes herself and carries on. This contrary movement leaves many of us half sick, and I am included in the group.

However, there are some remarkable things to be seen in the world, and maybe you and I would enjoy it more if we were together—and traveling first class.

> So much love to you,
> Sweetest,
> Dick

August 11, 1944

My Dearest,

It is mid-afternoon and very, very warm. I almost backed out of going to Toledo in this heat but guess I'll go after awhile.

I am really getting discouraged. I got a letter from the Child and Family agency in Toledo. The one in charge of adoption said she and the social worker who talked with me in her absence and the case worker decided they had better not place a child without the adoptive father being in the home. So suggested I table it for the time being and contact them when you get home. I suggest you write them anyway, maybe they will get an over supply of children.

At least we will have a bid in when you get home. I think I may contact the Lutheran agency in Toledo yet before I call it quits.

I feel a little encouraged about not hearing from you yet—Ms. Ballinger said it was over 7 weeks before she heard from Allen—he went to N. Africa. I've been fearing the length of time indicates a greater distance.

I got a letter from Mrs. Cash today. She says Bob is still in Greensboro but is constantly expecting to be shipped. Also got a card from Mrs. Howell asking about you.

I think I've told you this is the most continuous warm and dry summer I've ever known—My hand sticks to the paper.

The dry weather is hurting the corn and beans and there is less fruit. So Mother is canning all she can get a hold of—apricots and peaches are in the cellar now. I hope you are able to get fruit as well as other things you like. And of course most of all I hope you get home in time to help eat ours.

Darling, be good and take care of yourself. All my love, Sweetest,

> *Devotedly,*
> *Reva*

> *August 22, 1944*

My Dearest,

Now everyone is speculating on where you are. Bob Amundson offered to bet me that you are in Southern France—I don't think that is possible. I don't know whether I've convinced your mother or not but she had that idea too.

The 15th of next month we are supposed to start sending Christmas packages.

The family either asks me for ideas or want me to make purchases for them. My ideas are few so make your wants known. If you're not home by Christmas I won't have much desire to do any shopping—so I think I'll do ours pretty soon—It will be easier that way.

I took our camera up to the camera man here in town today. He says it is all right but it doesn't have a very expensive lens, consequently shows up defects easily and enlargements bring out defects. He made a few suggestions one being that your subject should be placed to throw a shadow. In other words the sun should not be directly to the taker's back but to the side just so it doesn't shine into the lens.

Evelyn goes to Lima to the Dr. tomorrow. I guess Bonnie and I will go along. I want Mother to go too. She has been having some ear trouble and I think she should go to a Dr. but so far she has declined. I think it may be just wax plugging her ear.

It has been two months since I saw you—a long time! I'm looking to the future and our happiness together.

> *Fond embraces and loads of kisses,*
> *Night,*
> *Ritter*

At Sea

Dearest Wife:

This is written in commemoration of our 7th wedding anniversary, Reva, and will inadequately express my sincere happiness and good fortune in being married to you. I should prefer to look into your eyes for a moment and then kiss you to express those feelings; since that is impossible, will you accept this letter?

I was too moved to write on July 3rd, instead I sat for hours watching the waves slip past the stern of our ship. I ran over our wonderful experiences: I thought of our hard times and the troubles we have encountered; and then I reflected upon the almost perfect peace and comfort which is ours when we are together. How our eyes light, and how solicitous we are of one another's welfare.

It is necessary, darling Reva, to refer to last summer and our second honeymoon.

Perhaps six years of living with you had to fade into history before my love matured sufficiently to leave no vestige of doubt. You are my fate, dear, and I am content.

This war is but a passing shadow, Reva, in our lives. If it should prove more, and I am not to see you again, then if there is any eternity, forever you are engraved on my soul's substance. But optimistically, I plan for the future, and I want you to do likewise. I hope that you will have a baby boy or girl waiting for me when I come home. If not then, together we shall secure the blessing of children in a family.

I love you, my girl wife, and each passing day confirms how engulfing my love is.

Even now I look into your lovely face, and with blurred eyes, pledge to you again my everlasting devotion.

Your husband,
Dick

August 29, 1944

My Dearest,

I am spoiled. I had received letters every day for five days. So today, when none came, I was disappointed. Actually, I expected it because I think I have all the letters you wrote at sea.

I received a letter from Rhea today which I'm enclosing. It certainly made good time.

I wish you were closer but maybe you are better off where you are and no doubt you are seeing more. The main thing is, I hope this thing is soon over and you can come home.

I get irritated when I listen to the news—all they talk about is the European front.

We are really too crowded here—you see, the folks have to use our storage room too. Otherwise I could spread everything out. I'll put up with it being jumbled up I think because surely it won't be so many months until we can get more room.

Bonnie asked me to go with her to a show tonight. It wasn't too good—a Phil Baker show. That is two shows in a row for me. I really enjoyed "Mark Twain" yesterday. I hope you get to see it if you haven't. Remember the paper that I thought you should get published? Do you feel any inclination to write these days?

There is a beautiful moon this typical fall evening. I look at the sky more than usual because I know you're probably looking at it too—and I feel just a little closer to you.

> *Goodnight sweetheart*
> *and Hugs and Kisses,*
> *Reva*

India
September 3, 1944

Dearest:

Five years ago today we were preparing to move from the Rabbi's house and you, dearest, had to do much of the work because your husband had an academic interest in the European fracas that had entered the stages of a formal declaration of war. That summer had been an eventful one for several reasons, primarily among them your operation and successful convalescence. We know now that if either that year or the following we had remained in Columbus, things would have turned out differently. However, we can console ourselves with the speculation that we have no way of knowing what would have happened—and it might not have been good.

What we have today is not good in one sense, yet it is in another. When we resume life together, our separation will have so strengthened our spiritual unity, that physical problems will no longer cause us the trouble they once did. Our sense of appreciation of one another will have been enhanced, too, though just this brief absence has created in me such an intense desire to be with you again that it seems impossible that it could be greater. When we meet again, darling, I just want to hold both your hands for a long, long while and look into your eyes. Your presence by me and in the same room is worth living for. Your presence in the same world is a good thing, Reva, and I am grateful.

It is a lovely Sunday morning here in India. I am sitting at the table looking out through the open doors to a green covered hill. The sky is leaden, as usual, though white, fleecy clouds can occasionally be seen against the blue background. American and British troops are sitting on the covered porch of our headquarters or crossing the street to the bazaar area. A hundred of them were intently watching, a moment ago, an Indian mongoose kill a cobra. That group has dispersed and now 15 or 20 are kidding an Indian who is putting his trained monkey through its paces for them.

Kenny Bayless sits across the table from me. He has been quiet all morning and I suspect is downhearted. I have told him stories and gossiped but nothing works. He just morosely reads the paper, refusing to write letters.

So five years of war are behind the Allies; soon three for us, the Americans; soon 1 1/2 for you and me. Even as I write, our Sunday paper, on the table by me, optimistically headlines:

Allies Sweep Through Flanders
Vincy Ridge Taken in New Advance
Americans 14 Miles from Reich Frontier
Allied Advance in Rhone Valley
Trapped Nazis Hide in Rumanian Woods
20-Mile Breach in Gothic Line
Finland Seeking Armistice?
Warsaw in Ruins as Poles Lift Nazis
New Bulgarian Premier

56

Tito's Troops Reach Belgrade Suburb

I presume that headlines, except in Germany and
Japan, are the same the world over and that the people
feel that no longer can there be any doubt about the
outcome—now it is a question of time. How much more
comforting that should be, dear, than the situation two
years ago, when we were confident but actually had done
nothing to justify that confidence. Several days ago I wrote
that 18 months would be the minimum time required to
bring Japan to her knees. That guess is predicated on the
assumption that the Americans will not attack the Philippines for 6 months. Should they now be prepared, but
merely waiting for the German case to be closed, knock 6
months off my guess.

We are confident, we British and Americans here in
India, and in a bored way are waiting for the end. We
know that serious work is in the offing, but the outcome is
so definite. Merely the stupid sun-god to set—then home,
wife, and love.

Ah, my dearest one —
Devotedly,
Dick

September 3, 1944

My Dearest,

*This has been a warm day and a super quiet one. I haven't
talked with your folks—they must have been away though, because
I tried to telephone.*

*I slept until about 11 o'clock, then took my time dressing. We
had a dinner to my liking. Then I drove to the P.O. with my
V-mail [Victory mail] to you. And waited for Miriam to call from
the bus station. She came from Fostoria in the middle of the
afternoon.*

*We continued to lounge the day away—it being too warm to
want to do anything. Bad school weather. Miriam looks better after
a few sun bathes and she coughs less.*

I picked up a "Lady's Home Journal" today which shows a couple of glass houses similar to those Tom used to talk about only not so extreme.

I don't really have any preparation for school but I suppose I'll have to get in the spirit of it anyway.

We have a teachers meeting tomorrow aft. and school a half day Tuesday.

Ray has a book I think you would enjoy. I'm going to get it if they have it here. It is composed of newspaper headlines and stories—each page looking like the front page of a newspaper and it begins with the 1700's. In the couple of minutes I looked at it I was fascinated with comparisons of 1917 and now.

The progress in the European theater is wonderful—we are supposed to have crossed the German border by tonight's report.

I'm afraid it is wishful thinking but I feel the Japs will be discouraged when Germany collapses and won't last long.

I don't like this double holiday. I hate not being able to look forward to the possibility of a letter tomorrow.

There is a beautiful moon tonight, My Darling. One of those full moons that gives a longing wife an extra touch of homesickness.

I keep telling myself that if I can stay out of danger, and if you aren't away too long that from your viewpoint the sacrifice will have added a wealth of material to draw from professionally as well as the personal satisfaction of having seen what you are seeing and will not have been in vain from a purely personal standpoint.

When I think you are living reasonably well and doing things which you enjoy doing and seeing I feel somewhat repaid for my loneliness. Lonely in the sense of the word that I am longing and waiting for you, my sweetheart.

And now, My Dear it is time for some shut-eye.

> *So Much, Much Love*
> *and x x x*
> *Ritter*

India—en route
Thursday, September 7, 1944

Dearest Ritter:

Today dawned as others, except today we move. It is safe to write this, for the letter won't be posted until the journey has been completed.

Ray came over to eat with us in our mess hall one last time. Both K. and I had slept through breakfast. We dressed Ray up in my corporal's shirt and dallied for an hour over our meal. Our packing had been desultory, as we weren't to fall out until 2:00. I had much too much luggage, but Ray helped me carry it.

Our Britisher helped us sweat out the hour and a half wait before the trunks came. We had a final tea and then the wave of a hand—and goodbye. It was strange how he grew on us—first he seemed gangly and ugly, but we later found his face pleasant and good to look at.

The convoy pulled out of the camp and through the suburb and then the city—with the crowds along the sidewalks shouting, laughing (humor, good, for the most part), and making the V-sign.

We were a little dismayed when we found car #5—Kenny and I. It was not 1st class, it was not 2nd class, it was not third class; the cursed (thing) boxcar was "lower class." You must understand, however, that no train in this country can compare with our trains.

The seats were of board, built in solidly, facing one another. The rest boards were just a foot above the seat level, catching me right in the small of the back. Our blankets helped and later in the day we piled our duffle bags between the seats and lay in a four or four and one-half foot enclosure.

Nothing was provided to help us hang up our helmets, cartridge belts, gas masks, musette bags, and suitcases. Five 10-watt bulbs burned feebly day and night from the ceiling—that provided illumination for the whole car. The toilets consisted of two box-like enclosures at either end of the car, with a hole in the floor and a water tap outside or along the wall ending about 3 inches above the floor.

Believe it or not, honey, it wasn't too difficult to sleep. I got at least 9 hours rest that first night.

To eat it was necessary for the train to stop. Our mess kitchen had the food ready and it was served from basins set on boxes out on the station platform. We squatted under lifts to eat, then I spent one hour waiting in line to wash my gear only to find the cold water wouldn't cut the grease of the chili we had eaten.

Beggar children approached our wash line, holding out their cupped hands or tin cups or pieces of dirty cloth with the ends looped to make a basket. I gave a large portion of my chili to a ragged little boy, who tried to hit a little girl who came running with her tin cup. Since his hands were cupped together and full of chili he couldn't hit her without losing what he had gained, so I finally got him to move away while I filled the old tin can of the girl.

The filth of this country, which I haven't stressed too much before, is incredible. Village after village—hovel after hovel—absolutely naked children—the fetid swamp odor over everything.

I think I'll close this letter, Reva, and continue the discussion tomorrow.

> Goodnight, my darling one,
> Dick

India—en route
Friday, September 8, 1944

My darling girl:

I slept well, though it is a little hard to understand why. Kenny and I put our bags between the two seats, piled the blankets over them and the boards, and doubled up on top of it.

We didn't eat breakfast until 10:00 and the train remained, on the main track, for two hours while we took the air.

Some of the country through which we are passing reminds me of the W. Virginia hills. Old, rounded, and green, they form the horizon on either side of us. Occasionally we come close to them and can detect the clouds nestling against the peaks. There is grass and all manner of lush vegetation everywhere. I cannot make out the crops, though the squared embankments apparently enclose small flooded rice fields. The corn crop is sparse, though apparently only about 6 wks. old. Everything in the field, except the rice, seems choked by weeds. Only oxen are used, though some of the plows looked as though they were of steel. The country through which we have passed so far was soaked with muddy water. The train often runs into rain storms. Usually we can let the windows remain up.

Little settlements are spotted about every mile along the track. They vary in size, but not in looks nor in action. When they hear the train approaching, every kid under ten grabs a baby and starts running for the tracks, his grubby hand outstretched, yelling "Buckshee"—or "Gimme!" They stand there grinning and yelling. Behind them both men and women adults pause in their work smiling broadly toward the train of G.I.'s. I cannot learn whether this is true of all trains, or just of ours. I suspect they have the same attitude toward all.

God only knows what a people living in such poverty have to be happy about, but they do not seem unhappy.

If anyone is in a hurry over here, including us, I have failed to see it.

Tomorrow I'll try to describe the types of homes I have seen along the countryside and anything else of interest which I think may be permitted to write.

I hope this journey is bringing me closer to you, my
dearest, for I want you very much.
>Devotedly,
>Dick

September 8, 1944

My Darling,

*This is my second letter this evening. We are going to Toledo
tomorrow and it is time I go to bed aside from the fact that this is
Friday and I'm somewhat tired.*

*I'm going to look for specially packed foods to send you—I'll
be disappointed if they don't have such things.*

*The Rev. Shepherds at Benton Ridge have a 7 week old baby
they got here in Findlay. I had thought some of seeing Miss
Enright (spell?) about the possibility. What do you think? I'm
sure you have to go through an agency anyway, and I'd want to.*

*I heard Dewey's opening campaign speech last night. He
blasted the present administration about their stated policy of slow
release of servicemen after the war and pledged police duty to volunteers. They answered today by saying they would release them as
soon as possible. Dewey had quoted Hershey (I believe) as saying
they would keep the men until jobs are created. Oh, me! What to
believe?*

*Do you remember Hilda Cramer from Liberty? She was a cou-
ple of years ahead of me in school. It seems to me you were some
way involved with her—took her home from somewhere or something—seems to me I recollect getting angry about it. The point
is this—after a few days' illness she died last weekend. She was
married and had a couple of children.*

*I am practically lying down writing this—it no doubt looks
it—surely wish you were beside me! You always are in my Dreams,
Dearest.*

*Got your clipping on Pat's pay and the Texans' vote on liquor.
I think the servicemen are probably saving more than civilians, not
because they make more but because they haven't the opportunity*

*to spend and they are more serious minded. I don't see how they
could be making more—that must be somebody's pipe dream.*
                         Goodnight My Sweetheart,
                         Hugs and Kisses
                         Ritter

India—en route
Sunday, September 10, 1944

Dearest:

Yesterday I took some snapshots. Kenny and I took
snaps of one another while standing in the wash line, after
eating. There are officers on either side of us. I'm afraid
we looked a little disreputable, in our fatigues, unshaven
and sweating. I located a little native girl who looked like a
dark-complexioned Shirley Temple, but had trouble getting her and her friend to pose, for a native policeman had
the children worried. Some of these little native girls are
amazingly pretty—though you never see a girl in the street
once her busts start to develop. At that point, they are
married, I guess, and when they next show up they have
the familiar child hanging from their dress. The transition
must be fast and darn businesslike.

While our food, served from a kitchen car, is substan-
tial, its flavor leaves much to be desired, so Ken and I are
using up our canned goods. The tempers of the boys have
been fairly constant, though Kenny has been getting in-
creasingly moody until it is hard to get along with him. He
just lies on his bench, occasionally cursing wildly at the
uselessness of all this.

For me it has been a journey filled with the new and different. The people (this is not true, of course), like the hills,
are ancient and unchangeable. Their huts differ little from
what they were two thousand years ago; their utensils are of
the crudest; the children either go naked, or what approxi-
mates it. They bathe in the dirty waters of their ponds: children and adults. They walk into the mud with their clothes

63

on. I've seen, from the car windows, full grown women doing that. This could go on for a long time—but you get the idea.

> Oh, my sweet —
> Simply I love you —
> Goodnight, darling,
> Dick

September 11, 1944

My Darling,

I was happy to get four letters from you today. Air-mails of August 29, 30, and 31st and September 3rd. That is second time—September 3rd. I wish my letters would get to you sooner. I also hope communications are just as good from your new station.

Since I have word from you to use your new APO I shall send your razor strop (an old one of Dale's) and your birthday present. It will be gift wrapped and sent first class mail. It should arrive next month but I'm going to send it now with the stipulation that you not open it until December 10th.

Thanks, My Sweetheart, for the picture, of course it doesn't do you justice but I liked getting it.

The news from China worries me but I certainly like the sound of the attack we recently made on the Philippines. Maybe I'll be able to cut 6 months off your guess of the end of the war. I realize, My Darling, that a lot of my optimism (sp?) is wishful thinking.

Getting back to your picture, are you as thin as it indicates? And do the bed bugs bother all the time, and have you had more than one attack of the GI's [in context, diarrhea]? How I hate to have you in that climate. Darling, do you think you'll be able to hold hands and look at me for long when we get together?—I can just feel Ritter collapsing in your arms. Oh, Happy Day! My Dearest, your letters are more beautiful than anyone could hope for. How I look forward to them and how sweet your love notes are. How much those assurances over and over again mean to your Ritter.

How will it be if I send you my O.E.A. and Miss Somer says I can have some of her N.E.A.'s and then subscribe to "Vocations" for you?

Mother and Mrs. Crawfis who live next door said if you know one or two boys who may not get a Christmas box to send them his name and address. Crawfis' only son died of cancer in the army here in the U.S. and they would like to take an interest in some homeless boy.

Again I say take care of yourself.

> *Much, Much Love,*
> *Night,*
> *Ritter*

Monday, September 18, 1944

My Darling,

I received your letters of September 2nd and the one started the 3rd and completed the 4th. I believe it was last Tuesday that I received your letter of the 3rd. Funny how they are sometimes held up.

I received a letter from your English friend Ray. It was a good thing your today's letter told about him or I would still be guessing. His letter was most interesting. He started out the letter with apologies for not answering my epistle sooner.

By the way the English censors must not be so strict. Your friend not only numbered his pages but told me all about the weather and that you had been to Bombay. I thought it must be awfully warm by your pictures with your collars open and sleeves rolled. The seasons are the same as ours, aren't they?

Have I told you about my boy that won't talk? Of course he doesn't know how to do much. It seems to me he should have been made to talk before this. He will talk on the playground and talk when he wants to go to the store or something like that. Last year the teacher just let him sit.

I thought I surely could get him to talk but I've tried being nice—ignoring him, getting tough and none of them seem to break his stubbornness. Of course he goes on the bus at night and

I'm supposed to be on the playground at recess and noon, consequently I have no time to spend alone with him. I noticed he voluntarily took two books home tonight. I make him turn in a paper whether he has anything on it or not and I've made him stay in at recess presumably to study. But don't be surprised if I adopt the method of leaving him sit too. Anything to suggest?

To more pleasant things, aside from missing just plain you, I miss you as a consultant.

Darling, you say the nicest things, of course I like to hear them. How happy I will be when you can whisper them in my ear. I do appreciate your devoted letter writing—realize you are a jewel, My Dear.

> *Much love and Many Kisses,*
> *Night,*
> *Ritter*

India
September 19, 1944

Dearest:

The boys have just walked out of the tent. We have shaken hands. Last minute pictures have been taken. It is sprinkling—just a trifle (10:10 a.m.).

The semi-muddy home is quiet for the first time in a week, but something rich and worthwhile has passed from my life. March, April, May, June, July, August, and most of September mark periods of training, moving, playing cards, talking, eating, doing details together. In the Army the same intimacy develops between or among men that is found in the peacetime relations of husband and wife. Cleveland, Bland, Bayless, and I have traveled 20,000 miles in one group and this company, by foot, train, truck, and ship. Now I am alone in a tent, in a foreign country, half a world away from my home. Tsk!

However, please don't feel bad over my condition, for Gil Schulkind was just here for a friendly talk and later today Al and Harry will be back. Lou Hiram expects to drop in this afternoon, etc. In other words, when one set of friends move on, another set takes their places.

6:00 p.m.

I didn't report for work this morning, for I wanted to say goodby in person. Those with permanent assignments were moved to the front areas in our platoon and the others were sent to another platoon. So at noon, and just preceding today's big rain, I moved.

Have I suggested that you continue to save cartoons for me? And I hope you are stacking up *Life* and *Time* in reverse order so that you and I can take a cabin in North Michigan, borrow Clete's trailer, load the magazines aboard, and spend a month looking over them.

I hope my packages arrive in America safely. It will be a great relief to me to know that you are receiving mail from me fairly regularly. If we had just stayed in the first camp a week longer your letters would have given me some indication of how our mail is getting out of India. By the way—a static address will be a luxury!

In another few days there may be another week's break in my letters to you. One thing you may be sure of, I am writing you a letter (at least one) for every day I am separated from you. When they don't arrive on time, they are merely postponed messages. Furthermore, I write everyday, but it isn't always possible to move the mail from the post daily, though I understand that that is the usual procedure.

No movie last night, so we returned to the tent, hid from the pursuit squadron of mosquitoes, and played "What's my name?"

Our tempers have been breaking quite often recently. Bayless and I think Si stupid and blandly tell him so. He proceeds to defend himself in a loud voice, proclaiming us educated bigots, and there he may have something. Cleveland thinks we are all too slow, and usually dashes off without us. Funny situation: Cleveland dashing off in a mad swirl this morning without waiting for me or Kenny, and I had to clean up the tent. When I reached the office an hour later, I found them waiting for me—but no work for Cleveland at all. A few minutes later he left in disgust. This afternoon he refused to come back! Poor Cleveland. What a temper he has, and what big talk of important people he knows. We definitely are not going to do anything with the Clevelands after the war. I don't want to get stuck with high falutin' talk and the check at the same table!

So the end of another five-page talk with you, my sweetest one, and God save your ribs if I had hold of you now.

> Ah, so much love and devotion,
> Dick

> India—en route (again)
> October 5, 1944

Dearest One:

This letter is really being written under difficulty—I'm sitting outside a barred office window on the station platform, trying to get enough light to write.

Last night I was more tired than usual, and it worried me greatly before I went to bed; however, I awakened this morning much refreshed. Desultory packing and checking out on my part. I met Cpl. Cross's brother, Red, who really gave me a tale of woe—about knowing so much about the work and still a private. (His extreme presumption perhaps one reason.)

I got the bright idea of catching a local to the train station—from which I must get my afternoon military special. It worked, though what I rode on was a coach attached to the rear of a local freight—and the coach was filled with Indians. Do you know, I think they ride for nothing—I did—and no one asked anyone for tickets. If that is so, and I think it is, such acts explain the crowded

condition of the passenger trains and the difficulty of securing coaches for troops.

The afternoon trip back to my freight yard, where I
now am, was not bad. Two American (?) soldiers stole
three or four dozen bananas from an Indian and refused to
pay. This caused some difficulty but neither the MP nor
the RTO representative did more than threaten—so nothing was done. If I hadn't been so low financially, I would
have paid for them myself. The boys charged that the British did that, but I never saw any such action; that still
wouldn't excuse us.

Large bunches of bananas hang from banana trees along
the route, and coconut trees seem blessed, too. Workers
are cutting green hemp, which looks like thin reeds, about
five feet high. The stalks are tied into bundles and placed
in water to soak. It isn't difficult to find water for every
other square yard has a two-yard square pond covering it
here in this area.

Some of my other companions were of a different ilk
than the 1st two mentioned, so on the whole we had a
pleasant time. I slept for about two hours, being the only
man in that compartment with his blankets.

Upon our arrival in the freight yard I hurried to see Lt.
Lutz, who told me that the boys had moved out last night.
So I've missed them. We had to transfer our things, of
course, and since I was late, I missed getting a place to
sleep, but may be able to use the floor. Ho Hum!

Fellows seeing me busily writing think I belong here
and come up to ask me questions. Since I lived here so
long I can usually answer them, too. Small satisfaction for
8 days of your life, though.

Just now I heard a child crying. That is worth recording, because it is a sound rarely heard in this country.

The mosquitoes are now gathering for attack—so I'll
save the rest of this page for morning. By the way, I foisted
Sunday, Monday, Tuesday, and Wednesday's letters off on

Lt. Lutz for censoring, so you should not experience too big a break in our correspondence.

By the way, (Now I wonder what I meant to say? written the next day.)

We are finally pulling out, about 10:00 p.m. I'm going to sleep on the floor of the coach and pray that the cockroaches aren't too active. (They weren't, but the next day about 4:00 p.m. one tried three times to crawl up my neck. The third was his last. If he were a bad Brahmin being punished for his previous sins I returned him to the soil from which he sprung. In a smeary fashion.)

Au Revoir, darling.

Dick

India—en route
October 6, 1944

Dearest:

The floor proved a fairly comfortable place to sleep, because I had plenty of room to move around in. We stopped quite often, though, and the mosquitoes had a field day. Eventually we ran into rain, but I was too tired to worry, and didn't get very wet.

The country we are passing through is fertile and filled with all kinds of life, human, animal, bird, and vegetable. Many of the fields are being plowed with yoked oxen, each team pulling a pointed stick through the ground. I saw one elephant working along the track this morning.

I've often wondered about it, but don't recall mentioning that while there are many ponds, there are few fishermen. That wasn't true of what I saw today. Not only were men, women, and children using poles, but they were also utilizing various kinds of traps and seines. The principal reason for so many ponds along the right-of-way has to do with the manner of securing dirt to build the roadbed. It was done by coolie labor. Each man or group digging from a specified zone. Sometimes the patterns this created look bizarre, indeed.

Bird life observed took a turn for the better. As a matter of fact, the profusion of species startled me. I saw falcons (?) as large as our American eagles. The cranes were so big that I rubbed my eyes in astonishment. Some of the fellows claimed these huge birds were pelicans. Maybe. One old grand-daddy was standing 3 1/2–4 feet, with a body as big as a large turkey. There were all kinds of plovers and water birds. Hawks abound in India. I saw one this morning with a bronzed body, which gleamed in the early sun, and a white head and neck.

We reached a large river about 1:00 p.m. and found that we would once more have to change trains. I looked for our freight but couldn't find it. While waiting three hours for the ferry boat, McClure (an electrician born and reared in Alabama but who spent the last 8 years as a contractor in Washington, D.C.) and I got some free tea. It was fearfully hot waiting in the sun but the tea was good for me, nonetheless.

We have crossed the river and are now jammed in unmercifully. It seems that we gather more men as we go, but don't pick up any new coaches. Right now McClure and I are in a small compartment with ten M.P.'s. Now we will have to be good—though both of us are of a good temperament, no foolin'.

You have traveled in America and know all about the shortage of red caps. Here one absolutely has to fight his way through the coolies—and I mean fight. One followed me almost a quarter of a mile to reach this train. Of course, I would have hired him if I had known how far it actually was. My pride interfered at the moment and I literally carried on.

Just outside the coach an Indian boy is playing an accordion while a little girl dances. One sees little troupes of this kind occasionally. They don't become very rich.

There are some foothills at this point, and since writing the earlier part of this letter I have seen another elephant and one more of those beautiful hawks.

My stomach has been insulted the last several days. Yesterday I lunched on five bananas. My evening dinner was a chocolate bar and later some tea. Today no breakfast, except for some Life Savers kept from the Red Cross gift on the boat. Lunch consisted of 3 crackers and some cheese. The Army cheese is very good except for the darn bacon they put in it. That is slowly turning me against the last meal item I enjoy in the K ration.

Goodness only knows what happens then. It's getting dark, but I doubt if the train moves out very soon. Before it moves I'll eat or rather drink a can of orange juice. That constitutes my supper.

Tonight I am going to have to try to sleep on a 10 or 12 inch ledge. I'll let you know how I make out.

> So much love,
> darling,
> Dick

P.S. Slowly but surely getting nearer your letters.

October 11, 1944

My Dearest,

I received your book reports of September 22nd. I intend to do some reading but still just haven't done any since school started. I guess I still haven't arranged my time properly.

This was a typical fall day, brisk and a little cloudy. I went downtown after school—saw Mrs. Grose and of course she asked after you. Also saw a soldier with a CBI shield on and three service stripes on his arm. Had a notion to stop him and ask him where he'd been.

Otherwise today was uneventful—in school and home at the usual time and school very much as usual. The only highlight: I

moved some seats, decided to move the slow students away from the
windows, thus remove temptation.

Several escaped from the Lima Asylum and two were caught
night before last in the vicinity of Center Street—Taylor, I think it
was. When I stopped at your folks this eve, your Mother had the
doors locked. I decided myself one ought to be more careful.

It is rather remarkable that more of us don't lose our sanity. I
was just trying to recall the time I didn't have something preying
on my mind. Don't worry, Dearest, I think I'm sane.

> It is time to say Good-night, my Darling
> So very much Love,
> XXX
> Reva

India—en route
October 13, 1944

My Darling Reva,

This is my second note to you tonight, my charmer, for
in thinking while alone endlessly and forever my theme is
you. How proud I am of you, darling, and how happy that
I have you to think and dream of.

I share the weaknesses of other men, and in some instances have faults beyond redemption, but in one respect
I have disciplined myself. I have done in this land as you
wished, and found that it was my wish, too. There is no
regret on my part for a physical want not satisfied. It can
wait until proper, complete, and marvelous satisfaction
comes in your arms and in your arms alone.

I should have written before on this subject, but I
wanted to be sure. Temptation is ever present, and here
there are in-bounds houses. The first question the taxi
driver asked us tonight was——. The soldiers on leave, at
least many with whom I have talked, spend a large part of
their savings on prostitutes.

This is a sordid matter; but I wanted you to definitely
understand what I was talking about.

Your faith and trust is great, dearest, and mine matches yours, but I know that you like reassurance. Well, here it is, little wife. "An humble and a contrite heart"—you know.

So, lie back, with your pretty face framed in your luxuriant black hair, and let me look deeply into those starry eyes of love.

Goodnight, precious,
Dick

October 13, 1944

My Darling,

No mail from you today, I understand so much Christmas mail is slowing up the other. Tomorrow will be the last day for that. I will mail your 5th box not including the one with Mrs. Crawfis' return address and the registered 8 oz. package and of course your small birthday package.

I decided that I needed to go out for an evening, so I asked Alleda Hall (Mt. Blanchard teacher) to go along to a movie tonight, then we decided to invite Margaret Gerhold. So the three of us saw "American Romance," a rather fascinating story including a history of the development of iron from the ore stage to the auto and airplane.

I try not to talk too much about you to people like Alleda who have neither husband nor boyfriend, but when Margaret and I are together it seems the subject of conversation is always coming back to Dick or Floyd. You and the war are our thoughts. We stopped in town for a sandwich, and sitting back watching the teenagers makes me feel old.

Surprise—we may be uncle and aunt again in the spring. This time it is my side of the family. Miriam thinks she is pregnant. The Dr. says she will be able to tell definitely in a week. I don't think it was planned exactly but Miriam says she hopes it is true. I do too, because I've been afraid she might have my experience.

If Miriam does have a baby, I'll be thrilled, but still it won't make my pill any easier to take. I've gotten so discouraged about the adopting business, but I do realize it would be more fun together.

I'm afraid to be too optimistic but both Margaret and I were excited tonight with the Pacific War news. The bombing of Formosa sounded good. She started me off with a pep talk and now I'm afraid I have the bug. Of course when I think of China, the wheel swings back.

It is 2 o'clock, so I guess it is time to go to bed even in Findlay. So my darling Goodnight—and remember how deeply your wife loves you. I shall dream of your tender embraces.

> *Devotedly,*
> *Ritter*

India—en route
October 14, 1944

Dearest Reva:

This morning's note failed to mention the bathroom facilities offered at our apartment house. Now this is India, of course, and one shouldn't expect too much, but the darn float on the bowl or stool wouldn't work and every time it filled you had to leave whatever you were doing and dash to release it. Some of the boys were remiss in their duty and consequently Sturke and I darned near swam while trying to shave. Tsk. Life in a plumberless land. To top it all, the proprietor blithely put on his hat and set off for the races, so for all I know, the darn beds have now floated away.

Our afternoon's program (now 6:00 p.m.) consisted of dinner at the Red Cross, a rickshaw journey to Newmarket, return to the RC, and then we went on the Red Cross conducted tour of the City. I'll send a printed copy of the places visited and write at greater length later about it. Suffice now to say that we were at the burning ghats, where we saw the burning pyres. Four or five had burned out and I could see nothing but ashes. Another was practically finished, but the pelvic bone was still there, but rapidly disintegrating. Another had just been started, and was roaring fiercely as we approached. The body was about 2/3's of the way up in the pyre, with his head and feet jutting out from the corded wood. They tell me that when the body burns through, the pyre, which is constructed over a shallow pit, collapses inward, carrying everything with it. Attendants then pile the unburned wood and body parts together and continue this process until, presto! no body. (No pun intended, either.)

Those ghats aroused my ghoulish interest, remember my research on torture?, but no one wanted to stay—so I had to leave, too. The Red Cross girl and her girl companion didn't even go into the burning section. There was a body of a girl (or boy) awaiting burning. It had a dirty white-brown rag thrown over it. Probably that of a beggar child.

This is a nasty letter, and time that I bring it to a close. I'll write on more tonight, if I have an opportunity. I have just had a nice chat (about the classification errors in the Army) with two musicians, Max Cline (grad. Cincinnati Conservatory of Music) and Hustes, who are with a touring troupe in this area.

Much love, darlin',
Dick

October 15, 1944

My Darling,

Of course Marilyn awakened early on Sunday morning and started teasing. I got up and since it was early, decided to go to church. But I still didn't make it in time and when I took Marilyn home I told Bonnie I was going back home to make some candy for you and seal it in a tin can. She suggested I make it there and she would help. We made two batches of fudge, one turned out too soft and the other too hard. When I stopped in later this evening to leave some cans for them to do the mailing it looked like your Mother had had better luck with her sea foam.

I stayed at your folks for dinner then went with the folks to Fostoria. Margaret G. and her son Tobey rode along too.

I get pretty heated up when I read and think of the scarcity of teachers and the type who are teaching now. People, like one of our teachers who hasn't taught for 15 years and threatens to quit unless she gets a $50 raise. She was coaxed to teach 1st grade with an offer of $50 more than the rest of us, then when the raise came the rest of us got $100 and she only $50.

To go on with my story, you, who loves to teach, has to be deprived of it to do nothing but wait and fight the bugs of India in the last almost 7 months now. No wonder education slips backward when we consider how little people in general and people of influence seem interested in its future.

I can't recall just what columnist—but I think Babson—recently said education hadn't advanced in the last 50 years and gave teachers a slur. I'd really like to open up and write a letter to My Dear Mr. Babson and tell him of the (lack!) of opportunity my Ph.D. husband has had to use his training since entering the Army. I am not a good morale builder, am I, Dearest?

But rest your mind now, Sweetheart. Your talents will be needed after the war. Take care of yourself, my Sweetheart. I love you so very much.

> *Goodnight, my Darling*
> *Hugs and millions of kisses,*
> *Your Ritter*

India—at rest
October 15, 1944

Dearest Ritter:

I am seated in a reclining chair under the porch roof of our basha—or Indian style barracks. The building is made of bamboo poles, split bamboo, and a thatched roof. Just to my left lies the mess hall, px, and post office, all in one building. Just in front a hundred yards or so lies the outdoor theatre.

And so at long last I have reached my parent unit—in this case the 12th Bomb 6 p.(m.) Hq., APO 390, C/o p.m., Ny, Ny.[5]

Here's the story. After my last letter to you yesterday I ran into Jack Solomon, Nick Shapiro, and Moe Glasier. The five of us, incl. Sturke, had ice cream, then Sturke and I rickshawed over to Capt. Lowell's apt.

Up very early—by 5:15—coffee only, for the Capt. failed to get us up, and Sturke's alertness saved the situation. We rushed to the downtown section to report—by rickshaw — and from there by truck out to ATC.

The plane took off at 8:00, and after two intermediate stops, reached the 12th. The thrills come on the take-offs and landings, and I had three of each today, so soon ought to be a veteran. In addition to eight or ten officers and men there were 3 women (R.C.) and much freight.

I doubt if lovelier patterns have ever been visible than those we saw from the air this morning. Thousands and thousands of green rice fields, separated by neat irrigation systems. We were low enough that the thatched Indian buildings could be seen among the palm, fig, and date groves. Miniature people, toy animals, and tiny carts move across this mosaic.

And finally our objective! We were nicely received and everything done for our comfort. This afternoon we went back to HQs for a talk with 1st Lt. Frankel, the Adj., and found that they had gotten Capt. Page's letter.

The bearer, native boy, made my bed and fussed over me a great deal. I got all my laundry off and sat down to write you this letter when a Sgt. brought up the basha pet baby monkey. I spent the next hour playing with the monkey and talking with the fellows, who are most friendly.

Sturke and I (just now) returned from supper—and what an excellent meal: creamed chicken! I ate two helpings. We don't use our mess gear, but eat from plates and set places at the table, with butter, jam, bread, and coffee or drink on the table. Tonight they also had hard candy in open dishes. Except for two G.I.'s all work is done by Indians.

Darling, Sturke is here to go to the movie—more later.

Goodnight, darling,

Dick

October 25, 1944

My Darling,

Today I received your V-mail[6] and two (regular mail) letters of the 13th. Your letters of the 14th and 15th haven't yet arrived.

Outside of knowing you were in Calcutta of course your whereabouts or rather my guess as to it covers a lot of territory. I should be wiser when I receive those letters. Funny the way they come, isn't it? Yours of the 16th arriving two days before the 13th.

When I'm feeling sorry for myself, I try to think of what I have to look forward to in the future—our love nest. I dream of you, our reunion, and our plans for the future.

Any news reporter reports that the Japanese navy suffered a crushing defeat. I hope that is true when the statistics are in.

I scored a victory today. My Robert, who has refused to talk, read for me. Miss Nesbaum suggested that a boy they had, had trouble until recently when he read for a teacher in private. I gave Robert a simple verse to study yesterday, and he agreed with a nod of his head that he would read to me the first recess. It worked. I had to tell him at least half of the words but he did it and promised to repeat it tomorrow.

I intend to find some more simple material for him. He often does a few simple arithmetic problems and today did addition. He is slow but makes few mistakes. He refuses to spell, so I decided to give him a few words to study. I think aside from his stubbornness, he fears trying to do something he can't.

If he continues to read for me, I think I'll have him learn something real well then hope he will read aloud. In the meantime, when he leaves the room, I'll tell the children not to act awed if he should talk. You see, they have never heard him talk during school hours.

Enough about Robert.

I have to get up early in the morning. Mrs. Hannon wants to fit my coat before I go to school, which means I have to get up not later than 6:30. I suspect you get up even earlier. Is heat the reason for work not being scheduled for the afternoon instead?

It's funny that the censor would question your use of classification numbers—as if I hadn't heard those particular ones no less than a hundred times.

> *Goodnight my love and much adoration from your*
> *Devoted wife,*
> *Hugs and kisses too!*
> *Reva*

Would you care to have one of your letters printed in the Republican-Courier [Findlay, Ohio's daily newspaper]?

I suspect that I am a little prejudiced, but I think your letters —which I love and cherish not only for their interesting descriptions but for the special meaning and love notes to me—would be a privilege for anyone to read.

November 1, 1944

My Darling,

Today I received four letters (envelopes) dated the 23rd and containing my letters from September 6th through September 16th. [Richard sent Reva's letters back home for safekeeping.]

I have been sending you funnies about once a week but will do it more religiously. I talked with your mother this eve. and suggested that I am sending the Blade *and they can send the Sunday paper if they wish. I'm not sure if she understood—so if you get doubles let me know. Between our phone, her hearing and my rapid speech—no wonder I'm not sure that we understood each other.*

A couple of days ago I mailed some funnies, today your enve-
lopes and an "Ohio Schools" and tomorrow I'm making an enve-
lope with an assortment of things in it.

I was at the Kageys' tonight—it made me feel very lonely
driving over there on Saturday night without you. I took about ten
of your letters along, selecting some of your most descriptive ones.
They enjoyed reading them and Glad says you should write a book.

I didn't intend for Ralph to tell you about the pipes, although
you probably guessed—I should have given him the dickens. I may
as well explain—with his help I selected three, one for Clete, one
for Miriam and one for me and had him send for them. They sub-
stituted one for Clete but I accepted it thinking you might like one
big one.

Then after canvassing the Toledo pipe stores, I found what I
wanted for your birthday (you're still not to open it until then)
and then felt proud of my selection when I showed it to Ralph and
he suggested the amount I must have paid for it was $3.00 more
than I actually paid. At that it was the most expensive one you'll
receive.

I had assumed that the topography was flat but I have a much
clearer picture of it. If sufficient territory is conquered would there
be a possibility of the airbase being moved up?

Do I understand correctly that you do not have a squadron but
work somewhat like you did at Selfridge? Of course you did tell me
that a lot of work consists of letter writing.

Darling I'm including a couple of pictures we took at the fin-
ish of that film, in the house. Poor as usual but I think a dark
background would have helped.

> *Goodnight My Precious*
> *Dream of me—much love*
> *and Devotion,*
> *Your Ritter*

November 4, 1944

My Dearest,

I received a letter in record time today. Your September 29th one and an envelope of your folks' letters mailed at the same time. I hope that you are getting mail more regularly from me.

I took you literally and I'm not sure whether there is any tobacco on the way to you or not. I had a couple of packages here and mailed them out immediately today. Could you use some vitamin pills? Please take care of your health my Darling.

I purchased Omar Khayyam *today but JoAnn isn't sure she can get* Finnegan's Wake. *It was only listed in an old catalog. It was listed at $5.00 and she thought it might be easier to get if you get to Calcutta.*

The neighbors offered us two tickets they weren't using tonight for the Findlay/W. Court House game. I decided I was too tired to go and Margaret was busy tonight so the folks went. They said the game was too one-sided, Findlay winning 62 to zero.

Alberta Hoffman and Anna Cole went to Arizona for Alberta's health last spring—heart trouble. Recently she had to have an appendectomy and had been critically ill since. Today the word came that she died. Ann just banked everything on Bertie. It will be an awful blow.

Your mother tells me you killed a poison spider. Please do be careful! Were the insects as bad near the mountains as in your present location? I was glad you gave me the description of the climate.

I can't seem to find much encouragement anywhere I turn. All predictions for the war's end are far too long. I'm planning on your being home by next fall. I just don't dare think of it being any longer now.

Darling, it will soon have been six months since I last saw you. Four of your pictures are facing me now. You are in four moods—how I love them, but how I wish you were beside me. (Of course you'd be in a tender mood.)

> *Goodnight, my love,*
> *Sweet Dreams,*
> *Reva*

November 10, 1944

My Dearest,

I received your letter of October 31st today. Naturally I was glad for that but expected more. Since tomorrow is Armistice Day, I doubt that there will be any mail. I wish it really were Armistice day.

I was interested in your description of the boys and will like more along that line. If you could only be looking forward to coming home in the immediate future!

Today was one of those blue days with regard to the war. Clara Jacobs and I held a gripe session during the football game, which didn't help. Mt. Blanchard won 34 to 7 against Arcadia. This was their last game—they were unbeaten.

I saw the moon coming up about the evening of the 31st too. It was a beautiful harvest moon, and like you I did an awful lot of longing and had to stiffen the chin.

I am sending your book in an overseas box. I called your mother and asked her if there was anything she wanted to send you. She gave me some cigars (which she has had awhile, hope they're not powder when you get them) and a couple packages of tobacco. I meant to get the box ready after I came back from picking those things up but I'm too tired, so will put it off until tomorrow.

My Darling, if I fail to tell you how wonderful you are, you should hear me tell others.

But most of all Dearest, I want to whisper in your ear "I love you." Dream of that and know how very much love I have for you.

Goodnight my Beloved,
Hugs and kisses
Ritter

India
November 11, 1944

Dearest:

I trust that by now my letters of the 14th and 15th have arrived; so much traveling and the handicap of having to wait for censorship make the arrival of letters in chronological order a possibility only. However, with only the exception of letters sent to the Tenth, your letters have come in order here to 390. Two came today, both dated the 29th, but one was written on Saturday the 28th, I'm sure, and the other on Sunday.

By now you should have all the information necessary to approximately place me, which is as much as you really need know, for most of the communities in this district are much alike and there is comparatively little danger from the Japanese, and that only from the air. His reconnaissance planes will have a swell chance indeed of spotting us, and even if successful, he could not manage the bombers to do any real damage. Furthermore, we now have a flank of supporting fighters that would knock the living hell out of him. The Navy from the East and the Army (British and Indian) and the American Air Force from the west are steadily pressing in upon the Japanese. His doom is blueprinted, and the mosaic will soon be completed. "Soon" here is used in a relative sense. I am done with wild stabs in the dark as to dates. Perhaps no man can determine that, but we can see the victory plan developing on all sides.

Today is Armistice Day. Twenty-six years ago the armistice was concluded and since then had been just an armistice, while one side thoroughly rearmed and the other dawdled in a "Blue Heaven." It is to be hoped that such an eventuality won't occur again, but I'm not as optimistic nor as foolish as I was in 1928. The Utopia will probably remain in the realm of fiction. Today I am too close to terrific problems to which no apparent solution is available to be sanguine about (if) a happy ending. To my mind, the chief stumbling block in reaching an amicable settlement of differences is superstition. It is all very well to be tolerant of what the other fellow believes, but where such beliefs interfere with proper sanitation measures, human lives, education, and all rational approaches to communal problems the matter becomes serious.

I have been very busy today with the matter of records for our new men. Tonight I played poker awhile but soon became bored. I quit 11 rupees ahead, though, and retired to read about 15 Winchell columns which Weinstein gave to me. Then just as I turned to this page the lights went out an hour early, and it doesn't seem that anyone is going to refuel the engine. So I'm writing by candlelight. Normally, the bugs let up at 9:00 p.m., but it was warmer today and so they cascade over me—not biting, but crawling over my face and hands and getting down the front of my open shirt. The chief nuisance is a little green rascal, streamlined 1/4 inch, with two tiny dots on either wing and a black tail tip to the wings which covers the body. There are hundreds of them. (I'm giving up for the night!)

The next morning –

I fooled the rascals by getting a goodnight's sleep—it is very cool these nights. The sky was not as clear last night. (I often spend ten minutes before retiring just gazing up.)

Pretty little girl, I send all of my love and devotion.

        Kisses, sweetness,

        Dick

November 12, 1944

My Darling Husband,

I am full of longing for you this Sunday night. I say over and over to myself, "Why do there have to be wars? The world seems very cruel." Then I realize that there are many less fortunate than I.

For example, I talked with Gyneth Downing this afternoon. She had a letter from her husband who is temporarily in a hospital. When he arrived there from Germany, he hadn't had his clothes off for 146 days. That doesn't seem possible. At any rate, she knows he is in combat most of the time.

I apparently was very tired this morning because I didn't awaken until eleven o'clock.

After dinner, I made my usual Sunday trip to the post office and picked up the Sunday paper, then home to read.

Mother wanted to drive around and look at a couple houses advertised, which we did, then we stopped at Deitsche's for ice cream.

This evening I cleaned off my desk, filed your latest letters after rereading them and made some clippings to send to you—funnies and sports. I enjoy doing something for you, Dearest, and I don't think I better depend on anyone else.

Mary Ellen asked us to keep Tommy a couple of hours for her Tuesday evening. Mother is going away so I expect I'll be kept busy. I think he is a little pill. I suppose most of them are at that age (20 months). She has heard from Warren (after 4 weeks) and thinks he is in France. As I think I told you, she is living in a furnished house on Morse Street.

Your folks invited me to go to Toledo with them today but I turned them down to sleep and be lazy. This is my week to drive, which gets me up ten or fifteen minutes earlier in the morning.

My darling, I miss you so very, very much, and pray that you will be home soon. Take care of yourself, my Precious!
Goodnight, Sweetest One,
Caresses and kisses,
Ritter

India
November 12, 1944

Dearest:

I forgot to mention yesterday that I received a letter from Berengarten in which he mentioned you several times and wished to be remembered to you. You see, dearest, even here you and I are inseparable, for I take you with me everywhere—on my desk, in my conversation, and in my heart. I am building you the best shrine that I know how.

Today brought your clippings of the 31st, which were more than welcome, and another letter from poor Elva who wants to be a Wac—what a shock that would give her.

Someone just put the "Song of India" on the phonograph. What cozy memories that recalls.

Tonight we saw a good movie program: Army films of the landings at Areua and Cape Gloucester on New Britain and "Summer Storm." The Army films were masterpieces of realism, and didn't hide anything from us. As for Lana Turner, George Sanders, and Edward Everett Horton in "Summer Storm," from the novel by Chekhov, I was simply bowled over. I have seen it before, but then did not appreciate the country scenes, the wedding ceremony, and the restaurant music. It is a morbid tale of a man enmeshed in an evil, but beautiful, woman's toils, and the sorry but inevitable end to which his weakness and her strength brings them. There is an atmosphere about seeing a movie out under the stars which I'm sure I'll miss when I return to civilization.

Today was another lovely Sunday that I put in that office, adequately busy all day long. Lt. Laughbon finally thought that I had gone too far in a statement I made in my letter to Jack Pockrasa, and I agreed with him. You'll find part of Jack's letter cut out—I did it myself! (Under his supervision.)

Gill, Wertheim, and Gutwold are going on leave to Calcutta tomorrow, but I hesitate to send for anything for Helen with them. Only the utmost skill can be used in buying a gift in India for a dollar. Most decent things start at 5 or 6 rupees and go on up. It wouldn't do any harm, I suspect, to pay a little more, though, for we have had quite a bit of the Bierys' hospitality. By the way, if you visit them, it wouldn't do any harm to pick up my books if you get a chance. The Bairs have some of them, too. There's a list in the address box.

Did I write that one of our boys got some packages mailed in July (6)? I think they are going to make a special effort on Xmas packages, but if they don't hurry, I can't possibly see how they will make it. Their system, once the packages reach this country, is stupid. The central mailing agency ought to check the addresses, but I'm sure that they don't, for they let the packages and mail traipse all over India before it reaches here.

There's one more letter left on this kind of paper, senseless, then fini! Oh, my pet, a very special kiss to you tonight. Goodnight, precious!

> Love you,
> Dick

November 13, 1944

My Darling,

Today I received your November 4th air mail. Naturally, I'm always overjoyed at getting a letter from you but today's sounded formal. Of course the fact that it was typewritten and short may have had something to do with it. I think possibly you had a gripe which you can't tell me. Open up if you can, Dearest.

You asked about Mary Ellen seeing Warren at the APO. They had a friend in the city where he called. She went there and he got a couple of overnight passes. After promising to keep Tommy for her, I see a native Indian (Hindu) is giving a lecture. I'd like to go, so Mother may stay at home.

I've almost given up trying to talk to your mother over the phone. At least five times out of six, the line is busy. After trying two or three times, I usually give up. Who'd have thought she'd have changed so much? I think her bird-raising friends talk to her often.

I gave Robert a first grade library book. He now can read the first page (one paragraph) smoothly. I taught him "was," "not," "brave," "very," "little," "Indian," and "boy." It remains to be seen whether he can recognize them in other contexts. He only knows a few words such as "he," "a," and "and." He acts proud of his accomplishment but still refuses to talk other than attempt to read.

Of course I should give him special attention in other things as well (numbers etc.) but just don't have the time. If I teach him a little reading, I will have done more than my predecessors.

I liked the little note written about you, for a paper I presume. B. A. Spy, I believe it was.

We had a discussion about Roosevelt's speech this evening. Mrs. Somers, Mother and I all agreed that it was not clear but sounded mushy in the last two news reels we've heard. At first I thought it was probably in its reproduction but since we've all noticed it.

Darling, here it is 12 o'clock again, still can't make it be eleven. It will be fun coaxing you to bed, and you don't dare object.

> Goodnight my Sweetheart,
> Hugs and kisses,
> Reva

November 14, 1944

My Darling,

No letters from you today, thus no bright spot in my day.

Mary Ellen came over with Tommy for dinner and Mother said she would stay at home and keep him while I went along to a class with her. The class is an 18-week course given by Dr. Herwig, Professor of history at Findlay College and Mr. Humphrey in Contemporary Problems, including postwar problems.

Dr. Herwig spoke tonight on the "Readjustment of the Home and Society." I thought her talk very good. She said that this is a changing era—the future is here and we can't go back to what we think of as normalcy. She sounded rather pessimistic on the length of the war. She of course placed emphasis on the family unit and mentioned some of the things it has to cope with at the present time.

I'm debating whether or not to take the class for credit. Next week she will outline the work for those who take it for credit and of course there will be a fee in that case.

My digestive system wasn't what it should be today, so I thought I'd come home—but I felt all right, so we stayed to hear Dr. Singh's lecture. It was good, but not as good as I expected. His tone of voice was the same all the time and that detracted. He spoke mostly of Gandhi and Nehru, making their point of view more logical. Of course he was anti-British but only moderately so. He said the educated people realize they are better off than if they were dominated by the Japanese or Nazis, but they aren't much concerned with the war.

He said the British would be better off to bargain with Gandhi and Nehru than possibly leaders who follow them. He also spoke of Churchill as a stumbling block in the Indian problem. I don't suppose you dare comment about this. I'll hear about it later, my Sweet.

We had a thunder shower with a lot of lightning about an hour ago, so you know it is rather warm. The patter of rain has stopped. I was in hopes it would continue until I was ready to go to sleep.

It's time, my Love, to say good-night.

All of my love and devotion,
Your Ritter

November 15, 1944

My Darling,

Another day without mail. I should be used to two in a row, then nothing, but I always hope.

I was so disgusted Monday. I had clippings ready to send and since Mother was going downtown, I asked her to mail the letter at the new sub P.O. since I wasn't sure about the amount of postage. The new sub is in the old Jackson block. As I thought, it was 6 cents and the man suggested that she send it air mail. She said she *questioned him, but at any rate, you know what happened. I got it back on Tuesday with postage due.*

I stopped in at your folks this evening. Your dad gave me a mystery to send to you.

Evelyn went to Lima (the Dr. says she needn't come back for eight weeks). Your mother, Gay and Bonnie went along.

We had a magnificent electrical storm last night. You know, you taught me to watch and appreciate the lightning. Of course, I want it in the distance. Some neighbors had both their house and barn set on fire by lightning this summer. The barn burned to the ground.

It rained quite hard during the night and some during the forenoon. Then the sun came out, and it was a very beautiful afternoon. It is getting cooler this evening.

Miriam writes that they are having trouble in Canada. I guess besides having a big coal bill, they just can't keep the house warm. They don't have storm windows and doors. I bet they miss their snug apartment.

We could keep warm, couldn't we, Dearest? I hope I remember when you get home that the petty little things don't matter.

I wish someone would encourage me on the length of the war. Everyone talks pessimistically now.

I got a letter from Leona yesterday—She wrote this joke: Have you heard of the longest donkey? His head is in England, and his ass is in Washington!

What a note to say goodnight on. Just remember, My Darling, how much I love you.

> *Lots of hugs and kisses,*
> *Reva*

November 16, 1944

Dearest,

My privacy is about as much as a canary's. I had thought of going over to your folks since I haven't stayed all night there, but of course I knew I couldn't sleep in the morning, and I may be able to do that here. We get tomorrow off, you know, because it's the first day of hunting—I guess our Superintendent is fond of the sport.

You asked about writing to Robert. I think it's a good idea. There is this difficulty, however. He couldn't read it, but I might suggest helping him read it. I'm trying to get him to read some-thing well, but I'm afraid he's memorizing it. He doesn't seem to know the words out of their context. He should be tutored, of course. Not having much time is not only a handicap as far as get-ting much across but a handicap when it comes to try to draw any-thing out of him.

We learned about the various types of homes (tepee, cliff dwell-ings, Chinese boats, log cabins etc.) in reading. I let them select any one they wished to draw. Then we voted on the best one of each group and I put them on the board. Only three people chose to draw the Arabian tent, Robert being one of them. I thought his was about the best and the children almost unanimously voted his the best. I really think they too were trying to encourage him, and you could tell he was pleased. One time when he was out of the room, I told them if he ever talked out loud during school, not to act shocked. One volunteered that he knew Robert's trouble. I asked him what, and he said the children used to make fun of him. He doesn't talk very plainly. But he will read quietly to me now with other children in the room.

I like the four pictures you sent, even though some were too light or dark. One shows your pipe up so plainly. I believe it was the one I mailed to you from Chicago. You do look thin, My Dearest—watch that. It seems so strange to think of you so far away, in a land of ox carts.

It will soon be over six months since I saw you—a long, long time, My Sweetheart. If the waiting were just behind us.

Darling, do you think that pencil and pen I sent you are lost? And the razor? I should at least be able to collect for it.

I love you with all my heart, Dearest One.

> *Goodnight, Precious,*
> *Hugs and kisses,*
> *Reva*

India
December 3, 1944

Dearest Ritter:

Denton, Phipps, Hosenkamp, a new S/sgt., and John and I are assembled in our compartment. Sturke just brought in some corned beef, and John brought out his gin. So my efforts at writing are going forward under handicap.

We just came from the movie where once again I got to see "The Mask of Demetrius," and by this time I am tired of seeing it. I recommend its excellence, but there is a limit to the number of grim, concentrated pictures of that sort which one cares to see in this theatre of war.

The boys are beginning to drift out of the basha, and this is good, for today I am not feeling any too well. I awakened with a headache, induced by too much close scrutiny of tiny figures. So this afternoon I took a couple of aspirins and rested for several hours. It was marvelous, and I had a good notion to stay in bed the rest of the afternoon. Nevertheless I did return, via the MP jeep, and didn't do much but stare at the grease board.

There's too darn much foolishness going on in here; I'll let this go until tomorrow morning.

And so now it is the next morning. One of those singularly lovely days that winter brings to this part of the world. The sun never gets very high on the horizon, but it doesn't have to in order to keep the atmosphere reasonably warm. Since we have no running hot and cold water, well, we just wash in cold. Soap lasts forever.

As I may have mentioned a day or so ago, the meals have not been to my satisfaction, so Saturday night I proposed to John that we go check the 82nd Snack Bar.

Sure enough we found a cheese omelet and piping hot cocoa. I ate two of the luscious dishes, tastefully primed with catsup, before my suddenly ravenous appetite was satisfied.

93

I suppose you have been wondering how much of the gin I had? Well, when I first tried to drink it I had to cough out the swallow I had taken. Later, I managed to get one drink, a faint gurgle, down; but really, I'm not cut out for that sort of thing. Too bad, too.

Today I shall do better when I write my daily letter, of that you may be sure.

> Ever in love, my darling, with you,
> Dick

December 5, 1944

My Dearest,

It is warm enough to write in bed again tonight—And again tonight my heart sank when I came in the house and found no mail. I thought surely there would be some today.

Your mother said Gay got a letter last week dated the 18th of November so that helped to convince me that the difficulty is due to transportation. I've just been taking it for granted that I'd get letters at least two or three times a week, but such are the trials of a soldier and his wife, I guess. I realize more than ever how one letter keeps me going until the next.

Mother and I went out to Findlay College to the class again. The general conclusion tonight was that we will have to maintain peace with force (a community army).

This wasn't discussed but I'm wondering if our present firm policy of not only hands off Europe for ourselves but for our allies is a good thing. Mary Emma fears England and Helen Reimund fears Russia.

Mary Emma was happy tonight. Nord is being sent to a Navy Rehabilitation school for training and then of course will be assigned in that work. She said of course she feared it might keep him in longer after the war is over.

The state inspector, a Mr. Garrison, visited Mt. Blanchard today. He observed the High School classes but only stepped in and looked around the grades. Everyone knew he was coming. I don't see much to it, one certainly couldn't give much constructive criticism visiting a whole school in half a day.

Robert refused to read for the children as he promised. I guess I'll have to work on something in our reader and see if that works any better. The stubborn little rascal!

I'm sending some funnies tomorrow.

Did I tell you Helen Reimund has a divorce from that boy that she married who was much younger than she? Now she is going with a former classmate of hers who teaches Greek and some other subjects at the College.

I keep vowing every morning when I have to get up that I'm going to bed earlier but here it is 12 o'clock again. What I should do is listen to the 10 o'clock news and then go to bed and write to you.

Goodnight, now, my Beloved. How much I long for you, and how very, very much I love you!

Tender embraces and kisses,
Your Ritter

December 6, 1944

Dearest Dick,

Ah finally—two letters today, November 18th and 19th. Needless to say, my spirits were raised considerably. Your letter taking me to town was most interesting and certainly next best to being there in person.

The women have a prayer meeting every Thursday afternoon in someone's home and some of them always have letters from their sons to read. Mother asked if she might take that one. I told her I was sure you wouldn't mind and gave it to her. In fact, I've sometimes been tempted to send your especially descriptive letters to the Republican-Courier but always decided against it without your consent.

I'm glad that you are getting a gas burner but now that I think over the things in your boxes I fear there won't be much useful in that way. I'm going to try to fix up some 8 ounce packages of coffee. By the way, how about a request anticipating your needs?

Only a few more days until your birthday. Naturally you have all my good wishes and my very strong wish that you are home next year and we can really celebrate. I hope you like your pipe and think of me with every puff. Possessive wife?

I got a letter from Helen Avery today, mainly about the children. Robin is wearing a truss and David has to have his tonsils out.

I didn't accomplish anything this eve. Of course before dinner, I enjoyed your letters but afterward for the first time lay down on the davenport and took a nap. I heard the Norths, Kay Kayser, and then the news at 10, which doesn't sound encouraging. Did a little hectographing then here I am in bed.

Kaltanborne, speaking from Paris tonight, said the experts don't think Germany will be knocked out before May. And it seems we are paying and paying in men as well as material. I'm sure the casualty list must be awfully high, just judging by our papers. If only Japan wouldn't decide on a last ditch stand.

My Dearest, it is time to say Goodnight. Take care of yourself, my Beloved.

> *Sweet Dreams,*
> *Devotedly,*
> *Ritter*

India
December 8, 1944

Dearest Sweetheart:

Well, here I am somewhere else again for a change. Just where I am I cannot write now, but I am very definitely here. I ran into a post in the dark a moment ago, and I found that as a substance I still react soundly.

Some of what I set out to do has been accomplished, but no tobacco! Here's the sad tale of the weed: Wednesday night the big Px [Post Exchange], servicing this whole area, was closed for a week for renovation. Tonight the local Px was closed. Tsk.

Maybe by the time I get back to the 12th they will have some welcome packages for me?

My adventures today have been exciting to me—though I suspect an experienced flier wouldn't have been very much impressed. I've had my first ride in a bomber. I sat right beside a loaded waist gun and wide-eyed watched the swirling patches of earth from the gun window and from the floor, through which another window had been placed.

Complicated radio and attach armament left us little room, and the bomb bay went off the front of the plane from the waist.

These medium bombers have little wing expanse in proportion to their weight, and consequently have to go with terrific speed to get into the air. They come down the same way, too. Since one's conception of speed can be gotten only from comparison of the moving object with one that is not moving—to me, as a spectator in the afore-said moving object—the takeoff was (I hate puns!) a moving experience.

The two motions each appear at least twice the size of those employed in cargo ships and make a relatively more severe sound vibration within the plane. I was so concerned with talking myself into a reasonable attitude that I didn't notice, however. To be very frank, I think that I'm afraid—it isn't just excitement that thrills me—it's downright cold chills. I quote statistics to myself. Dozens of planes, most of them with full bomb loads, take off the field every day; and there are weeks on end with no irregularities. Aha! my yellow streak takes over—but there are some minus figures in the calculation after all. And so it goes, I carry that darned two-edged debate on until sheer weariness forces me to drop it, or I get my feet on the ground again.

I'm afraid I'm not an earthquaker, but an earthworm.

There were six of us in the waist and rear of the bomber, one of whom was Capt. Kier. The Capt. is a very outspoken man, who, while waiting for some minor repair work to be done on the cowling of the plane before we left at 10:00 a.m., spoke as follows to the 1st Lt. pilot, "I hate these 25's [B-25 medium bomber]. I wish I could have taken some other plane."

The pilot's eyes narrowed as he replied, "Well, if you don't like them, why don't you walk."

Capt. Kier looked at the man in the leather jacket a moment, then, "Damned if I wouldn't have if it hadn't been so far."

Fine stuff, indeed, with me already shivering out there in the warm sun of a very beautiful day.

Just as I climbed into the plane I heard the pilot tell his co-pilot that maybe they could show the Captain a thing or two. Brrrrrr.

And they did.

The trouble was, I was along, too, and whether I would or no, I had to be shown, and I didn't really want to see at all.

We shot like an arrow into the blue of the Indian winter morning. I watched the earth recede with great satisfaction. When in a bomber, the higher you are, the better. I heard a vast sigh of relief and settled back—just 30 minutes—and presto! we would be there. Then, without the slightest warning, the compact, heavy ship nosed over and darted toward the ground. The speed was so great that we were thrust sideways at a 45 degree angle. Our faces were immobile, though one corporal cracked his lips trying to grin reassuringly (not this corporal!) but I just stared, transfixed, at the approaching checkered fields. As the very earth met me through the window in the floor of the plane, we leveled off (naturally, you know that had happened or I would hardly feel like writing this) about 30 feet above the railroad track. For several miles we roared along practically sliding on the tracks, then shot into a climb that took us high in the sky.

Again I relaxed with a vaster sigh than before.

But all was not over.

I observed one of the fellows reach for the earphones with an expression of real concern on his face. Then he and another soldier started making signs to one another.

There was no point in trying to talk, not a sound could be heard above the roar of the motors. There was a violent jolt from the left motor, and it quit dead.

The sergeant next to me grabbed a parachute and tore at its clips. All of us did likewise, though I had never had one on, and didn't know the first principle of getting into it.

At that moment I decided to learn fast. Damned if I didn't, too, for I was the first completely buckled up, beating Capt. Kier in the maneuver. Not one single thing flashed through my mind as I grappled with the 'chute except the numbed and pointless query, "Why did I take this trip today?"

Well, as you have probably guessed, it was all a joke, and the pilot had deliberately shut off the left motor. We came shouting onto the landing strip of this field in great shape a few minutes later. I say in great shape advisedly, for I never want to be in the same condition again.

Fate, in the form of a witless ambulance driver, intervened to make me miss the return trip, so tomorrow I'll go back with a different pilot. One whom, I trust, hasn't been needled by a superior officer just prior to the takeoff.

We waited two hours for transportation to the station hospital, and made it just in time to miss the regular noon meal. However, the mess Sgt. had an Indian waiter fix me up a plate of salmon salad, green beans, scalloped corn, apple sauce, sliced pineapples, and hot coffee and I made out very well.

The x-ray of the chest, the only item in a physical checkup which can't be done at our field, took just a moment, then I caught a ride back to the field and the Service Sgt. with whom I am spending the night. I chatted with the 1st Sgt. (Kelly from Steubenville) and a very fat corporal in shorts for an hour, then set up my cot and mosquito netting and dozed until 5:00.

The meals here are served by Indian waiters, but tonight's was a washout, any way you look at it. Viennese wieners and stewed turnips. Ugh! So I ate two and a half slices of bread, drank some coffee, and filled my hands with hard candy from the jar in the center of the table.

I wandered over to the movie area—it is a simulated quarter bowl, with an open air stage, and watched a half-dozen shorts with interest. Then, Benny Fields and Gladys George in "Minstrel Man" flashed on the screen and I stood amazed (as I had when at Dum-Dum a month or so ago) at this horrible caricature of a motion picture. Hollywood could not have been serious when they made this picture. It is the worst I think I have ever seen. Yet, Gladys George once won an Academy Award, and Fields is from a famous family of actors. It must have been the picture I smelled.

My hands are just beginning to thaw out, for it gets chilly in the evenings here. I'm writing this from a desk here in the Headquarters building.

This morning, when I came off C2, Lt. Frankel kindly permitted me to take the jeep back to the area, to enable me to make the ship in time.

And, so, pet, that just about winds up the description of today's activities. I was disappointed in one other matter, aside from the tobacco, for I had assumed at the hospital that I could get my teeth cleaned. No dice. I'll have to go to the General Hospital for that.

Now, I'll try to sleep between woolen blankets, without benefit of sheets. Perhaps thinking of you will make that a comfortable bed—in truth, darling, today's journey, as with all my moves, was made with you uppermost in my mind.

So much of love to you, dearest,
Dick

India
December 14, 1944

Dearest:

Fol de rol in the compartment again—with Sturke yelling "Chop Chop" in the window, Hosenkamp making rude sounds through the partition, Phipps and Wells in the compartment with John insulting them freely—and I sit hunched up in the cold evening air, laughing at the show and making preparations to write to you, even as now.

Today I have felt so much better that the working hours flowed smoothly and rapidly. I brought my grease board up to date and then tackled some odds and ends that required cleaning up.

A huge truckload of packages came in but none for me. However, Windham got one, and since his came to me, I had the pleasure of opening it. Shaving materials, toothbrush, tooth powder and paste, 3 games, foot powder, 3 packs of cough drops, candy, two packs of cigarettes, and some magazines made up the parcel. Of all that stuff I kept the foot powder, the cough drops, the toothbrush and powder, some of the candy, and the magazines. The rest I distributed around fully—but mainly to fellows whom I thought might not get packages of their own.

Tonight there was a show in this area, but since John and I saw it last night, we drove in the truck (utilities truck) to headquarters. I spent much of the evening laying out a sane accounting system for checking of your letters and packages to me, my acknowledgment, my letters to you, and your acknowledgment. I think I've finally worked it out. Incidentally, counting tobacco you have notified me of, and all Xmas parcels of which I know, I have 39 pack-ages on the way—some 22 of them being from you. Oh, my darling, there's a loving and provident wife, indeed!

One of the most desired packages on my part is my un-derwear—so that I can put on my OD's [olive drabs]. I am actually getting real chilly in the mornings and late eve-nings, and I'm afraid I'll not be able to shake this cold un-til I warm up a bit. They tell me, though, that the weather breaks and gets warmer in January—the sun seems very low in the south, but still gets quite warm at noon, pro-vided you stand in its rays.

Well, sweetheart mine, I'll ring off again, dreaming of my darling as always.

> Goodnight, precious,
> Dick

Long P.S.

Capt. Seeger has been uttering scathing remarks about men who wear glasses and fail to carry their prescriptions with them. Specifically he was referring to Lt. Laughbon, but the indictment touches me, too. So, my little darling, will you or Dad go to Barchent and get said prescription and post to me? I suppose he will be reasonable about it. In the case of men like myself, whose eyesight isn't bad, the Army won't furnish glasses, so we must have civilian sources make us new ones.

Will you check in the file to see if you got a V-mail from me dated October 21st?

You haven't reported it. It may be the letter you thought was missing on the 25th. I wrote two letters on the 21st—one airmail, the other V.

> Love,
> Dick

India
December 15, 1944

Dearest One:

Hello, darling, how are you ten days before Christmas, I wonder? I've been trying to guess when your vacation starts; since today is Friday, I suspect that school continues on through next week. No doubt your letters that are on the way—some of them should come this weekend—will tell me all about it.

Before I forget, will you see what you can do about securing Radio Tube #1-H5(G) for a Philco? T/Sgt. Ives said the (G) wasn't important, that 1-H5 would be sufficient. Do what you can—and if one isn't forthcoming, why the repaired one still works. Should you get a tube, send by the fastest route, ma cherie.

Today brought letters from Lou Herion and Tommy Joyce, the latter enclosing 3 rupees which he borrowed September 20th. Lou sounds very much in love with Fern, so I suspect that we were wrong in thinking there was a lack of affection there. At any rate, Lou is almost lovable in his letters—one surely couldn't guess his character—or rather, the other side of his character.

The mail brought Miriam's Christmas parcel—the one mailed September 15 which you have been inquiring about. I noticed that it had been rerouted several times and once hit an "Unknown." So I put it next to yours and will open them both Christmas eve.

Tonight, dearest, I returned to the office with Denton (John) and Kenyon (John) and wrote several letters— added to the four I wrote at noon and earlier in the evening that means that I am feeling better—much better.

We got in a large consignment of Px supplies, but no tobacco. However, I was able to buy all the fruit juice I wanted, so purchased a full case of 24 cans. Now I can guzzle it regularly for almost a month, already having 4 or 5 cans on hand. In addition I bought a case of Pabst Blue

Ribbon—which aids the conviviality of the atmosphere more than somewhat. There were 4 dinky cigars available for each man, but even a horse would have turned his nose at such hay. Capt. Seeger has a box of Robert Burns small cigars that he has kept open on the desk for us the last several days—they are much better.

I got in a game of poker at the Club this evening, but the lights kept going out.

Largely because I never had an opportunity to win a hand I lost Rs 14.[7] Tsk.

You will get this letter about Christmas, I presume. God grant we do not have to spend another apart, but if we do, precious one, the thought of you will give me courage to carry on. I hope only that I can prove worthy of your steadfast and unwavering love. I have always been in love with you, Reva, from the first May morning in 1930 when I became aware of you, but I never dreamed how all consuming, how complete, that love would eventually become. In the fullness of time is more than a phrase with us, my dearest wife, it is a fulfillment. When again circumstances permit us to be together how well and truly we can consummate that love. I rest content in the knowledge of you. Christmas this year will indeed be Christmas in my heart. All is not lost in this world. Its evil and folly cannot bury the spirits of people like us—we must and will have our way.

Goodnight, darling, goodnight.

All my love, ever,
Dick

P.S. 8:30 a.m.—the 16th—the mailroom boys had the November 17 (2 packages) tobacco waiting for me. Thanks!

India
December 24, 1944

Dearest One:

Tonight, Christmas eve, I have already opened my packages, the eager beaver that I am. I have excellent news for you, sweet, for today brought 6 packages to my desk — that's right, 6 packages—Santa Claus for sure!

Three were from you; really four, for one had Ruth's name on it—but yours inside.

One from Clete and one from the Church of God.

Two of your packages contained my OD's—shirt and trousers, the latter having some clippings enclosed. The third Reva (!) package contained nut tidbits, some socks, wash cloths, towels, handkerchiefs, and candy. The fourth may have had some of the welcome dry goods in it also; a September Journal, several wrapped small items, peanuts, and 2 cans—one of which contained cheese. You see, when I made the list at the office, I didn't unwrap any of them, just unpacked them and replaced the items in the six boxes in one large box so that I could carry it all.

The Church had a really lovely package, with several church papers enclosed and eleven gaily wrapped items. They sent such things as soap, candy, comb, handkerchief, etc.

Clete's package was the only wooden box which I got, and it was the only broken one. Nothing was smashed in, however, except the Mennen's powder—which had scented everything very nicely. His package included a Middleton Tobacco kit, a pack of Raleigh, popcorn, candy, a comb, and 2 Life Savers.

Your December 8 letter arrived today, as well as your clippings of December 2 and 6 and a package containing Old Mariner and Blue Boar Tobacco dated November 24.

In the distance I can hear Christmas carols. It will soon be time for the Christmas Service program to begin—so on with the Quiz. Will be back later.

Well, my darling, it is now 11:00 and the big program is over. Lt. Fox and I were the Hq. contestants, pitted against 4 officers and 4 enlisted men from the four squadrons. Lt. Seale, our Spc. Services officer, presided. Lt. Goodman, his assistant (who later offered to get me a job in New York schools), offered each contestant team a choice from an envelope, the class of question determined the specific question which Lt. Seale read.

Well, to cut a long story short, we came out second, missing 1 3/5 questions out of ten. The type I answered? Such questions as the world's largest artificial lake; the length of time it took Moses to reach the promised land (a trick question—he didn't reach it!). The questions I helped miss were 1/2 of what John Alden's wife's name was (Priscilla Mullins. Yeah! I know—I knew it, but couldn't think of it at the moment); the three gaits of a three-gaited horse (we got trot and canter, missed walk); and all of the quotation taken from the Cadet's prayer—since neither of us had ever heard of it.

Oh, yes, second prize was thirty rupees, which Lt. Fox and I divided. Later, as I sat with Capt. Seeger and Lt. Husak during the terrible movie, "Gambler's Choice," Lt. Husak answered my criticism by telling me that at least I had been paid 15 rupees to sit through the program.

Lt. Steegman figured in the presentation of medals and a trophy to the winning softball team, of which he is the pitcher. Though I was talking with Capt. Robinson, the chaplain, at the time, Steegman came up, put his arm around me, and gave me explicit directions on how to reach his basha to get some of his scotch. P.S. I didn't go.

After the movie, Kenyon, Jakinjin, Phipps, and I went to the Club, but a scene of disheveled revelry met our eyes—so we said hello to the boys who could still recognize us, and then wandered back to the basha.

The boys in the next compartment have just yelled out an invitation to come over and help them eat some

cheesed and buttered popcorn which they have just prepared. (15 mins. later) It really was good—indeed, we
contrive to keep reasonably happy in some fashion.

The lights went out just as I started the second half of
this letter—and so this is being scribbled by lantern light.
Kenyon went off to (high) mass (Xmas) down the road,
while I elected to finish this letter.

Merry Christmas!

It is now the next morning, for I stopped writing when
my pen ran out of ink. There has been so much to comment upon that I have had difficulty in remembering everything that I want to say.

I'm smoking the pipe Miriam and Ray got me, and I'm
saving the beautiful cherry-stain Weber of yours until later
in the day. You have all been so thoughtful and kind that I
am overwhelmed. Please thank everyone for me!

Dearest one, I had one of those confounded headaches
most of the day, but a nap at noon with the meal skipped
seems to have set me up fairly well.

I appreciate all of the stationery which you provided
me with—and thanks for Steinbeck, too.

I'm afraid that I had better draw this rather incoherent
letter to a close—so dearest Ritter, a thousand Merry
Christmases to you, my darling—and all my love,

     Ever,

     Dick

          India

    December 28, 1944

Dearest Girl:

Well, here I am having a chat with one of—nay, sahib,
with my favorite person again.

Good old CQ night is back with us—and what a time
for it to come. You recall some time ago I mentioned the
fact that a show came to the camp? One woman and a half
dozen men? Well, tonight, there's a big USO outfit in

camp, so filled with glamor and talent and equipment that it took three planes to get them here. There are five girls in the show, among other things, and where is good old Dick when all of this pulchritude is being exhibited? I'll tell you, he's safely ensconced at his desk at headquarters. HO HUM!

There's one good derivative from the ghastly business, however, and that is the fact that everyone is down at the 81st baseball area (where a special stage was constructed) and the phone hasn't rung once. No matter if it rings all night long, as it did the last time, I can't be any worse off than I was then. We have a lot of men due—and I'm definitely expecting them in the middle of the night. Another good feature about tonight's work is that Capt. Goodrake is the OD, and he's a very capable young officer, not to speak of his being a handsome young man, too. I'm pretty sure that no matter what comes up, when I try to awaken him for a decision he won't mutter, "Do what you like," and go back to sleep.

This afternoon Capt. Seeger got a candy-eating streak. He took a piece of everything offered him, was still hungry about 4:00, so wandered into Lt. Laughbon's office, returning with a large piece of sticky peanut brittle. He courteously offered me a piece of the messy looking concoction. I said, "No, thanks." Next he turned to Lt. Husak, who also "Nay, Sahibed" him. Rather meekly he approached Phipps' desk, but was rebuffed there. Looking rather disgruntled, he turned away with "Ah, the hell with it!" Coming as it did, so unexpectedly, it struck me as being very funny, and I started the laughter which was still going on when we broke it up at 5:00.

Our truck-bus driver, Harry Pearson, wrenched his ankle over Christmas, and now we have a new driver, who failed to show up at all this evening, so that I had to hitchhike with my bed bundle over my back and my hands full of mail. Harry got relieved just in time, though, for he had been getting harder and harder to get along with. His poor befuddled mind, operating on 0 wattage, was frustrated by the strain of constantly having to meet deadlines. His conscientious effort to do his work well was, I believe, the real reason for his disagreeableness.

Last night, after leaving the office, John and I had omelettes together, then I settled down to read the local (Findlay) papers. I hoped that I could out-wait everyone in the club, for I wanted to play your record, but I couldn't and had to give up just as the lights went out.

Of course, when the lights go out, so does the phonograph, which is operated by electricity.

However, I'll find some opportunity to play the record when I am the only one to hear it, if I have to abduct the player.

Well, darling sweetheart, I presume that I had better try to get off another thank you letter or two tonight. I lay my worship at your feet, my love, and seek only to hold your hand.*

> Ever yours in deepest devotion,
> Dick

*I doubt if you could hold me to that—but at the moment, just the comfort of your hand and presence would fulfill my life and make it complete.

> D.

> India
> December 29, 1944

Dearest Ritter:

Well, I was lucky last night, for no phone calls came through to disturb the tranquility of the night. Before retiring I had an opportunity to talk with Captain Greatrake for about 20 minutes. Among other things I mentioned how unusual his name was, and he confided to me that it aroused so much attention while he was in grade school that it almost gave him an inferiority complex. He went on to say that by the time he had reached high school, that he had ceased to be sensitive over it.

From all that I could gather, the USO show was a success, though each man reacted according to his nature. The girls came into our Mess Hall, a moment or so after I left last night, and ate with the boys. Most of those I talked with thought that made the officers angry, but that is an assumption—for I haven't talked with the officers about the matter. Nonetheless, after the show, and the actresses were making their last appearance in CBI so they put on an extra one for the lads, they disappeared in jeeps with officers—from the 83rd, I heard. Conjecture ran the full gamut of each speaker's imagination. Ha! You would be amazed at soldiers' camp. Frankly, I think the boys consider them a high class camp follower. (Note that I'm not giving an opinion, for I don't know. I'm merely recording what the fellows tell me.)

There are two views concerning the appearance of a white woman among men starved for feminine company. One is favorable in that it assumes that the morale of the men is raised. The other takes the opposite view, that such appearance is a disturbing factor, and actually makes the boys dissatisfied. I rather incline to the latter viewpoint myself, though I haven't any evidence that it makes much difference one way or another.

Definitely some kind of entertainment is needed, for if the fellows don't get it they are going to sit around and mope, or drink, or worse.

I personally think that a well-organized entertainment program would provide more opportunity for the boys to actively participate. You recall our visit with the Wallens to the barn just outside Delaware? That's the sort of thing I refer to. However, here lack of space and equipment are serious factors, though there is no real reason why space couldn't be found, and the equipment made by the men themselves. There just isn't anyone to engineer it, from what I can see. Special Services brought in two dart games, which got considerable play. Sturke and I have had a lot of fun at noon playing dart baseball, and we've provided entertainment for those watching our antics. But out of six darts only two are usable, and there is a very limited space in which to play.

Such innocent, but satisfying, pastimes could use up a lot of energy if there was someone charged with seeing that the equipment was kept up and room for the fellows to participate. A pinball machine would be an excellent idea, too, or something on that order. One of the difficulties encountered by Special Services is the rough usage given the radio, phonograph, and other equipment. I do not ever recall any orientation in such matters —and the boys get careless, and need to be reminded of their responsibilities to the other fellow.

Tsk. Such a way to begin and continue in a letter to the one you love best in the world.

Today was a day of leisure for me. I just got in under the wire for breakfast—and ate my fried eggs slowly, drank my fruit juice and coffee the same way. Then, not to upset my routine, I shaved, which thoroughly awakened me. I had brought back a flock of Sunday School papers and some *Newsweek*s and *Times*. I dragged out my easy chair, sat with my back to the sun, and read until 11:00.

At one I went for a haircut, returned, showered, and washed my hair. Read a little longer—watched the planes, both in the morning and afternoon, as they circled above the landing strip, and went to bed at 4:00. By 5:00 I was up again.

Tonight John and I got the truck, decided against looking up "Destination Tokyo" which is playing at one of the squadrons, and came to the office. There I promptly set up your portrait—which pleases me immensely. Sturke is CQ,

John is sitting at the Captain's desk, and the three of us have been chatting on and off all evening.

Sweetheart, old Sturke has been in here spinning a top which someone in the mail room gave him. He wants me to tell you about it. While throwing the thing he almost put out Kenyon's eye. He claims (S) that he is going into his third childhood, having given up all hope of marrying.

This interminable chatter must terminate, for it is 10:40 and John is anxious to go, so I'll say a fond good night, my precious one.

> Ever yours,
> Dick

December 30, 1944

My Darling,

I told you in a previous letter that Grandma was failing—She died at 6:15 this morning. According to Aunt Alma, she had little suffering. The funeral is at 2 o'clock Monday (New Year's Day) afternoon at Miles Funeral Home.

I know that it doesn't sound well for me to talk this way, but I know too that you are interested. Aunt Alma remains the boss to the last.

I sat in on the conference of decisions this morning since it took place in our living room. But after a few comments I decided the only way to get what you want is to pretend you want the other thing. Even Daddy did some complaining and felt bad that he wasn't called last night.

Our family purchased a $10 spray of carnations. They should be nice. They didn't get the casket but they did get a compromise. They wanted a mahogany but were glad to get the oak instead of a brocade one (the cheapest). I guess I better stop before I sound like an over the fence gossiper.

Your December 19th letter arrived today. Maybe some of these slow letters are coming by ship. I also got a nice letter from Kenny Bayless. He received the box Mother and I packed, his first. I still hadn't written him. I shall answer soon. I'll send you his letter when I do. He made me feel good by telling me how much you talked of me and how much you love me.

I drove downtown this eve to get some tobacco to have on hand to mail the first of the week. The drugstores close from Sunday noon to Tuesday. I stopped by your folks' and your mother invited me to supper. I accepted and after supper she read several of your letters I had along.

I saw "Heavenly Body" too and felt very much as you did about it. Just tonight I read about camouflage the movie stars use and they gave as an example: Hedy Lamar has artificial hips made in all of her dresses. So maybe the real Hedy doesn't even have ecstasy.

That reminds me, Bonnie has some pictures to send you, an especially good one of your folks and one of me in which I look like I'm pregnant. The scales don't say I'm gaining weight. I must need a new girdle. That is the picture I mentioned in which I have on my homemade hat. There isn't much hat!

I should carry a writing pad with me. I think of so many things during the day I want to tell you or ask and then feel when I'm writing at night I've forgotten half of them.

I'm so anxious to learn if you got any Christmas boxes before Xmas. You certainly ought to get my first ones. I sent some to you before sending that box to Kenny.

I almost forgot an important thing. September and October's bonds came today. I was on the brink of writing about them. I guess patience is the word.

It is after two o'clock. I must have stopped often between paragraphs to think about you and how much I miss you.

> *A big, big hug and kisses,*
> *Ritter*

December 30, 1944

2-Ritter

What an evening— . . . Jahnigen is a man after my heart. We started out by discussing some things which didn't please us in general and we ended up with the

113

damnedest haranguing (we were in agreement) that you ever heard. How I wish that I could transmit it to you, but I'm afraid that I'll have to keep it for my little notebook. So many folks have wanted me to write a book, that, contrary to my earlier views on the subject, that I am now seriously thinking about it. However, if I do start work on it, it will hardly be the jelly-fish stuff that I have been reading in the periodicals from the States. This will be a forthright statement of the picture from the little guy's viewpoint and he is the only fellow that really counts. Stupid, bull-headed, ignorant, profane, and uncouth, the little guy isn't the dope that a lot of people have taken him for, and all over the world there are a lot of paleskinned little guys who are beginning to see things in a new perspective.

Personally, one of the principal points of irksomeness is that I didn't want to get excited about anything at all, I just wanted to get back with you and live quietly ever after —but I am beginning to get hot under the collar . . . very hot under the collar. (I'm hoping that my sense of the ridiculous comes to my rescue.)

Well, darling one, New Year's will soon be here, and I'll soon begin my eighth month of overseas duty. You see, I just completed six the 29th, but between the 29th and 30th I finish another month, for we get credit for the month that we sailed from America in, and that was June. Of course, as things now are that doesn't mean much, for the boys are going into their 31st month overseas—those who are still with us of the original group. However, soon all the replacements will be in and everyone will be happy, except the fellows now approaching their 20th month. I just hope that the time is going as rapidly for you as it is for me—for I kept dreadfully busy all the time—and the days pass in swift succession.

You know that I can hardly wait to get back to you, don't you sweet? Chasing the hours and days past—even though it means chewing up my earthly days that much faster, is my sacrifice in that direction. Just don't languish yours out too much, my wife, but get out and among people and laugh (save your love) and enjoy yourself.

So, Ritter, another day is fast coming to an end—all my love goes out in ether waves to you—that you know.

> Goodnight, precious, your own,
> Love,
> Dick

December 31, 1944

My Darling,

Since it is 2:30 a.m., it is actually 1945. I suppose you have had your New Year's dinner and are back to work.

I went to the funeral home to see Grandma and then to Mary Ellen's. She lives on Tiffin Ave. Since it is slippery, I hated to leave the car parked in front, so I drove around on the side street. (She lives on the corner.) There is an incline there which forms a little ditch.

To get to the point, I got stuck. Just then, a boy came along. By rocking the car and him pushing I started forward but the incline caused the car to slip. The front wheels were on the road and the back wheels were in the little ditch. I thought I was in trouble but Mary Ellen brought out a snow shovel and little piece of a rug. The boy shoveled out in front of the back wheels, put the rug down and I was out.

I decided after that I'd take my chances on the Main Street. I try to keep the car in most of the time and if I'm gone for the eve. Daddy puts it away when I get home. But on eves like this, when he is in bed, I leave it out because I don't want to fool around in the alley at night.

We went to the 9 o'clock show and saw Jean [sic] Tierney in "Laura," a mystery. I thought it was a pretty good one. I picked the right suspect but serious doubts kept arising in my mind.

Then we went back to Mary Ellen's and she had a regular meal for us. At twelve, we drank a toast (apple juice) to our husbands' quick homecoming. When army wives get together, the conversation constantly comes back to our husbands and the war. I'm sure that was four fifths of the conversation.

Vera's husband is in Italy and Betty's and Mary Ellen's husbands on the Western front.

Unless it does a lot of melting tomorrow, I doubt if we can have school Tuesday. We still had quite a lot of snow and I believe it snowed a couple inches tonight. It is very pretty out. The snow stuck to the trees like the night we walked from Habels' to Lanes', where we'd park our car.

During most of this snow, it has been pretty out because it has stayed cold but today it was warm enough that it was awfully sloppy. It must be thawing a little now, though, because I hear it dropping from the icicles on the house.

Goodnight, My Darling,

(Wasn't it nice that I got your birthday wish to me in yesterday's letter?)

And now to a happier New Year,

> *All my love and devotion,*
> *Your Ritter*

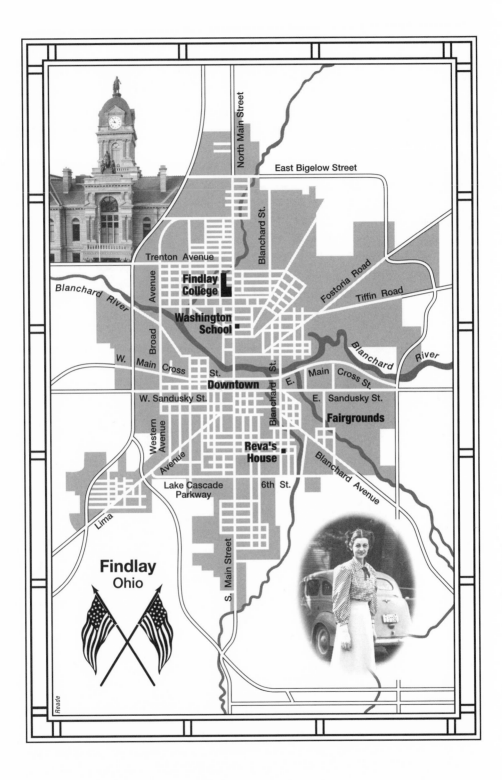

North Main Street

East Bigelow Street

Blanchard St.

Trenton Avenue

Blanchard River

Fostoria Road

Tiffin Road

Findlay College

Avenue

Washington School

Broad

Blanchard St.

Blanchard

River

W.

Main

Cross

St.

E.

Main

Cross St.

Downtown

W. Sandusky St.

Blanchard St.

E. Sandusky St.

Fairgrounds

Western

Avenue

Avenue

Reva's House

Lake Cascade Parkway

6th St.

Blanchard Avenue

Lima

Findlay
Ohio

S. Main Street

Reade

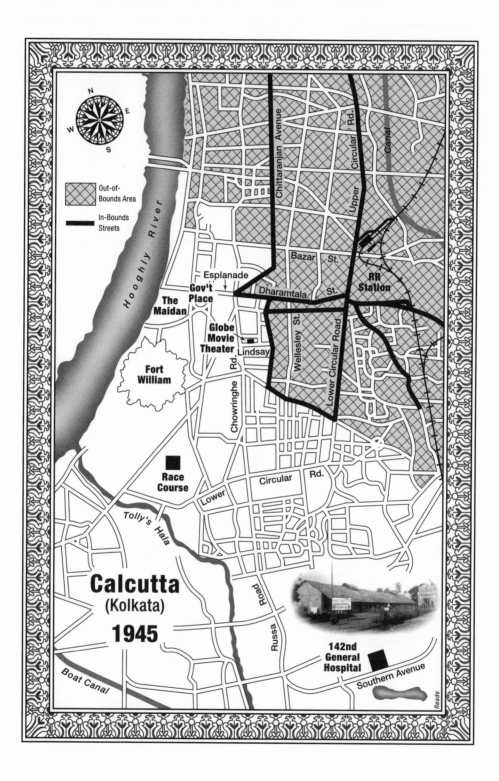

Calcutta (Kolkata) 1945

The Taj Mahal in Agra

Part Two

1945: Serving in India

Sir Winston Churchill said it couldn't be done, but before World War II ended, Allied forces connected the Burma and Ledo Roads, creating a supply route from India across Burma to China. On January 12, 1945, a 113-vehicle convoy —headed by Brigadier General Pick—traveled on the Ledo Road from Ledo, India through Burma to Kunming, China. The convoy crossed several rivers by ferry, climbed steep grades, was held up for as many as three days while Chinese troops drove away lingering Japanese, and took nearly a month to travel eleven hundred miles.[1] However, arrive it did, on February 4, 1945, the first of thousands of vehicles that would carry tons of vital supplies that couldn't be flown in to China before the war ended.

Conditions were intensely challenging. The Japanese killed over 130 of the engineers who worked on the Ledo Road. Construction accidents, crashes of supply planes, diseases and drownings took other Allied lives. The cost of the road was said to be "a man a mile," and the mission took twenty-eight thousand engineers and thirty-five thousand native workers.

Perhaps most wretched were enemy sieges that took place during the monsoon season. In reviewing the CBI theater, we read accounts such as the following:

> On one occasion Japanese soldiers dressed in Chinese uniforms beckoned to a company of replacement infantrymen. The Americans walked right up to the Japanese and were cut down with machine guns. Fifty of the replacements became mental cases. Some quit taking their mepracine tablets[2] in order to get malaria or deliberately wounded themselves—shooting off toes—to escape combat.[3]

The ATC, beginning in December 1942, started flying supplies to China when the Burma Road was closed. By the end of 1943, the ATC had carried 12,641 tons of supplies; in the month of August 1944, 34,641 tons were delivered. The total of ATC deliveries from December 1942 until V-J day was 721,700 tons.

In India, one country away from Burma, Richard may not have been fully aware of the overall drama. According to many CBI veterans, as they played their individual roles in the war, they were not necessarily informed of the bigger picture. Whatever the case, Richard's 1945 letters barely mention the Ledo Road. Nonetheless, like Merrill's Marauders who were carving out the Ledo Road, Richard was plagued by insects and in his February 9, 1945 letter, joked about them. The months wear on and Richard's mood becomes one of resignation and ennui. He fills the page with accounts of poker games and "mini reviews" of nightly movies shown by the army to entertain the troops. He describes the men's reaction when a movie fails to appear. While he tries to find humor in the situation, it is clear that he is in the doldrums about his position in the Army. As depicted throughout the early 1945 letters, all the men relied on movies and poker games for entertainment. Richard was not alone in his moodiness. No doubt, many felt as he did that they might better serve their country if they were fighting real battles.

The spring of 1945 finds Richard feeling listless. He worries that he might be coming down with dengue fever,[4] and he finds India's weather unusually oppressive. His ennui deepens as time goes by. The only action seems to be that of the calendars rattling in the spring winds. The men perform various missions and maneuvers, leading to Richard's speculation that Allied forces will soon be moving nearer to Rangoon, Burma. Conjecture and rumor abound. It does not help morale that no one knows anything for sure.

Meanwhile, Reva keeps Richard apprised of events in America. In her letter of April 12, she writes about the death of President Roosevelt. At the same time monumental events were happening on the home front, a major change occurred for her husband. At last realizing that they could utilize Richard's expertise in psychological counseling, the army commissioned him a Second Lieutenant.

Richard's buddies celebrate his promotion at the officer's club. This time, Richard treats the entire gang to drinks. Alcohol seems to have been the all-purpose medication, serving to treat both doldrums and celebration. Although he joined in the drinking, there is no evidence that Richard imbibed heavily. Nor is there the slightest evidence that he participated in mixed company dances or dating. He often reassures Reva on this point. After the war, Richard rarely touched liquor.

After his commission, Richard's assignment to the neuropsychiatric ward of the 142nd General Hospital in Calcutta followed quickly. Lieutenant Beard's routine included studying case histories and interviewing, as well as leading therapy groups. Although he occasionally treats interesting cases, Richard laments the slowness of time. Even though his talents as a counselor are now being used, it is not enough to make Richard like his situation. The crowded activities of the day, he observes, serve only to hasten the seeming eternity until he and Reva will be reunited.

The tone and content of Richard's summer 1945 letters are more upbeat than they were during spring. In addition to ongoing commentary on the entertainment movies, Richard shares some of his cases with Reva. He sprinkles his missives with pep talks. Though addressed to Reva, his cheery paragraphs seem also to buoy up their author.

In the face of war, however, the good moods never last very long. In early August, Richard focuses a letter on the dropping of the atomic bomb. He describes an impending sense of doom. Even winning poker hands fail to boost his spirits. Though the war is ending, he fears that the army will hold him in India indefinitely.

The surrender of Japan is announced to the staff of the 142nd General Hospital at 8 a.m., August 15. Richard's letter that day conveys to Reva his excitement at the news and the surprising reaction of his patients. Mental fatigue and melancholy characterize later August letters: clearly, his charges are wearing him down. Since illness carries a priority, the neuropsychiatric patients parade into his office with ever more imaginative illnesses.

Despite an optimistic beginning to September, it turns out to be a downhill month for Richard. His weariness with army life deepens. His roommate Gus, often drinking to excess, quits speaking to him. On September 10, Vienna sausages are the main course at supper. Richard, nauseated at the sight, likens them to "earthworms." Only by gazing at Reva's portrait is he able to refrain from starting on "the two quarts of good whiskey in the closet." Richard's letter of September 18 complains of the scorching heat and unpredictable downpours of Calcutta.

Even good times shared with co-workers don't help. Richard reaches a new low. The weather remains gloomy. He gently chides Reva for her reminders of how much she misses him; they darken an already bleak mood. He wards off sadness, fighting himself as never before. Using his gold wedding band as a symbol, Richard fortifies himself with uplifting thoughts of his and Reva's love.

In late October, during more gloomy weather, men are gradually being shipped out. To his chagrin, Richard is not among them. On October 23, Richard's "worst day of psychiatric experience," he recounts the emotional warpath of a patient who accidentally ran over a Hindu boy. As this patient is being restrained, Richard receives a call about a patient discharged a week earlier who was brought in during the night and might be dying. Before leaving the ward after visiting this patient, he is taken by a colleague to see yet another far-gone case. As if to erase the horror of seeing men driven to madness, he focuses his next few letters on the natural beauty of India and recalling romantic milestones with Reva.

His October 24 and 31 letters reflect his despair and en-
suing lethargy over not being sent home. He apologizes to
Reva that so little changes that he can barely find anything
about which to write.

Less than two weeks later, there is much to report, all of
it macabre. In his letter of November 10, written while he is
the O.D. (acting officer of the day), Richard relates a deadly
stabbing. The same day, he recounts, the corpse of a man
who had been listed AWOL is discovered in the latrine of
Ward 53, which had been closed for a week. Obviously, not
only Richard but everyone at the 142nd General Hospital
was ready to "quit India."

Barracks of the 142nd General Hospital. Under the supervision of
Lt. Colonel D. B. Peterson, MC, Chief of the Psychiatric Section, the
142nd was known for success in psychological rehabilitation. Part of
the treatment involved such activities as supervised shopping and sight-
seeing tours, regular exercise periods set to music, and part-time use of
a swimming pool in Calcutta.

"To the Loveliest Girl in the World, My Wife—Dick, Calcutta, 1945"

India
February 9, 1945

Dearest:

Per my usual fashion, when given the opportunity, I am starting your letter early tonight. That is a good idea in two ways: first, should I get real busy I'll have had my chat with you; second, it provides me with a chance to write half a letter to you, spend the evening accomplishing other objectives, and then finishing your letter with a final word to you.

About the mail. I received your January 26 letter today, as well as clippings postmarked January 24 and the Miss Somers' January copy of the NEA mailed January 17. So you did handsomely by me today, as indeed you did yesterday. My January 29 issue of *Time* arrived also, and a carbon copy of a general letter issued by Rhea Burrow.

Further, I got quite a surprise when a heavy package filled with fruit cake, candy, and cookies came from the Misses Floro and Dorff. It had been sent to my temporary APO [Army Post Office] and so had taken a long time in transit—however, the contents were in excellent shape. I brought some of the items along to eat while CQing tonight.

Now that it is definitely warmer and rain is threatening, our friendly pests, the bugs, are back. It is interesting to observe how the bugs change in kind and character from one season to another. At the moment I am being particularly annoyed by a brown bug, about a half inch across, through, and deep. It infiltrates through the bamboo lattice works and goes careening around the room. I've already killed a half dozen of them. The ever present mosquito is here, but I've seen very few of those small blue bugs. Just as I was about to write that the huge, inch long, half inch wide beetles hadn't been seen recently, I heard a buzzing by the door, and sure enough, there was one, appearing for all the world like an overloaded bomber struggling through the air.

A moment ago I checked with Capt. Frankel on the appearance of the OD, or rather his lack of appearance. The Colonel came out of the door at the same time—and it seems that no one had noticed that there was no OD. In the meantime (it is 7:45) the Colonel and the Captain have been missing their supper.

I have a lot of letters that I should tackle, but I don't feel ambitious tonight. Instead, I think that I'll rather ration myself—one letter, your clippings, another letter, the NEA Journal, etc. Okay? See you in a couple of hours, sweetheart.

I've had an evening of excellent fun, inasmuch as I have done nothing but take my time writing a few letters, reading a detective book, and poring over your letters. Among the letters which I wrote was one to Ray and Miriam and when you read the copy which I am sending you, I hope you do not think me too severe in my dealings with Ray. I really enjoyed the twitting which I gave him, but I'm not too sure that he will. However, read his portion of the 1-6-45 V.Mail which they sent me and see if you don't think that he deserved it. After all, I could have just let my punches fly, instead of pulling them as I did. In some fashion, though I presume it's folly to try, I must cure him of that habit of talking down to me.

He does it to everyone, I realize, but it particularly irks me. While I recognize his brilliance I refuse to concede, on the basis of the evidence which I now have, that he is a better thinker than I. Furthermore, I know a lot more about a great many more subjects than he. And when it comes to questions of world policy, I don't consider that his performance of the past two or three years grants him the slightest right to even open his mouth. Tsk. (I imagine that I'll continue to split infinitives right to the bitter end!)

It is now quite late, and I presume that I ought to say goodnight. There was a slight mixup at the 81st on the OD question, but one put in an appearance around 8:00. About 10:45 I heard someone open the door to the Stat room and enter. I was amazed to hear the Colonel's voice asking if the OD had shown up. Lt. Steegman dropped in for a few moments today. One more mission, then home for him. He expects to leave about the 20th, he said.

I note that in an earlier paragraph I remarked about the absence of the little blue bugs. I take it all back. I have killed so many of them that there is a heap by my desk.

Well, sweetheart, I sent you another big brown envelope today filled to the brim with letters, service papers, and copies of my letters. I hope you find it interesting.

All my love to you, cherished one, and I repeat, what fun to sleep with you.

Goodnight, darling Ritter.

Dick

India
February 14, 1945

Dearest:

To my Valentine—my Love.

It was the middle of the afternoon before I realized that the 14th was Valentine's day and that I had an unopened gift from you awaiting me. I went to the footlocker immediately upon my return this evening, and with great delight found your snapshots and the leather snapshot container.

Indeed it was too bad that the camera blurred on your shots when Ray's turned out so well, but I got great joy from them anyway. Thanks so much, honey, they mean a lot to me. I'll be looking forward to those pictures which you and Margaret took recently. Too, I hope you got some snapshots of the extreme snow—that should prove interesting in future years.

Someone told me that they were having a show in the 82nd area, and so I walked over that way—sure enough, they were, but it was the same one I saw last night. Upon my return to the basha I pored over a November copy of the Reader's Digest. "Rajah of the Soil" proved interesting, though I'm afraid none of his methods have infiltrated to this community. I boasted to Capt. Seeger that Sam Higginbottom had chosen Ohio State's College of Agriculture when he returned to the States to learn agriculture. This started Lt. Husak, Capt. Seeger and me to talking about buildings, campuses, Ohio's state office building, etc. You recall that Capt. S. is from upper N.Y.? And went to Cornell!

As I predicted, the music of falling rain and the rumble of thunder lulled me to sleep last night. This morning we awakened to find the rice paddies partially submerged and the drying ponds given a new lease on life. Where the boys had worked so hard leveling and scraping down a tennis court, a smooth placid lake lay, disturbed only by a croaking frog.

This afternoon, Lt. Scanlon, our medical administrative officer, came in to confer on some forms which he is making out for our Medical Corps officers. He spent the whole afternoon with me.

My darling, I hope my flowers reached you—or that it was possible to get flowers.

With each petal I bless the sacred moment that brought you into my life. You are my love, my existence.

> With your name on my breath,
> Goodnight, sweetheart,
> Your husband,
> Dick

India
February 16, 1945

Dearest:

When we were kids we used to play a game of "rathers," which called for no energy but imagination. Right now I am confronted with the problem of would I rather have it cool with no bugs or warm and buggy. Thinking back over the last several days I realize that when it was cool I complained of the cold, and when it was warm I complained of the insects.

Why all these rumblings? Because last night it turned cold again and I'm chilly—there are no mosquitoes around, however. Since the bugs send me into such a rage I guess that I'll vote in favor of the chilly weather, despite the discomfort which it brings to me physically. In India it is probably healthier when it is cooler.

Your letters of January 31, February 1 and 2 arrived with the good news that Dale wouldn't go for at least a month. With world events moving so rapidly toward a military climax surely the States won't continue to draft older married men in essential situations.

The clippings of January 30 (?) came, as well as the February 5 *Time* and two *Republican-Couriers* (November 14 and 24)—or 27.

So you are still out of school? What a remarkable situation has developed—I only hope for your sake that you don't have to drive to Mt. Blanchard in June to make it up.

Concerning your question on what to do next year. (I've already written, but as you point out, some letters don't get through.) First, do as you like or think best. Second, my advice, for what it's worth: Sign with Mt. Blanchard. Let Kinley know that you are still interested in Intermediate work. If he offers you a job before August 1, take it. Should I happen to get back before the year is out you could find a substitute teaching job better in Findlay than in Mt. Blanchard, I should think.

An amateur band is doing a nice job of entertaining us with music in the Club. I am writing at a table on which Sturke and Winter are playing checkers—either one of whom you could defeat easily. It finally dawned on me—the band—I mean. The G.I. show stayed over a night and the fellows are down here putting on an impromptu show.

The lights are still off in the bashas—water in the generator, but I presume that they'll be on again soon.

Tonight we had a movie, the G.I. newsreel showing scenes taken in Myitkynia last August. It was interesting beyond the ordinary to me, for as it showed fighter planes dive bombing on the last Japanese installations, I could make out the bend of the river (Irrawaddy) and one or two buildings which miraculously survived, around which I have strolled twice this year.

The principal feature, Judy Canova in "Louisiana Hayride," was an amazing vehicle of irrationality. It just doesn't seem possible that anyone could produce such a picture and expect people to accept it seriously. Even Judy's voice was distorted to get a "cute" effect.

Well, sweetest one, it's high time I bring this to a close. I have been very irascible today, and have gone around saying mean things about people, but this chat with you has restored my good humor.

So much love, pet,
Dick

India
February 18, 1945

Dearest Ritter:

Everyone is so despondent tonight that it is very pitiful to behold. Groups meeting in disconsolate clusters, dissatisfied expressions, and various mutterings occasion concern on all sides. The reason? Well, it is Sunday evening and there is no movie! Someone slipped somewhere and we are left to our devices—and very poor devices they are.

Tonight I joined one of the poker playing groups and played for a couple of hours, but grew bored after awhile—I did win ten rupees! despite poor hands. (But then, I always get poor hands!)

So when old Sturke came wandering along looking like the wrath of God incarnate, I joined him and returned to the basha. There I found Frank and John comfortably ensconced under the light. Our generators are working again, but asthmatic coughs indicate that all is not well.

It is difficult to know when one is well off, but at the moment I am very dissatisfied with my position. Of course, I have had a nice vacation, but it is hard to work at 20% of your potentialities all the time. Then there is the question of toadying to officers with a fourth of your (my) background, education, and ability. There is hardly an officer in the place, outside of their technical training, who comes within a mile of me in ability to organize, analyze, and explain. As I say, it is a little difficult to remember, month after month, that the U.S. government has seen fit to utilize a highly trained man as they have me—and reward him proportionately. If our country and homes were in desperate straits, and I had a rifle in my hands, and grenades in my pocket, and were battling to save my home and your honor and safety, it would be a different matter, indeed. But when the need is so great for trained educators and men who can speak a piece well and convincingly, and the government sees fit to throw all that away—then indeed, I question the wisdom and fruitfulness of the policy.

Now that I have that hot chestnut off my hands—let me hasten to add that I know you are aware of the folly of the whole business and that you agree. It just does me good to let off a little steam to you occasionally. If I don't you will question whether my personality has not changed and I assure you, it hasn't.

The mail was disappointing. Letters came from Sgt. Alvarez and Bill Iluas. The latter told of a 6-months extension of his deferment and of a letter from you.

It has been cloudy today, and is definitely warmer out. Even at 10:00 o'clock in the evening it is still too warm for my sweater! (Look at the way I speak of poor Ken's sweater!) More rain, I suspect.

My sweetest gal—how pleasant it is to dream of you and your treasures. Keep this for me.

Ever in love,

Dick

P.S. I mailed another brown envelope today. They've been numerous lately, haven't they?

D

March 25, 1945

My Darling,

The weatherman has gone completely crazy—Another summer day in March. I don't know what the thermometer said today, but I was too warm in just a suit this afternoon.

The folks went to Aunt Edna's today so I was alone. After getting myself some lunch and reading the Sunday paper, I decided to take a little drive. I have just a bit of extra gasoline which won't be the case this summer.

I drove out to Wordens thinking I'd ask Lucille how she likes Arlington. Lucille was at Whistlers for the day, but I stayed and talked with her mother for awhile. Mrs. Worden didn't know anything about the vacancies but says Lucille reports that it is a nice place to teach.

She suggested I talk with the Supt. I hate to go over Mr. Ray, though. If I don't teach all year, it wouldn't be worth the possibility of creating his enmity.

Lucille has been having trouble getting mail to Glenn in Sweden. Of course he likes it much better than Cairo. He boarded the Grisholm and interviewed all the Americans being returned to the

U.S. He said they were lean but happy. The Germans (our war prisoners) were fat but sullen.

He has sent Lucille some nice things from Africa among them a couple of decorated brass jugs. Some girls don't ever seem to get anything. I suppose their husbands either don't have the opportunity or are thoughtless and maybe I should add, penniless.

I felt lonely today and hated to come home. In fact, I hate for the summer to come—then I think more about the things we would normally do together. It seems easier to keep occupied when it is cold. As I started to say, I drove by Mary Ellen's. She and Tommie were outside and came and sat in the car for awhile. Tom almost drives me crazy getting into things and I don't go as often as I might otherwise.

I miss Margaret. Of course, she can go without taking Toby in the eve. and then she keeps him out of things better than Mary Ellen does Tom. It seems that little boys are quite inquisitive though.

I am happy to report to you that my cold is about gone except for the hoarseness I get after talking quite a bit. The last stage was a nasty cough which was stopped with some cough medicine loaned me by your dad. I'm glad to get it licked. Those hanging-on kind wear a person down, as you know.

> *Goodnight, my Sweetheart, my Beloved Husband,*
> *So much love,*
> *Your Ritter*

P.S. Drew Pearson says the European war will be over in April. Uncle Ben says the Japanese war will be over 6 months later. Hope they're both right.

March 28, 1945

Dick, My Darling,

Lucky day—three letters from you today. That and the CBI insignia in beaded work are quite attractive.

I ran into some bad luck on the pictures of the boys you took. It seems there is a paper shortage and they will make only two of each print. I had planned to get 10 of those you were in for the family. I wanted even more of the one of you alone which I think is very good. I see no reason why I can't take them someplace else but that will all take time.

Of course I ordered two of all of them and will send those as soon as I get them. If you can do with any less than you first asked for, let me know.

I am anxious to get the pictures you took in the village, but of course they didn't come today. I am also anxious to read the paper you are writing. The children will be pleased to get your letter but you really should not go to so much bother. (Editor's note: The children Reva refers to are her fourth-grade students.)

I am taking Jean and Marilyn to school with me Friday. They are having Easter vacation. I thought of taking just one of them but decided that they ought to get along under those circumstances.

I called the Arlington Superintendent, Mr. Rost, tonight and made an appointment to see him Monday night. Lucille had told him that I saw Mr. Ray, who was not favorable to making a change. So I suppose when he (Mr. Rost) said on the phone to-night that I needn't say anything to the other party that he was referring to Mr. Ray. I'll be lucky if I keep out of trouble, won't I? It does seem silly to do so much fussing over something so temporary.

It sounds like Kenny has been having quite a time. I still have a little hacking cough myself, one of those things that have to wear themselves out, I guess. Everyone seems to have that kind this spring. Two of the other teachers have lost their voices this week.

Miriam writes that Ray has the flu, the spring kind that isn't supposed to last long.

It is still like summer out. The trees are budding and some fruit trees are in blossom.

I hope it doesn't get cold enough to hurt them with the food situation as it is. Rationing of meats and fats has been tightened. I read about the black markets flourishing.

War casualties must be very high. I don't think the number in Findlay is any small figure. Of course I don't know many of them,

but often some of the other teachers do. A number have been from
the group that were sent to the induction center when Dale was
last spring. They were mostly all put in the infantry at that time.

Another evening gone and nothing worthwhile accomplished,
but another evening nearer your homecoming.

> Goodnight, Dearest Husband,
> All my Love,
> Ritter

March 30, 1945

My Darling,

It is quite late, so I'm only going to start this letter now and
finish it at the beauty parlor in the morning.

Marilyn and Jean visited today and although they were good,
the children were very much interested in them and made the day's
teaching hard. Bonnie had invited me to go with them to Ralph
Long's (army) going away party. I really wanted to stay at home,
but didn't want to appear unappreciative of her thoughtfulness. I
enjoyed the evening though and won high ladies prize at the table
of Hearts.

Marilyn could do some of the 4th grade work and did better
accordingly than Jean.

Jean is more timid than Marilyn too. Marilyn almost talks too
much when she gets started, but she acknowledges introductions
etc. better than Jean. As much as she's gotten around with her ba-
ton twirling, you wouldn't think Jean would be so timid.

I got both your letters of March 16 today. There is never a
time that most women aren't glad for reassurances, and from my
own experience, and quoting Dorothy Dix, "voiced pledges of love
from their husbands." I look forward to your personal letters. They
serve as road signs for my proper mental attitude. I have been quite
successful in focusing my thoughts on our many happy experiences,
our life in Toledo and our future plans. If my thoughts sometimes
drift to things I would like to erase, I remember that I love you
completely, that I never deep within me doubted that you love me,
that my life without you is empty and meaningless, that you have

told me how much a part of your life I am and that all those things leave but one answer.

These months that are slipping away from us are most difficult and for me aging ones (or is that a mind set?) but if it is any comfort, we should be wiser homemakers because of them. I am sure that my sense of values has improved for the better.

All my Love, Dearest Husband,
Reva

March 31, 1945

My Darling,

Your envelope of March 16th came today. While I was downtown, someone from the post office called and said I had a registered package there from you and they thought maybe I'd like to pick it up since otherwise I wouldn't get it before Monday. Nice of them—I'm sort of a regular customer. I don't know the man's name that telephoned. He may have known you. I think it was Mr. Rantz who told him where to call. A couple of the men that I thought were grouchy at first now that they recognize me are almost friendly. The one at the parcel post window most of the time is quite accommodating.

The latest package I sent you was postmarked March 22. It contained an assortment of things. I have some stationery ready to mail tomorrow.

Today I delivered the Easter cards I'd fixed up and your 1-anna⁵ coins for the nieces.

Marilyn was pleased. Jean and Evelyn weren't at home, so I left them with Mrs. Cameron. I talked to Linda a bit and she jabbered back some.

The brake went down so near to the floor that I feared the fluid was leaking, so I stopped in at Foran's, the brake man. He said that it just needed adjusting, which he did for $1.00.

I am going to pick up Mary Ellen and Tom in the morning and we are going to the Church of God. So I'll be seeing some of our old friends.

*One of the Fellers girls, Olive, I believe, who is now Mrs.
Miller Fink, is teaching or rather in charge during the afternoon
at the day nursery. Mary Ellen has the forenoons and Mrs. Gunn
is cook—all three service men's wives with one child. It makes it
convenient for Mary Ellen since she can take Tom along and still
supplement her income, which needs to be supplemented. The high
cost of living is hard on people like her. Eighty dollars just isn't
enough; working is almost a necessity.*

*Wouldn't it be wonderful if we could really celebrate Easter,
having the war end?*

> *Goodnight, My Own Dearest,*
> *All my Love,*
> *Ritter*

India
April 9, 1945

Dearest Ritter:

The frolicking wind blows wildly and irresponsibly
through our compartment at this 5:30 afternoon hour.
Our pinup girls are dancing on their heads or really kicking
up their heels in wild abandon. Still no rain and so our
lives are talcumed with dust at all hours of the day and
night.

Already I am on top of my work again, so I had most of
the afternoon to devote to my own devices. However,
Heckman from the 434th came in for awhile, and we
tossed odds and ends around. Mac from the 81st called to
pass the time of day. Our outfit has missions every day, but
it is hard to escape the conviction that we are just biding
time. It wouldn't surprise me if we moved nearer Rangoon
—although there is serious question in my mind if that
would put us in a better striking position when such matters as gas and bomb supplies are considered. Many of us
think that no move will be made until Rangoon falls—but
everything is speculation, you understand, and no one
knows anything for sure.

Lt. Laughbon and I have put in for guidance work of a personnel and educational nature. That's all we know about it. Yesterday a radio [*sic*] from 10th came in asking for such personnel by name, experience, etc., to be answered by radio. A long radiogram went out yesterday afternoon—so if I send you a change of address soon you'll know that I'm finally headed for war, for which I am trained. I was sent in as available without replacement, which upset Capt. Seeger. However, Smerken, who has been transferred to the Air Inspector's office, and a 275[6] in the 83rd, now working as a 502, could be utilized. Don't hold your breath on anything, though, my dear.

I played a little poker this evening, but with mediocre luck. Rupees 25 in 12 hands in 4 hours—the last 8 in the last hour. Excellent! Someday I'll quit that game for marbles.

> Much, much love, dearest, hugs and kisses,
> Dick

April 12, 1945

My Darling,

Even though I've expected it, I was shocked at the news of the death of the President. And now, as I think about his physical condition, his complete confinement to his wheel chair, his thick speech etc., surely there was reason to do more grooming of Truman.

I hope that Truman proves to be a better man than we think. One of the things which has impressed me is his lack of education, which may not be important in the filling of his position. It seems to me the main thing to be affected will be the President's influence with other powers.

I mailed your shorts this evening. The man at the post office commented that I was a pretty regular customer.

This school day was as usual. It was warm, but not enough so as to interfere with work.

141

I finished the washing of the car tonight which was washing windows and scrubbing the rust spots off the back bumper.

Then I went to the Central Church of Christ to hear the preacher Mother and Mrs. Somers have been talking about. I neglected hose washing etc. but the folks think if I can go to the movies, I can go to church. It isn't that I object to going to church but I rarely go anyplace during the week and I have company (Margaret) to go to a movie with and of course they (the movies) are the most relaxing thing I know to do. I hope that you are in favor of attaching ourselves to a church when we settle down. But of course I resent pointed suggestions. However, I realize I don't hold my tongue when I have suggestions to make.

But why rehash the insignificant difficulties presented by wartime living? They do fray a lot of people's nerves though, I suspect.

Next to having you home, I look forward to our home—our own things and in a place where we cannot only find them but use them. How about you, my Sweetheart? You may miss Junior (bearer) though. I promise not to take his place.

What war news I've heard sounds like we are really rolling on in Germany. A little news, talk of the President, and music are the only things on the air all evening.

Take care of yourself, Dearest. Here are my love and devotion wrapped up.

> *Night Darling,*
> *Your Ritter*

India
April 13, 1945

Dear Ritter:

It is a miserable, rainy night, with pitching black clouds crying their distress over Mother India's rice paddies. But in the enlisted men's club a spirit of revelry abounds, for tonight your husband is paying for all drinks.

Joe Knapp, bartender, climbed on the bar and shouted, "Five cases of beer and all the mixed drinks you want on Lt. Beard," and so my appointment as an officer in the

United States Army was confirmed and ratified by my buddies.

This is the secret I have so zealously kept from you, not because I didn't want you to share in my anticipation, but because I did not want you to undergo another heartbreaking disappointment if the commission failed to come through. A week or more ago I had given up all hope, and so permitted my name to go in for this educational and vocational project about which I have written you.

Now can be revealed the reason, the real reason for my x-ray in December, my trip to Tenth AF HQR in January to appear before the direct commission board, and my frequent appeal to you to have faith. It is ironic that one month after I gain my sergeantcy that I should become a 2nd Lt. (By the way, how does it feel to be an officer's wife?)

Today was like other days, except that I shamelessly kept to my own correspondence and affairs. It's true that I had little to do, though. Rain threatened all day and Friday the 13th, which Lt. Husack remarked in particular, stayed dismal.

About 3:00 in the afternoon Capt. Frankel came into the office with a smug look on his face. He wandered around awhile, finally asking Lt. Husak to step out—he had something to show him.

In my case, for a change I had been working, and after smiling at Capt. Frankel I resumed my task. Both returned and before I understood what had happened, Capt. Frankel had ordered me to stand and hold up my right hand. He then swore me in as an officer in the U.S. Army, while the whole office force filed in with big grins on their faces. It was difficult for me to control my voice; I don't recall that I was particularly elated; rather extremely surprised.

The business of resigning from the Army and resigning (signing again) as an officer, took just a moment, then Lt.

Husak and Major Wegner whisked me back to their dwelling (a brick building) for a toast, previous to which Lt. Husak pinned the gold bar on my lapel.

The trip to Basha #20 for my things was an ordeal, but all of us drank beer and got very merry. Junior snapped into a smart salute as I rounded the corner to the infinite delight of Ken and Mac.

Lt. Husak took me to dinner at the officer's club, where we are served, and most of the officers (I know them all) came over to the table and congratulated me.

Afterwards, I made preparations for free drinks at the EM club, then returned to Lt. Husak's room where I am staying. Major Wegner, Lt. Seale, and Lt. Husak and I just finished a brief get-together while drinking a little beer. Lt. Husak is now reading the January issue of *Esquire,* and I am writing this to the woman I love more than life itself.

What does this mean? Well first, it means that I leave the Group shortly to be assigned to a hospital in Calcutta. Oh yeah, my commission is as a clinical psychologist.

More details will have to wait until I learn more. Naturally, my primary hope has been to use this as a means to get back to America where 62 general hospitals are operating.

The next morning.

We've just had breakfast and arrived at the office where I am finishing this first letter to you which I'll have the right to censor myself.

I spent most of the evening at the EM club where my total bill came to about 275 rupees, but it was worth it. The boys were even nicer than I thought they would be. In fact, they couldn't have reacted with more wholehearted good humor. My last act was to have omelets with Mac, Ken, Yennie, Seguin, and Jack Williams. (Link trainer boys.)

Well, sweetheart, I've got some things that must be done—will write more later.

> Ever in love with you,
> Dick

April 17, 1945

My Darling,

Your letter of April 8 came today. It was almost 5:30 when I got home, so I telephoned daddy to bring home the couple of flashlight bulbs which you requested today.

No luck, they are out of the screw type. I'll go downtown after school and look tomorrow night. If I can't find any will send the one I have in your flashlight. It is almost new. I have a couple batteries—They aren't too new but I guess we'll have to take a chance on them. My supply depends on what Gambles have.

Mrs. Stephens called tonight to tell me that you sent her a copy of the letter that you sent to my 4th grade. She was very much impressed with it and said the children will surely be thrilled. You've made a hit with her—said she'd like to hug you when she read that letter and then she continued on in a complimentary tone.

It is still cool and windy, though the sun was out today.

Margaret called me to go with her to a show tonight but this weather brought back my hoarse voice so I decided to stay in and get my rest. So far, I haven't developed the cold that accompanied before and I don't want to.

Margaret hasn't gotten a telephone call yet from Floyd so decided not to try to stay at home any longer. I doubt that I would have given up yet but unless he has a long layover in Hawaii I doubt that he would get through.

President Truman seems to have made a hit with the press. The war news isn't encouraging to me. Sounds like the cleaning up will take time in Germany. And I don't like the sound of Japan's suicide plans. I wish they could see the folly of hanging on. I should think Germany would be a lesson for them.

Contracts were given out today with "salary to be announced later." What is the use in issuing a contract on those terms? Mine is for two years. I can't understand why some of the girls stick around so long with a setup like that. Now is certainly the time for them to change. I'm only putting in time and am interested in my career only as it affects me now. I want to soon be just plain housewife Ritter again and Dick's best girl every night. But as for girls like Myrtle (she's been at Mt. Blanchard four or five years) without any other very definite prospect, I'd say they are in a rut.

You asked me about the mailing time of the mystery books you received April 7.

Your November date is probably right because I know it was quite awhile ago. Apparently I forgot to write the date down. I always report to you in my letters but often neglect writing down things of small value. As usual I depend on your bookkeeping. I just plain depend on you.

How I wish I could lean on you in person!

    Goodnight My Love,
    XXX Ritter

April 19, 1945

My Darling,

The children were delighted with your letters. As they read, I heard little giggles every once in awhile over the room. After I had given them an opportunity to read them themselves, I read the letters aloud for the benefit of the poor readers. They enjoyed every bit but were amused particularly in your description of the natives brushing their teeth, washing themselves and washing their clothes. They liked the line about a big smile for their favorite teacher.

Then I gave them the coins you sent, and I'm sure they felt like they'd had a big day.

One of them asked if you'd like a letter from them. I said, "Of course he would." That suggestion immediately won the approval of all. You can see how big your letters went over because writing letters doesn't usually have their approval. So tomorrow each student will write you a letter. I must warn you that we haven't done much letter writing, and I see where I'm going to spend the rest of the English period spelling.

Can you believe it? I got letters again from you today, your letters of April 5 and 10 and your story "Under the Village Palms." Of course the story was well written even though the subject was revolting. It gives me a very unpleasant feeling reading it, which speaks well of your writing. That of which you write sounds worse than our stables. Do any GIs go there for its intended use? They must be plain crazy and I do mean crazy if they do.

My voice is better tonight but I'm not completely rid of this cold. Guess I'll have to take some sun baths as soon as it gets warm.

Time to say goodnight to my Sweet Husband.

> All my Love,
> Ritter

April 21, 1945

My Darling,

I'm so excited, I'm sure I won't make sense. Both your letters of the 14th came at eleven o'clock (the mail comes early on Saturday), and I've been like a dog chasing its tail. Of course I'd be more excited if you were coming home. Which reminds me, when you come home, be satisfied with the trains. I'd rather have you take them than planes.

Finally I'm getting around to saying CONGRATULATIONS! My Lieutenant. Now I'm sorry you sent that money home. I'd send you some but I suppose you'll have more before it would get to you or you would have asked for it.

There are a number of reasons why I'm glad you have a commission among them, your better living conditions, your change of work which you will probably enjoy and I'm hoping this work will be farther back of the zone of activity. Such little things as censoring your own mail (that feeling of privacy) are important too. And then the fact that so many of our friends are officers is not to be overlooked. Although neither of us would admit it, didn't we feel we were being talked down to?

Ruth King has a little 22-month old girl from the home (up for adoption), who Evelyn fell in love with and now your mother. She must be nice since your mother thought it a good idea for me to see her. She says she is pretty and dainty. I hate to let a good opportunity slip through my fingers, so I may try to see her. Her parents are separated and they don't want her.

I had lunch this noon at your folks'. I called them first to tell them the news. Then of course I had to drive over. Your mother asked me about putting your promotion news in the paper and I told her it was being taken care of by the Army, according to the information from you.

I am anxious to know about your work. Our mail should go through better to and from Calcutta. Today's letter surely came in record time though. I got mail every day this week.

This is the first that has happened. I'm keeping my fingers crossed about next week.

Leo U. at the bank this morning asked me to send his regards and of course I had to tell him about your commission. You've earned it, my Dear, and at least you've avoided the grind of OCS.

Take care of yourself and be careful of the big city. I understand that an officer's wife has more to worry about in some respects. That wasn't meant to be nasty. I have my faith.

> *And you have all my love,*
> *A kiss and an awfully tight hug,*
> *Your Ritter*

April 22, 1945

To My Dearest Husband,

You asked for reassurance in your letter of the 12th. I can think of no better way than to say it. You are my Life! No matter what is in the foreground, you are always in my thoughts. I constantly plan for our future together. My love is always strong, my longing never lessens. Your letters are my strength and I mark time until the day I will again be in your arms.

Your reassuring letters, your thoughtful gifts, and your every day letters are so much more than most army wives have. I know and appreciate that.

> *I am your Ritter*

> May 1, 1945

My Darling,

Your letters of April 19 and 20 came today. By now, you probably know what things are going to be like at the hospital.

I notice in today's paper that Howard Wilson is home on leave for 20 days. Florence said she would be thankful if she could just have him home for one day and not have to worry about him. I agreed in one sense but I certainly want you to stay when you get home.

Going through the business of separating again would be almost beyond endurance. But I guess we army wives learn to appreciate minutes with our husbands when the Army is gracious enough to give them.

I don't mean to gripe when I realize we are getting a break but I do so begrudge the months of separation that are slipping by.

Everyone felt so sure that Hitler would give up today—Well, apparently he did, as his death was announced. I certainly don't take any stock in that unless he was shot by his own henchmen. They certainly are playing some kind of a game. That probably being to split the allies. Do you think Russia will enter the war against Japan?

You can see or guess that I'm leaning on one elbow. Good-night, my Lieutenant. It does seem nice being an officer's wife, but it is you, you, you that I love.

> Hugs and kisses,
> Ritter

Calcutta, India
May 9, 1945

Dearest:

We suspect, from the lightning flashes around, that it has been raining somewhere, for an hour ago it turned cooler, and now we will sleep in comfort tonight. It threatened rain all day, but none materialized here.

Today cannot be considered one of my better days. In the first place, I couldn't get the group therapy class to respond. I've lost 4 of the original 12, and 2 more were missing because they had appointments. That left me with six, only two of whom would open their mouths. The humidity was 85% the other day—probably more this morning. Then, since we meet outside, the crows proved a real nuisance, holding San Franciscan conferences in the palm tree under which we were seated. (And to think I kept an Indian boy from killing a wounded crow, or kite, or raven [or whatever they are] yesterday.)

Then the last conference I had this afternoon was with a 26-year-old patient who has gone to pieces from psychoneurosis induced by incest dreams and a subsequent guilt complex. He asked me why he had them and what to do. Apparently I failed to take fully into account his moronic intelligence, for after I explained why he had the dreams and the action he could try to take, he left in fair spirits. During the interview we had been interrupted many times by Indians flying steel plates off a truck. Whatever the cause, just as I left the office he returned. He had lost control of himself. He declared that I had hurt him; upset him; didn't believe him; made fun of him; and he didn't have to stand for it. I was pretty annoyed, but I agreed that he didn't, indeed. Then I asked, "What is it specifically that you don't have to stand for?" He began to stammer a little, finally trailed off into silence. I dared not point out to his twisted mind that the deliberate misconstruction of what he had asked me to tell him was symptomatic of what had driven him crazy in the beginning.

The failure was my own fault for being too eager to try to effect a cure. In his dreams he had relations with his mother and sister, both responding. That would be enough to make most men a little uneasy, but since dreams (subconscious desires repressed by the conscious mind) of that sort are fairly common, only one who had actually done something about it would be particularly guilty in his reactions. All the evidence pointed to relations with the sister, probably when she was quite small, and I suspect without her consent. At any rate, I muffed the problem, and in psychiatry it is far better to do nothing than it is to do the wrong thing. My reassurances apparently hit a sore spot in his martyr complex, for I said upon his return to the States, if he would accept the fact that his dreams were no different from those of thousands of similar cases he would soon be alright. (Tsk! Tsk! What a stupid waste of a teacher's time, when he could be working with strong, young potential minds!)

But most of the cases are much more promising than that. Interesting items are not lacking in this business.

This morning I had my inlay reset. Friday afternoon I have my teeth cleaned and scaled. Later will have four (!) cavities filled.

Yesterday I learned that since we hadn't gotten the May allotment request in early enough, that no deduction would be made for that month, so your first check will be for June, which you won't receive until July. Sorry about it, pet, but maybe the money can be used for the Christmas gifts. If I decide differently, I'll send you a money order. Ok?

Tonight Gus and I saw Errol Flynn in "Objective Burma" and after a slow and typically Hollywood start, the picture became quite good. It held the interest of everyone despite the fact that there were no women in the cast. If

151

the scenes taken from the planes weren't actually Burmese, I can only say that when I looked down on Burma, that's the way it looked to me.

Letters today from Kenny Bayless and Jimmy Joyce. Maybe one from my darling Ritter tomorrow.

A fond goodnight kiss and clasp,
Your devoted husband
Love,
Dick

May 11, 1945

My Darling,

I may finish this letter in the morning. It is now 12 o'clock and I've had a very big day.

I spent all evening until 10:30 getting a permanent.

Margaret talked with one of Floyd's friends from Australia en route home and he is very optimistic about an early end to the war. He emphasized the might of the Navy, of course.

It sounded like you needed to be a patient yourself with a cold and the GIs. Please be careful. Your work sounds interesting but possibly depressing at times. What type of lecture do you give?

Does the club include both men and women? Apparently being an officer gives one the ability to take care of oneself.

This sounds rather silly but your being an officer sort of affects the status of this point system coming up. One of the girls at the beauty parlor said last night, "Oh, it doesn't concern officers' wives." I know they consider me very lucky. Of course Margaret was very glad for your change and we gloated together about our husband's promotions. Floyd is chief petty officer now and really expects to become a warrant officer.[7]

I think it was hard for her to realize the living conditions you had. Floyd has always lived in places with conveniences very much like the U.S.

I will buy the war bonds you suggested. I intended to do it today, but I guess I'll wait until next week. We are supposed to get paid then unless they hold up our pay until the last week.

*I haven't mailed you a box (candy etc.) since March. Since the
February box didn't arrive in very good shape and I don't have
much time, I'll wait until I get back from Canada to send another.*
I love you! I love you!

> *Your devoted wife,*
> *Ritter*

Calcutta, 1945: outside the tailor's shop. Like many other American soldiers stationed in India, Richard had suits and jackets sewn to
order.

May 13, 1945

My Darling,

Three packages of brass came today, all postmarked April 5, one with your return address, Mac's and Kenny's. I believe that makes all of them. I opened all three—there were trays, lamps, ladle, spoon, bell and pitcher. I am very pleased with them. In them we have something unusual and something to be proud of. Imagine Mother's comment when I pulled out the pitcher, "I wish it were full of cider now." I think that shoemaker's bench idea of mine is just right for those things. I'll wait until I open it all to decide on the trays to give our folks. Like you, I particularly like the crudeness of the brass—too, it makes it seem more representative of the people you've described.

Your mention of the little girl spurred me to do something. I haven't yet seen her and of course Ruth doesn't want to give her up. I called Miss Oren, who's in charge of the home.

She says that she is a sweet child, isn't up for adoption yet but she thinks she will be. Miss Oren says they have a waiting list (same story) but suggested I come out to the home and file an application. I told her I was teaching and couldn't come until Saturday. She is not sure she can be there then and I'm to call her at her home before I go. I noticed her interest was greater when I told her I was a teacher—that always seems to carry weight, doesn't it?

I didn't tell her that you are in the Army and overseas. That so far seems to have been the catch, so I thought I'd tell her that when I see her. The fact that you are an officer may help some. In Toledo, they questioned the financial end. I thought too maybe they'd be reasonable about the Army. The thing that aroused my interest was your mother's encouragement. The child seemed really to have impressed her. The parents are divorced.

I should be able to tell you more if I get to see Miss Oren Saturday.

It is 12:30 a.m. again. I think the fact that it gets dark late makes the evenings go fast. It gets dark before you know it. It is still way too cold.

> *A big hug, a big kiss.*
> *All my love,*
> *Ritter*

Calcutta, India
May 16, 1945

Dearest:

Today I opened your unusual, unexpected "game" box and found those six darts.

What a clever idea, sweet; Gus will get his carpenter to work on a target and he and I will have great sport with the darts. Frankly, you shouldn't have deprecated your gift. Do you, and of course you did, recall what fun I used to get from throwing darts? Tonight I practiced by opening my wardrobe and throwing the darts "Cupid's arrows" into the back of it. They worked well. How thoughtful of you to have hit upon that idea.

Now, I am wondering if you got your roses and sweet peas, or if the one letter I wanted to get through was again late? If they failed to arrive, at any rate, sweet one, I know you had the ivory cribbage board. Did it come up to your expectations? I was inordinately proud of that board, caressed it, fondled it, dreamed of tossing it on the bed, sitting cross-legged thereon playing cards with you. Wonderful! Yeah, wonderful!

All day the thunder growled in the distance like a surly dog. Tonight it came closer, with brilliant etchings of livid flame writing acrostics on the tumbling clouds. But no rain—though they called off our outdoor movie. Gus went to his shop. I returned to the room. I wrote a personal letter to you which I'm sending to Toronto. By the by, your May 29th gift went first class today, though I'm afraid it won't reach you before you leave for Canada.

155

The group therapy class grew to 16 in number this morning, which makes it almost unwieldy. I cannot adequately tell you how much it takes out of one to try to keep such a class going for 1 1/2 hours. Teaching will be easy after this. Perhaps I concentrate too fiercely; will have to learn to take it easy. Staff meeting this afternoon at which I earned the Cols. displeasure for not being there on time. However, he called a 2:00 p.m. meeting at 2:00 p.m., and I was doing work where he couldn't get in touch with me. So I told him. I think maybe I am supposed to be psychic. The remainder of the afternoon was spent in interviewing.

Tonight I exercised the plastic cards in a relaxing game of solitaire, breaking it in the sixth hand. The cards are hard to keep in shape in this country—too damp.

Capt. Haden, the Adj., dropped in for a half hour earlier in the evening. He had some decided views on the way things are run. To my amazement, by the way.

Happy memories of this day, sweetheart mine.

> Ever in love with you,
> Dick

P.S. There are three thin bundles of copper on the way, sweet, mailed April 4—listed Kenyon, McGraph, and Beard.

> Calcutta, India
> May 21, 1945

Dearest:

For the third time in an hour a cat has raced frantically past our door, meowing her heart out. She doesn't stay long enough for us to ask her what is wrong. Gus came to with a start, swore, said, "Birds, dogs, cats! All we need now is the braying of an ass." Since I had been talking quite glibly, I shut up.

All is well here in Calcutta. It was hot today—I received your July 3rd gift, sweet—group psychotherapy—board meeting all afternoon.

Petty and Gus are pulling such corny jokes that it is almost impossible to concentrate. Their idea of humor is pretty darn basic—but it is honest and I salute them for it—but the salute is a trifle low.

After tonight's surrounding rain storms, the air is quite cool. So much so that I am wearing a robe.

I like the concluding thought of most of your letters—in my arms. How I do wish you were, little girl. That will be the day.

> Ever in love with you,
> Dick

P.S. Give Mimmy [Reva's sister Miriam, who was expecting] my cordial best wishes for an easy time of it. Do not hold Ray's hand.

> D.

> Calcutta, India
> May 23, 1945

Dearest:

It is, or was, a remarkably warm and stifling day which turned reasonably cool as evening drew on.

As usual, I hold a group psychotherapy class, but this time I spoke straight from the shoulder about some of the things that might happen. After the class, I had my 2nd success in 24 hours, for a very tough-minded boy broke down, cried that he wanted to get a load off his mind. He followed me to the office—weeping—confessed that he was a coward. Sounds almost like evangelism, actually it is confession. It is remarkable what clearing one's conscience can do.

For the remainder of the business day I attended an N-P [neuropsychiatry] staff conference, wrote reports. 1st Lt.

Myers, one of the older (iron gray hair) nurses, has been telling me of her experiences as a public health nurse for a suburban Pittsburgh school previous to the war.

She has been overseas over 2 years, I think. She says that she spends most of her time in her room or with other nurses. The inference is that she prefers not to fight her way out of situations constantly. She reminds me a little of Miss Cummings, who used to be Hissong's secretary. She is more interested in her work than in men; though to be fair, those nurses I have met on our wards have all been pretty dependable.

Captain Robinson, Protestant Chaplain of the 12th, looked me up today, talked for a half hour, left some items for our chaplain here, Major Coburn, which I later gave him.

Robinson spent some time visiting the boys who are here from the 12th. He means all right, but is ineffectual.

Our G.I. barbershop has 5 chairs improvised in it. I managed to find time for a haircut this afternoon. Clean surroundings make a difference in the confidence one has.

Last night, about 2:00 a.m., I was awakened by a hideous racket just outside my window. Alarmed, I looked out. Someone was running up and down the porch dragging a careening rickshaw. Bicycles were being knocked helter-skelter. The boys seemed to be having a great deal of fun.

Tonight Gus and I saw "Music for Millions" with sweet Margaret O'Brien, June Allyson, Jose Sturbi, Jimmy Durante, Marsha Hunt, Marie Wilson, Hugh Herbert and an excellent supporting cast. We were finally impressed with the entertainment quality of the picture. The scenes between Margaret and Jimmy were inimitable. I hope you saw it.

> My sweetheart,
> My everlasting love to you,
> Dick

May 25, 1945

My Darling,

When I got home from school this noon there wasn't any mail, none since Monday so you know how I felt—But the sun shone after all, your letter of May 16th came this aft.

Don't wear yourself out teaching. Take it easy. I don't know what to do about getting you socks. I am sending that 6th pair and some envelopes tomorrow.

I'm sorry the book didn't arrive for May 16th but I'm glad you think you'll enjoy the darts. My flowers were beautiful and the cribbage board too—I'd surely like to play you a game now.

I decided to open the rest of the brass tonight since I won't be home the 29th. You shouldn't have bothered sending me something else—if it doesn't arrive before I leave I'll look forward to opening it when I get home.

All the brass seems to be here but the large spatula shipped April 4th. I have the small one. I had daddy look in the furnace thinking it could have gotten in the packing papers but he said there were no signs of it.

The brass is very pretty. I don't know what is my favorite. The different sizes and shapes of the bowls are interesting. The big mug is especially so.

I went out to see Miss Orem this afternoon. She is not as business like as the others I've talked with. Do you know her, she is elderly and rather thin? I doubt that much investigation is made about the child's parents. Dr. Nurnburgh [sic] at Bowling Green does the intelligence testing and the probationary period is one year.

She must have something in mind or she wouldn't insist that I put in an application before I go to Canada. She says she has several nice little children (I saw the pictures of three) but she can't get their parents to give permanent commitments.

She says the child Ruth looks like me. Your mother says not and flatters me by saying she won't be as good looking. Your mother often makes remarks like that—her love must cover my blemishes. Your dad and mother say she is pretty though—I'd

159

surely like to see her but Ruth is so determined to keep her that I won't make any trip there.

Miss Orem didn't commit herself but rather intimated that if she comes up for adoption we'd have a good chance of getting her. I gather that she makes the decision. I gave three people as references whom I thought would be sure not to neglect a reply.

Mother, about a year ago, received a letter inquiring about Rev. Shepards—they got a 3 wk. old baby.

Your mother thinks that maybe the Kings would be allowed to adopt her especially now that Leonard's mother died and they'll be getting an inheritance. I certainly wouldn't think so.

She (Miss Orem) sounded lenient about the home—I told her frankly our set up and she didn't seem to think it would be necessary to make any changes here. Mother doesn't either but I feel hemmed in now — .

Here I go. I'm going to have to throttle the enthusiasm I'm inclined to get. I must remember that the child isn't even up for adoption yet, that I might not be impressed with her, and that I'm not sure we're being favorably considered.

Do you think we'd be fairly safe if her I.Q. were reasonably high and she were given a complete physical? There I go—but I do want your answer to that.

We talked with Miriam again tonight. She says she thinks the baby is going to look more like Ray. It has a wide mouth (I hope not), a turned up nose and blond hair in little ringlets all over her head. Miriam said she is getting along all right and her voice sounded stronger.

It is raining a nice steady rain now—I wish I could lie in your arms and listen to it.

I have a lot of odd jobs to do tomorrow including getting my hair done. I dread my train trip coming up. I think it would be fun to travel on a train with you if it weren't too crowded but I don't like looking out for myself.

> *Goodnight My Darling.*
> *Love and a lot of Kisses,*
> *Your Ritter*

May 25, 1945

Dearest,

    I have signed and sent in an application the same as this—as soon as they have received this one with your signature they'll substitute it in their files for the one I've sent.

    Miss Orem didn't think I should wait that long to get in an application. Sounds like she might mean business. If you want to send this direct to her, here is her address.

    Miss Haley Orem
    The Hancock County Children's Home
    2515 N. Main
    Findlay, Ohio
    Make any corrections you like.
                    Much love,
                    Reva

Calcutta, India
May 25, 1945

Dearest Ritter:

Today the wind decided to frisk briskly, thus blowing huge blankets of dust over everything, including the sacred bodies of officers. One can, and does, take a shower, but the disconcerting thing is to examine the sheets on the bed. Here it is observed that the white cloth has aged, sallowed with the passing of the day. The whole surface of my bed has formed a delta for fruitful breezes to drop their burdens. If I perspire tonight I should have no difficulty in sliding out of bed in the morning.

Continued weather report: vivid, streaked lightning bill-boarded a storm to the southeast, but it passed around. Spotted clouds obscure the moon, but the day's heat has been moderated.

My darling sweet—I miss you so much. Last night I just lay there (on the OD's bed) imagining you were beside me. What I said to you was meant only for your ears. What we did concerns no one but us. Ah, Ritter, it will be worth

Snake charmer: for a rupee, he'll make his cobra dance.

waiting for. Each spent hour now, gilds the future in a blush of happiness for us.

> I love you, little one,
> Love and kisses,
> Dick

Body being cremated: an adult body will become ashes in four hours.

Calcutta, India
May 25, 1945

Dearest:

I wrote last night's letters in the humid heat of Ward 45. From that time on until 2:30 my shirt was never dry. At 11:00 I decided my jeep was untrustworthy, so picked up another at the motor pool. I went to the Club for awhile, laughed with some of my friends because the OD may not touch liquor. Drove Petty and Gus home. I chased various and sundry beebies away, broke up Clinches (gently, go gently, OD, for love is very fruitful in this clime), chased couples from trees (under them, of course), pounced from my jeep upon entangled clusters in rick-shaws and taxis. In the latter open cars, saw some impas-sioned kisses which resulted in considerable admiration for the staying power of the participants.

Caught a wandering patient, checked all of the nurse's buildings to make sure that they had signed in by 1:00. Since it was 1:45 when I got around, it still didn't surprise me to find 5 still missing. (Too bad I couldn't make a bed check to be sure.) Did bed check of enlisted men's bar-racks—2 men unaccounted for. Names, but no bodies. Finally, by 3:00 a.m., joined the MOD and SOD in the room where three beds are provided for the OD's. Slept fitfully until 6:45. Up and at 'em again.

Ralph's gift of Thurber's book showed up and I snatched moments to enjoy it.

Otherwise I had a group therapy class this morning, took a 3 1/2 hour noon, sleeping much of the time—returned to the office for the numerous vexing questions and interviews which form an important part of the day's work. Miss Ambushe had some nurse friends in this morn-ing, and a Red Cross worker took our pictures. If I get a print, I'll allay your perhaps fears with a look.

Dressed up for the first time since I've been here this evening, and when I checked myself in the mirror, darned if I wasn't almost handsome. The bush jacket fits as well as anything can fit (me), and is itself resplendent with russet buttons, various gold insignia. I think you would approve. Believe me, it would have been perfect if I could have set out with you for the Great Eastern Hotel.

An open touring car taxi dropped me at the door of the Hotel—just inside was a large room with tables scattered around for the guests to deposit their unfinished drinks. A step or two and I heard someone call my name. Then the boys were around me: Gebilaro, Clark, Knagen, Kiell, Brown, Glassier, Frahm (I hadn't expected to see knot-head). That was all; there were 10 at the table, and two new men whom I barely knew. We had a drink or two, a great deal of talk, then we went upstairs to the big dining room. Uniformed waiters, polished floor, balcony, two-storied banquet hall, golden-amber tints, huge chandeliers, and a multitude of ceiling fans gave the impression of air-conditioning and luxury.

The meal, itself, was hardly worth shouting Hosannas over, esp. when Rs5 [5 rupees] were considered. Soup, chicken, and dessert, with the tiniest demitasse cups for coffee that I've ever seen. But the big item was the exchanging of reminiscences. It was good to see the fellows again. Big good-natured Frahm, now a sergeant, was especially in good form.

Gib asked about you several times.

About 9:30 we broke it up—I returning by taxi to our Club, where I encountered Petty and some nurse friends he was buying drinks for. After letting him buy one for me, besides a cigar, I rescued him from the feminine onslaught —took him to the Brks [barracks].

> Dearest Ritter—all my love, sweet one,
> Ever in devotion,
> Dick

Calcutta, India
May 27, 1945

Dearest:

I've been playing poker all evening instead of answering letters, but I'm happy that I've been accepted by the officers, and consequently feel that the time was well spent. As you may have guessed, officers are much more cliquish than EM, and I was a little concerned. Of course, I had Gus and Wes Petty, but I wanted to get in with a little of the higher brass, not only for reasons of profit, but because more avenues for personal pleasure are opened that way.

Gus is a fine roommate, but headachy Petty acts and looks like a goon, and I didn't want the odium of association only with him fastened on me. I believe that has been definitely broken, for these fellows called for me—I didn't seek them. Good.

My hatred for the Army hierarchy has not been lessened, but I have no desire to bang my hard head against the wall uselessly. In other words, my principles have not changed essentially, but, with mental reservations, I have found it necessary to modify my behavior. I do not like to walk a rail fence, but I can do it as well as the next fellow.

Three letters from you gladdened my heart—May 15, 16, and 17th. May 16 our day.

Right you are, dearest one. Fifteen marvelous years* with you—at least 3/7's of my life has been worthily spent.

Ever yours,
Dick

*[Editor's Note: When they met and fell in love, Richard was twenty and Reva was sixteen. Richard is referring to their courtship and seven years of marriage.]

Calcutta, India
May 28, 1945

Hello, little sweetheart:

Because of and despite your mission to Canada I hope
you are enjoying yourself fully. If everything goes well
there is no reason why that shouldn't be a very pleasant
vacation trip, indeed. If Ray and Miriam are still there we
shall have to plan to drive up after the war. "After the
war," makes a nice phrase doesn't it?

Are you as intrigued as I by the sidestepping negotia-
tions which are now going on among the world's great
powers? France is back there scrambling like everything
with politicians of dubious color in the saddle. Here, as
you will be able to see from the clippings I am sending
you, the Indian press takes every opportunity to make the
imperialistic powers look silly. Some comedy!

My love—seven years ago tomorrow!

To you—my tenderest caress.

Yours,
Dick

Toronto
May 29, 1945

My Dearest Husband,

*No one ever had a better husband than I have and no one ever
wanted their husband near them more than I want you this minute. Your simply gorgeous bouquet of Talisman roses with a few
sprigs of baby breath arrived this evening. They brought the mist to
my eyes when they arrived but now in my room as I look at them
on the dresser it is no long mist but a shower.*

*Our seventh year has been one of strengthening our love in
spite of our separation.*

*And my Darling I can say tonight that your gestures and re-
peated assurances of this last year have made great strides I find
recently toward the healing of that deep wound. Only I know what*

that means but suffice it to say the emotional struggle which only I can control with your help occurs much less frequently. I think the best indication that I am becoming the conqueror is that I have (am) writing about it. And now I speak of it because I'm sure that you were aware of it and even though you know it is not a question of love, other emotions involved are vital to our happiness and no doubt it is the kind of assurance you like to hear.

I had a tiresome trip today—We went to the hospital as soon as I arrived. Miriam seems to be doing well and Jill too. She looks very much as all very tiny babies do. I will say she did look nicer than the couple of other babies I saw—I think the fact that her hair is nicer has something to do with that but of course you can't tell what that will be like later—My wish for next year is to be snuggling up in your arms, My Love. Tonight each rose bud says Dick loves you and I breathe back Ritter loves Dick so very deeply.

Night My Darling
Your Devoted Wife,
Ritter

Calcutta, India
May 29, 1945

Dearest Reva:

You asked why I had white roses delivered to you on May 16. It was a sentimental and romantic gesture in which the traditional meaning of the colors of flowers was invoked.

But to my way of thinking I could as well offer a white rose upon the altar of my love for you each day.

Purity is as much a lovely characteristic of your being today as it was the first time I touched your hand in 1930. By some miracle, your contact with life—with me—has not coarsened you—has not marred your virginity. As I reflect upon you and me in the car under the moonlight, in the front room listening to "Moonriver," and in the bed we have shared I am aware that I have approached you each time as a man who knows his love for the first glorious union of body and soul.

How much our separation has meant to me I dare not put on paper. Perhaps, just before I sail for home, I may try. But rather by far that I be permitted to demonstrate in a real way what I mean. You will not have to cling to me, you are me.

Perhaps in all this I am idealizing, but I think not. This low, weary year has given me time to consider many things, the significance of which has been blurred in the past. Clearcut, sharp and pure, etched against the certificate of our union as a palm tree silhouettes against the blue of a late Indian evening, is the world-crashing, world-engulfing, between-you-and-me eternal fact: I am so glad that you married me.

Goodnight, precious Ritter. I'll help moisten that pillow soon, from which I have so often seen your large brown lovely eyes watching me. They are looking down on me now, Reva.

In devotion,
Dick

Calcutta, India
May 31, 1945

Dearest Ritter:

Let's see if I can recall the names of the men I played poker with tonight: Major Shaw, Major Wills, Captain Batista, Lt. Whittaker, Lt. Knapper, and Lt. Levinson. We had a pretty good time, though I was out 100 rupees about 10:45. By 12:00 I had a handful of small notes which gave me a profit for tonight of 57 Rs. Luck just hasn't been with me, but I like the game and the atmosphere is pleasant at the Club.

The hot weather brought circling storms, but outside of vivid flashes of lightning, nothing happened.

Last night you recall that Gus wasn't back by 11:00. When he did show up at 12:30 he was a drunken sinner, claiming that I should be ashamed for not celebrating his

15th year in the Army. Of course I wanted to know, sar-
castically, just what there was in that to be celebrating, but
it was lost on him. He had carried a drink all the way from
the Club for me, but some captain in the command car
had grabbed it, drank most of it. While explaining, Gus
drank what was left, to my relief.

Just before lunch a Major Johnson, a flight surgeon
from the 20th Bomber Command, came to see me about a
couple of patients. He stayed on to tell me many details of
the 20th's B-29 experience about Japanese suicide rams,
evasion by various means of fliers forced down (this was
interesting, but I can't repeat it), etc. They take an interest
in their men that no other outfit has shown.

Just one thought, Ritter, I love you.

Kisses,

Dick

July 15, 1945

My Darling,

*It has been a very gloomy day—rainy and cold, about 50
degrees. Did I tell you one day while we were gone it was 43 degrees
here? We actually have only had a couple of weeks of the usual
summer weather. I don't like to swelter, but I don't like this in the
summer. We should have had a furnace fire today but instead either
froze or sat around the gas grate.*

*I awakened late but decided to carry out my intentions of go-
ing to church. The congregation was small but I saw a lot I know.
Mrs. Althaus asked if you got the letter from Michigan. I talked
with Mrs. Bair, Mabel Frazer, Mrs. McDowell, Gyneth
Downing—and her mother, Nanny Hoblugar and Rev. and Mrs.
Linder.*

*The paper boy must have gotten rained out. We didn't get any
Sunday paper today.*

*Even the children seem to have acquired the independent war-
time spirit. I should think jobs would be getting tighter with men*

being released and some war plants closing. However, I suppose
industry will take its place.

The radio reports that Japan is getting an awful pounding
from the air. What does she expect to gain by hanging on?

My darling, a long hug and a tight one! So much love!

Your Ritter

July 16, 1945

My Darling,

Your very sweet love letter of July 3rd came today, as well as
your letters of July 5, 6, and 7. I am excited about the dinner
ring. What finger are you having it made for? And what is the
name of the stone? Really, Dear, you shouldn't be spending so
much money on me all the time. You're spoiling me!

I purchased your hair tonic and green soap tonight. I also
bought a shaving bowl (Yardley's). It will be only a few months
until Christmas box time. How about some suggestions? How do
your needs differ from last year's? The thing that perturbs me is
the scarcity of pipes.

Mary Ellen and I rode to Bowling Green with Helen Reimund
today. She just walked in to see Dr. Prout saying she is interested
in teaching English, and before she left she had interviewed
Hissong and (I think head of the Department) Smith. She said
she is sure they have several vacancies and she thinks she will get
the Freshman English job. That is what she wants—5 classes,
Monday, Wednesday, and Friday. Shuck is still there although the
army almost took him this spring—lucky guy.

We stopped uptown in Bowling Green and had very good fudge
sundaes at Alspach's. Mary Ellen did some shopping and I bought
a little calendar for my desk. I thought it was a bargain, 50 cents
for a little black leather one.

Tonight I went to a home nursing class that I'd signed up for.
I've missed the first two classes so I have some work to make up.
We learned how to make beds, which I already knew except for the
fine points.

171

Margaret has been away for a couple of weeks. I hope it warms up so we can go out to the pool for some sun when she gets home. It was warmer today but cool enough to wear a suit.

Thanks My Darling for your lovely, lovely letter. I adore you!

Hugs and Kisses,

Ritter

July 19, 1945

My Darling,

Your letters of July 10th to 11th came this afternoon. It sounded like you are working too hard. Let me know if you've been cured of your old breaking out. If you haven't, please do something about it at once. Mrs. Amundson's mother died of a skin disease, which brought to my attention again that skin trouble isn't to be fooled with. Promise me you won't neglect it!

I didn't exactly forget that you sailed the 29th. In fact, I thought you may have sailed the 28th. There were so many anxious days last summer and every time a letter didn't come, I thought you'd sailed. Then when you actually had, it took me several days to convince myself. It has been a very long time since that Sunday night you last held me in your arms. I hope the long stretch is over and the one ahead is very short.

I washed my hair this afternoon then, with kerchief around my head, went down to Gambles to pick out some record albums before they go on sale tomorrow. I decided to make you (perhaps I should say us) a gift of five albums, since they are so reasonably priced. I'm not sure that the selection is a good one but I tried to pick out the best of what they have and I figured I couldn't go far wrong at that price. I'm enclosing the list.

I was having trouble getting my wave in front so I drove around by Bonnie's for her assistance. I got it and the wave went in fine when I combed it tonight. Much to my regret, Bonnie found a short gray hair in my head yesterday. I believe that is my first. I hope the second waits a long time to come. Bonnie consoled me by saying she had found several of her own. I'll like you with gray hair, but not me.

The weather is finally warmer and it was a typical summer day. I much prefer a little extra heat to the cold we've been having.

Goodnight, My Darling. Don't work too hard, save up for that heap of hugging I want.

Love and Kisses,
Your Ritter

August 1, 1945

My Darling,

No letters from you today but a package came—the purse and horse picture. I think the picture amusing, poor horse. My next time up town, I'll find out who does framing. I was and am most elated over the purse. It is outstanding and smart looking. I thought you said it was alligator trim but isn't it snake? The leather is good and the trim sets it off. I have no idea what most things you sent would cost here but my guess is that this purse would cost no less than $25.

Just plain leather purses cost nine or ten dollars, and I saw two alligator ones, one was forty dollars and the other, fifty. I wouldn't think there would be people foolish enough to pay so much for a purse but apparently there are. However I shall enjoy feeling ritzy with mine. It was a good thing it arrived when it did, as mildew had just started to work. Olive oil took care of it. If you have occasion to send any more leather, it would be a good idea to oil it before mailing. Then if any mildew formed, it wouldn't be likely to work into the leather.

My Darling I do appreciate all the things you send and I know how much time and effort it takes as well as money. I showed my purse off to the neighbors and Margaret said she has one to show me that Floyd made. Mrs. Bruchlacher says you surely look out for me.

I don't very often tell Mary Ellen about the things you send because Warren never sends anything probably because he isn't where he can get anything.

In the latest Time *Magazine, I read that quite a few physicians will be discharged but those with specialties, such as psychiatrists, who have already been in the Pacific area a long time will have the least possibility. Do the psychologists get rotated?*

Helen Biery is in town, and I'm going over to see her tomorrow afternoon and so the days roll around and it will soon be time for school to start.

I better get to sleep. I'd like to get up and clean up my room before it gets warm in the morning.

Goodnight, My Sweetheart. I love you so very much, My Precious.

> *Your longing wife,*
> *Ritter*

Calcutta, India
August 2, 1945

Dearest Ritter Sweet:

Your July 24 letter came today making excellent time. In view of the remarks you made, and in lieu of the 23 July communication, I can at least conclude that your folks bought the Fred Zoll place at 215 E. Lincoln. Despite its cost, I think it is a sensible buy, particularly if you move soon. I remember the house vaguely, but you must send me a snapshot of it. At the moment, I am concerned with the terrific amount of moving you will have to do—so sorry, dearest, that your wandering husband insists on gathering junk.

Once home, I am going through that stuff pretty fast—will give away or discard most of it.

Sheer folly to keep it. Particularly the book reviews, in view of the work that I shall do from now on.

But I like to reflect on the peaceful hours you and I enjoyed clipping and pasting those same reviews. Our ambition floated in a tiny orbit, would that it could return to that cycle.

Have you noticed what a euphonious relationship "Ritter sweet" has to "bitter sweet"? I am very fond of bitter sweet, and as for Ritter sweet—hello, life and wife!

You must keep your head high, my lovely lady. Let us be the kind of people whom our children will remember with love and admiration. Let our weaknesses be amiable, our strengths steadfast, our courage boundless, and our hope faithful. Let us love life for the sheer joy of living. We can be so thankful for what we have if not another drop passes our lips. And if, as I am confident, the future is bright, how very glorious it will be! I admit that there are moments when this weak flesh would falter, when the petty annoyances of existing seem overwhelming, when the contrary wills of men of evil intent are like a threatening cloud on the horizon. All this, yes, I admit.

But there is a further heritage of the spirit that bids me stand erect and unafraid; that would have me walk into the storm; that will not let me lie supine before an inarticulate fate.

Whatever waits just beyond the veil of the morrow, for that I am prepared. I want you to see the sunrise with me.

What happened today? Very little that I can recount of interest. Mrs. Wale froze me all day and courted the Col., and Milner. An hour in N-P conference with the Col. this afternoon—dictation for an hour. That about covers it!

Tonight Gus and I saw Laurel and Hardy in "The Bull Fighter." The best parts were taken by the bulls.

Gus is beside himself with joy, for the engineers will build his photo laboratory.

Since his arrival, he has been waiting for the British to do it, but they move slowly, or lack the men, or something. The commanding general in this area finally commanded that it be done.

> My love to you, sweetheart,
> Ever yours,
> Dick

August 8, 1945

Dearest Ritter:

It has been several days since I have used the little fellow (the typewriter), but I notice that it still types with gusto . . . whenever I hit the right keys.

There has been just one subject of conversation anywhere in the hospital today; that is right, the atomic bomb. I was pretty sure that they would succeed in splitting and harnessing the atom, but I had hoped its power would be less than what had been predicted. Apparently it is even greater than first guessed. Unless the stories are all propaganda, the effect of the first bomb ever to be dropped has been terrific. It matters little now whether the Japanese quit or not; we can proceed at a methodical rate to obliterate them with almost complete safety to ourselves. Furthermore, there can be no objection to its use since the Geneva Convention does not mention it.

But in another sense the atomic bomb fills me with a sense of impending doom.

Now all the Jules Verne stories about mankind being wiped out are more than theory. It could be done. There will be no question about international amity now . . . either we have it or we have nothing.

The USA has the upper hand on this atomic bomb; surely it will have sense enough to keep it. But what our scientists have done, so can those of other nations. In a few years, those who were first will have no particular significance. Nevertheless, the short time goal which I first note is that of getting the war over with and that will make possible the attainment of my ONE goal, getting back to you. I doubt if it can be done by Christmas, but it isn't outside the realm of reality, as it was several weeks ago.

I am sure that I am catching a slight cold, which is not making me any happier or easier to get along with. I worked hard all day, but found that the morning program kept getting out of order.

Tonight positively nothing, except to drop flat on the bed and sob with relief . . . I intend to dream of you. Just you, sweetest girl . . .

      Love and devotion,

      Dick

August 9, 1945

Sweetest Girl:

Since I am reasonably sure that you are writing me an optimistic letter tonight, I want to counter with one which I consider optimistic myself. I think that I will surely win that bet from Gus, if not in the letter, at least in spirit, for now it may not be necessary to man an invasion to assail the beaches of Japan proper—as though anything Japanese could be proper!

But now I am sure that we will not be separated for more than two years, and with luck, since the British would like to see us out of here, it may be less time than that. If we just knew for sure exactly how devastating the atomic bomb can be—if it really does obliterate everything within several miles of where it strikes. If so, it shouldn't be too hard to methodically destroy the enemy with little danger to ourselves, in case they decide that suicide will be the face-saving operation necessary to restore their national honor, while it effectively removes them for all time. Swell!!!

With the Russian advent into the war, the India warehouse becomes obsolete to all intents and purposes. It was practically obsolete before, now it becomes an established fact. We knew that we would not be here long, under any circumstances, and now the length of time yet remaining seems surprisingly short. Of course, the Russians may not have announced to our government their anticipated move, so that we may not be in a position to take full advantage of this opportunity at once.

What happened today in my life? Nothing of particular importance. It rained today at 6, or at least it was raining when I awakened at that hour. During the morning, it rained again, but not furiously, as it ought. The Col. was too busy to see me today but I managed to get all my dictation out of the way as well as an occasional interview.

Tonight Gus and I went to see Ruth Hussey and some other people in "Bedside Manner" but it was so bad that we left before it finished. We stopped off at the club a moment, but there things were so crowded that we couldn't find seats. I did speak to Col. Peterson briefly, while Gus was buying himself a drink, then we came on back. I still have a cold and I am still tired, heaven only knows why.

Goodnight and sweet dreams, my darling wife.

> Ever,
> Dick
> In love with you
> Love and Kisses XXX

August 12, 1945

My Dearest,

I so want to wake up and hear that the war is really over! This suspense is hard on the morale. You are probably going through the same things. I'm anxious to get your letters telling me your ideas about how soon you will get back home. I suppose the rumors will be thick there, though.

> *Goodnight, my Beloved,*
> *So much love and devotion,*
> *Your Ritter*

August 13, 1945

Dearest:

I am writing this near the witching hour of midnight. By the way, I wonder what is especially magic about that time of day? For my part, light of my life, the grand, overwhelming moment that I once again see you, after the cruel months, will be burned forever in ecstasy in my heart.

Today? Well, it has been marked chiefly by the fact that your August 3 letter arrived.

What excellent mail service recently. There is no point in thinking of its continuance, for it is sure to fall off again. I think you will find that the picture of the horse grows on you after awhile. I may buy one more of the ancient Indian watercolors, this time more in keeping with the typical Indian spirit.

Of course today was Monday, and as such should have been a group psychotherapy day, but I decided against starting it then; think that I'll begin it Wednesday now and run over into next week. I spent the morning in interviews, doing a half-hour's dictation which brought me up-to-date.

I fiddled away the whole of this afternoon in reading over new cases and in talking an hour and a half with a radio singer who is embarrassed because of his big breasts!

Believe it or not, that just about does it. He is so sensitive that he won't undress before anyone else, always has to shower alone. With that goes impotency but for some perverse reason, he isn't worried about the latter. At any rate, he was an interesting patient and told me some of the hardships of entertainment units, of which I already had some conception.

He knows and likes Tony Martin.

Tonight the gang played poker and I won a few rupees, but quit early. It will interest you to know that poker bores me now, even when I win. Gus played for 3 1/2 hours this evening and lost only 19 rupees. He is doing much better than before.

War news? From what has been said, even the end of the war will hold us indefinitely, and as Major Bryce said tonight, for some reason the government seems more interested in returning auto mechanics and others to civilian life than they are professional people—so—despite the desperate need for teachers, I haven't heard the faintest murmur. Here we can blame our teachers' organizations, universities, and other such institutions for not yelling! There is such a thing as suicidal patriotism. I think they are guilty of it.

My dearest wife, keep your faith bright, honey, and soon, despite hell and highwater and red tape, I'll be holding you in my arms.

> Ever yours,
> Dick

August 13, 1945

My Dearest,

Everyone went out fishing this morning but Marilyn and I—we decided to sleep in.

The boys went fishing again this afternoon. Incidentally, their only luck today was a few little ones.

During the time I listened to the radio this morning they said in a couple days after the war is over they'll announce the plan for sending the boys home from the CBI—that those who have been there the longest and those not needed will be home first. Some by Thanksgiving and many by Christmas. I felt encouraged to have them mention the CBI in particular without commenting on any others. Sounds like your theater will be the first.

The radio announcer speaks as though the war is really over and a holiday may be declared tomorrow. I am a thankful girl—and now to be in the arms of my Beloved.

> *Hugs and kisses,*
> *Ritter*

August 14, 1945

Dearest Ritter:

"Unconfirmed" is the anticlimactic word to all we have been hoping for these last few days. No doubt, great questions of state are holding up responses! and our own atomic bombs cannot be dropped on Tokyo, for instance, without destroying our men who are prisoners of war. It is a harsh decision that faces American leaders, this wholesale wiping out of a people. If only it were given us to see more clearly.

Your August 4 letter reporting receipt of the ivory shakers arrived on schedule today. I'm glad you liked them. How very happy it makes me to know that in a small way I can add a sparkle to your lovely brown eyes.

Some people have rich, generous lives, with emotions at the flood-tide, and happiness in abundance because they know the secret of sharing and giving and doing.

Such a one is Bonnie . . . warm, impetuous, foolish, kind-hearted, lovable sister. But sister Gay's life is bleak in contrast, sterile, unfruitful, unwarmed by the commission of thoughtful deeds for the sake of a smile. Bonnie has Marilyn. Bonnie has much that Gay has never had, could never have. To my sister Gay, then, to whose children I do not send gifts and letters and cards, I sent those shakers. You will see that she gets them soon, won't you, honey?

And dearest wife, when anyone does something for you, the touch of your hand, the fragrance of your presence, the light in your eyes, is no small reward. These attributes which I ascribe to you are not imagined by a fond husband but are confirmed by the evidence of 15 years of living with you and by the hundreds of people who have known you—not one adverse word have I ever heard!

Sometime I must write on the theme of Reva and Dick's relationship and what I think it has done to both of us and for us. To what heights you might have gone if you had not fallen in love with a small, erratic, earthy person like myself, whose mediocrity drags in the dust!

This morning I spent in writing out an account of my Group Psychotherapy classes for the Col. who wants to send it to Delhi with his monthly report to Major Mays of that headquarters. While I think it wasted motion, I did work out a comprehensive outline; Mrs. Wale typed it. Incidentally Pilgrim came over yesterday and wanted to know why I hadn't written out promotion data for him. I doubt if anything comes of it now.

A conference with the Col. over 4 patients this afternoon and several personal interviews. This noon, a boy in tears brought in a letter from his sweetheart, in which she broke with him. He has had 25 months overseas, and she now wants to be "just good friends." (Both are Jewish.) Another young man, also Jewish, handed me a 13-page letter from his father. It was a dignified response to an attack by the boy in which he condemned his father for his parents' separation. I believe that letter is literature. It revealed deep injury and sorrow, a father's pride and joy in his family, in his wife, the agony of watching a lifetime of work crumble while he was powerless to prevent it. He stands alone now. The mother is schizoid and paranoid and Pilgrim thinks the boy is too.

Mrs. Wale gave me quite a lecture on the meanness of the American army in making the Anglo-Indians work on a holiday and V-E day. Wanted to know if she would be expected to labor on V-E day? Said she would be damned and docked before she showed up. While she was in the process of working herself into a frenzy, I was futilely trying to inform her that a 2nd Lt. had little to say about American army policy in this theater; that I agreed that she should have time off to celebrate, etc. Between my secretaries and my nurses, life gets complicated, albeit exciting, much of the time.

Tonight Gus and I ate with Col. Peterson but we had had a couple beers and were very jolly. Two nurses joined us and we slipped out, leaving the Col. in possession of the nurses. Gus and I saw Fred Allen's movie, "It's in the Bag" in which he kidded everything Hollywood. It was fairly clever but horseplay at the end hurt its effectiveness.

Benny, Ameche, Victor Moore, and others helped add variety too. To quarters to read and write.

> Ever in love with you,
> Dick

August 15, 1945

My darling Ritter:

And so it finally came, that day for which we have been waiting, that preliminary day, the one that had to dawn before we could anticipate our reunion, our rebirth. The enemy gave up, and perhaps gave us several more months of joy. Yet much depends on what move is made by those who control the hospital. I am not sure that I would have been better off in the 12th. Our safest outlet would be to stay here for several months, then ship home when the theater is cleared. I look forward to that as a solution. I can hope.

Assorted celebrating is in progress (11:30 p.m.) in our area and the club held open house. I had expected to dress and go over about 10:00, but Gus had started drinking early in the afternoon and passed out about 7:45, just outside the door of our room. We dragged him inside but he kicked the furniture and swore, so we let him go. He promptly lurched through the door, vomited, and lay down on the ramp. Shirtless, the mosquitoes could get at him. I tried to cover him, but he knocked everything off. I got assistance from the guard at 10:00, to get him inside, but he was truculent, wanted to go to the Club.

I told him "No Club," but it wouldn't have made any difference; he couldn't have walked 50 feet. He stumbled out the back way and was gone for an hour—so, being my brother's keeper served a useful purpose. It kept me from the club.

My drinking has been confined to a minimum—a little at noon, at 4:30, and at 6:00.

Then, I quit. The stew tonight was atrocious, but I bribed the bearer to bring me 3 dishes of delicious ice cream—with chocolate syrup.

Obviously, since the surrender announcement came at 8:00 a.m., little was accomplished today, and we gave our patients permission to stay in the wards—a pretty concession, since normally they have to be out from 8:30–11:00; 2:00–4:00. Despite the splendid activities program built up for them, they don't do much. My people were sicker today than before—Imagine?! (Illness carries a shipping priority.)

The Col. was very rough in the section meeting today. Stressed saluting and making applications for regular army (God forbid!) All of us civilians think the R.A.[8] boys are afraid we will leave them with all the work to do. Ha!!!! Gladly. Incidentally, I was 15 minutes late, but the Col. didn't snap at me. We had a victory retreat this afternoon.

My everlasting love, precious sweetheart.
　　　　　　Dick

August 18, 1945

Dearest:

Today has been a long one, with darkness and rain shutting out the sunshine and leaving our part of the world in gloom. It apparently affected both Gus and me, for we decided to stay in tonight. After a brief nap, I went to letter writing. It is now after 1:00 but I don't feel sleepy.

I interviewed, dictated, and interviewed more the whole day—or rather until 3:30. At that time, Ruth Firsching came to the office to talk and stayed until 6:30. I think I said in yesterday's letter that she was going to a wedding. Ruth reminds me of a 20-year-old Gladys Reed Kagey! Her popularity in Calcutta and environs is incredible.

Gus (hooked nose, tow-headed, pig-like face, Dutchy) is unhappy. Tonight, trying to get to sleep, he suddenly rolled over, said, "I skiddy boo (do you suppose he got that habit from me?) I want to go back to the states." He has tried 3 or 4 dates, but I doubt that any of the girls he likes cares to go on with him when they can have their choice of more attractive men. Fat, unwieldy Mary Wieland casts sheep-eyes at him, but he ignores her. Ho hummmmmm.

It is now 1:30, honey, so I had better say goodnight. I love you, precious!

Dick

August 19, 1945

Dearest Ritter:

I cannot recall that I wrote that I received your August 8 letter yesterday, which made the eighth straight day in which I had received a daily letter from you in the proper order.

Then today the spell was broken, and I got no mail at all. I am so used to hearing from you daily that I am definitely spoiled and a sense of loss has accompanied me the whole day.

These days have no significance, and I drive myself at work, upheld only by a feeling that I ought to do my duty . . . despising in my heart the men who come before me but in me lies their only hope and it is not fair that I feel as I do.

Perhaps whatever powers there are left some vital elements out of their souls, for they are not strong men, not even moderately so. They sit and look, then talk of scandalous episodes which should be turned over in their breasts but not spit out for everyone to hear.

These men are spiritual nudists and what I see is not good to look at. I am to help them regain a degree of self-confidence and a modicum of insight, but to a man they usually reject any and all suggestions, preferring to dwell in the darkness of their own misery. They face the future with fear, and the past is filled with ghosts of incomplete and unsuccessful efforts.

This afternoon Gus and I took it easy, napping and reading comic papers. It was raining when I first awakened this morning, about 6:00 but I slept on until 7:30, went to breakfast about 8:00. This evening Gus and I went to see Fred MacMurray in "Murder, He Says," and it proved to be a rather funny satire on murder-mystery-adventure pictures, with several clever situations. We got back a half hour ago and I went to work on this letter at once. I have 15 unanswered letters to go, having worked pretty hard this week in cleaning them up, but my good resolutions for this afternoon came to naught.

That is the day, honey child, and I will see you in my dreams.

> Ever in love with my wife,
> Dick

August 20, 1945

Dearest:

I have just come from the Lighthouse movie theater, where I saw a movie in an air-conditioned modern building. Its theme was an English play, produced and directed by Lawrence [*sic*] Olivier and starring L. Olivier in "Henry V." The first half hour showed us the play as done in Shakespeare's time (1600), then our imaginations were invoked and the scenes thenceforth until the conclusion were played straight. The Technicolor was magnificent. At times, when models were used, the distant castle and rolling meadows were lovely, unearthly. The campfire scenes, the dreams of the famous charge of the French knights at Agincourt in which they were cut to ribbons by English bowmen will not soon fade.

Against the film was the difficult English dialect, the use of much of Shakespeare's original dialogue, which is hard to follow if the lines aren't well known. Despite this, if it comes to America, you must see it by all means.

I began a class of group psychotherapy this morning in which 17 men are enrolled.

I'm not too serious about the business, however; I expect to try to maintain a level of interest only. Since no constructive benefits ever came out of these classes that could be evaluated, why not try this approach?

Clare Spranger told me today that she thought one of my former patients was going to strike her for a moment. It seems that he refused K.P. duty. He's a shell-shock case from Burma. Touchy business, much of this. Lou Battista returned my breast obsession case—and so I'm stuck with him again. The only breast obsession I ever had was with yours, pet, and I've still got it! Hmmmm. How I want to take advantage of your offer to share your side of the bed.

Threatening rains circled us today, with some falling here. But tonight the moon is shining. We came back in an open taxi—swell—if you had just been beside me, Reva.

That's all, honey. I start each day with the thought of you, and end it so.

Ever in love,
Dick

August 23, 1945

Dearest Ritter:

Tonight I saw something which amazed and delighted me: a moonbow. It followed a freshet which had shut off the bright moonlight temporarily. As the clouds cleared in the east, a perfect arc, varying from light gray to a tapering lead, bridged the avenue of the west. Lovely, and rather eerie.

What of today?

First, a letter in each of the day's mail deliveries pleased me immensely. August 11 and 12. You were at Russell's Point when you wrote the 12th, and you and the kids had just returned from an abortive peace celebration. If you stayed there until Wednesday, you had a real opportunity to celebrate. One thing about this rejoicing. I have never had the slightest doubt at any time that we would win, and I just haven't felt like yelling and shouting.

When one goes to a football game, there is usually a good chance that the other team might win, but in this little game, neither of our opponents had a chance once we got into the fight. If they hadn't been blinded by their own stupidity, they would have known that as well as I.

The day has been routine for the most part. Just after Gus left me a note that he had gotten tickets to the Lighthouse Theater for Friday night, I learned that I was to have AOD Friday. By scurrying around, I got that changed to Saturday . . . which I won't like particularly. Gus was gone for the noon and evening meals, taking pictures of patients coming in by plane from China.

Tonight I went alone to see Danny Kaye in "Wonder Man" done in Technicolor. It was very good, I think, but our equipment couldn't reproduce the sound loudly enough so we had to enjoy the comedy in almost complete silence. After picking up our jungle ration, Lord Calvert's, I walked slowly home in the moonlight, thinking of you.

Goodnight, my dearest wife.

Love and kisses,
Dick

August 24, 1945

Dearest:

Today has been a day of contrasts in the weather, first fair, next stormy. The temperature stays about the same. Clammy, warm, moist, bathing, sweaty, watery, steamy—I don't mind it particularly but most people do.

As usual, this week a Group Psych class. For a change, some of the boys admit they get something from it. This surprises me; arouses the cynic, and causes me to reexamine the fellows who so speak. I am becoming as crass as Pilgrim about the "boys."

He says they are damned spineless yellowbacks!

The nurse is bothered constantly by a procession of them with complaints like these:

"I want some APC's[9] for a headache." "My back hurts." "My joints ache." "I've got a breaking out here (they point), what's good for it?" "Can't someone do something for me?" "I'll blow my top if I don't get out of here." "I couldn't sleep last night." "I had the worst dreams; awakened tireder than when I went to bed." "The back of my neck aches . . . What about an x-ray of my ankle; I think it is swollen. Look how my fingers shake (spreading the fingers for all to see them tremble). I want an eye consultation. My ear hurts. I itch all over. I want to see the Lieutenant. I want to see the Major. Someone had better do something for me." That's the way it goes . . . the whole day. In addition, many of them are on regular prescribed medication programs. And these are fellows that have been cleared of organic disease by Medical Services.

What fun!

Tonight was a big night. Gus and I took our time. Bathed, relaxed, then drove to Karnani for dinner. We had a whiskey and soda or two at the bar, wine with the meal of chicken-fried steak. Then we proceeded on up town to the Lighthouse to see Deanna Durbin in "Can't Help Singing." I liked the fountain in the closing scene! Deanna's singing and a lot of Technicolor were wasted on one of the worst films I've ever seen.

Clouds partially obscured a brilliant full moon. We stopped at the club for coffee, drove past the lovely lake, whose border of trees was mirrored in its bosom. Placid, calm, restful. Calcutta going to sleep.

Your August 13 letter rejoiced me with its timely arrival.

> Goodnight, my love,
> Dick

August 26, 1945

Dearest Girl:

Good old gloomy Sunday . . . the whole darn day . . . every bit of it . . . gloomy. And just awhile ago, it rained like the seven hells had broken loose and heaven had sent all of its fire departments to put out the blaze. However, the rain did let up in time to let Gus and me go to dinner about 7:15.

Just as I finished my letter to you last night, I was commenting to a patient on the fact that it had been a quiet evening, and I hadn't taken my duties too seriously. I laughingly rapped on wood, but I should have hit it a terrific lick, for just then an MP walked in and that started a four-hour mess that carried over the next day.

It seemed that an Indian girl had been raped by two GI's and that the Gurkha[10] guards were yelling for vengeance. I found the girl in the Receiving Office, a pitifully huddled figure perched at the rear of the building on the pavement. When I checked the barracks in which she was supposed to be, no one knew anything. I called the downtown MP's, for the interpreter said that she had been assaulted, or said she had, in the mouth, vagina, and rectum. They sent out two CID men who located one of the soldiers, who confessed that he had had, in company with the other men, relations of the type so unhappily described.

Then, in the rain, I had to find a gynecologist for the examination. We secured a nurse, opened the operating room (about 1 a.m.) and gave the girl a thorough examination.

It was as she said, but the question was, had she struggled and screamed as reported? If so, where had she gotten

G.I. gum and handkerchief? It was my opinion that she had gone willingly enough but put up a fuss when the men didn't pay her. I was pretty angry with the fellow we had caught, the dope! He could have saved me a lot of trouble if he hadn't behaved in such a niggardly fashion. She, the girl, turned out to be a Hindu widow, which under the Hindu laws, is damned near a prostitute's level, to keep body and spirit together.

Someone hit a bearer on the head at the club . . . otherwise, no excitement. Major Schnitker and I had late dinner together and enjoyed some good talk on "the hell with the army." After my final round, which went smoothly, I had coffee with some of the enlisted men. To bed at 4 a.m. Work went as usual this morning. Read papers and napped this afternoon. Decided against seeing "The Great John L."

But very much in love with you,
Dick

August 27, 1945

Dearest Little Girl:

I cannot say much for this day, nor any other day that does not see me on my way to you. You have asked me not to tire myself out, but this you must not do—for it is my one sure method of therapy for the blues. If all else fails to arouse my spirits, the drugging effect of sleep erases everything from my mind for a blissful while.

As ever, I am still nervous, albeit I cover it nicely by easily slipping from one situation to another without too much fuss and too much hurry. This is deceptive, and does not reveal how agilely my mind is dodging from pillar to post . . . but naturally I know. Nor does it discover to others the vague unrest that has stirred in me for years. I had thought that perhaps India would help me gain insight, but I have learned nothing here that I did not already know. If anything, I find issues somewhat clouded by the incredible things that I have seen in this part of the world.

There are so many people here that just watching the crowds makes me very impatient. Where are they going? Why? Not even their grazing sacred cows, whom they reverence but let starve, seem as aimless in their goals.

Last night I was at the club for awhile; Petty, Pilgrim, and Dols were there. Petty bought me a drink. I do not envy his headache, but I do the fact that he sails this week.

Well, today during the last session of Group Psychotherapy, I was on the ball and delivered myself of some rich sentiments. The class was large; about 21 and they seemed to enjoy it more than before. But I am glad that it is over in a week or so. I despise the stuff, what with airplanes whamming over the hospital and trucks grinding by and gabbling natives working around the area. It does no good to yell at the latter, they just look at you, turn away, and continue their damned gabbling.

Though tired, I played poker with the boys for awhile, but the game was slow and boring and after losing 21 rupees, I returned to my quarters at 11:00. There I finished Donn Byrne's *Hangman's House,* which I highly recommend to you.

> Night, precious sweet.
> Dick

September 1, 1945

My Dearest,

I'd make a good war wives sad-sack. If it isn't the car, it is something else. I got my suit (the new one I bought in the spring) from Kroger cleaners today. When I was putting it away I noticed a not large, but bad, three cornered tear and dark spot between the button hole and edge of the jacket. Most perturbed, I took it back. They are sending it to be rewoven and claim the repair won't be noticed. In the meantime, I do without it for a couple weeks.

I got my hair done this morning. I have quite a few new hairs that are an unruly length.

In about a month, I'll either have to get a new permanent or let it grow and continue rolling it or possibly start braids. I doubt the latter. I never have been able to get you to say how you like my hair best. How about telling me now?

Margaret is trying not to get over-excited, but she is washing up Floyd's civilian shirts. I expect to celebrate V-J day tomorrow by going to church and, I hope, being lazy.

> *Night, My Darling,*
> *Devotedly,*
> *Ritter*

September 1, 1945

Dearest Ritter:

So beginneth a new month.

Last year I was still in Bombay.

The year before I was in Washington, Pa.

Next year—in your arms, and the place won't count!

Well, that is something!

We have one more month of this rather uncomfortable weather to endure, then the season will become nice. If our work lets up sufficiently, life shouldn't be too onerous, especially if I can get out to the golf course several times a week. I will begin golfing this Wednesday, unless something interferes.

Today, Saturday, I went to the general meeting which is held weekly in the conference room. This morning, after an incredible interlude of an hour in which the RA doctors, with the exception of Peterson, proved that they couldn't read English in attempting to interpret a directive, an English lieutenant, who had been a war prisoner in Siam since January 1942, spoke to us.

He told of the general bad conditions under which they worked, the lack and poor quality of the food, positively no medical supplies except what they bought themselves, etc.

Since he was an officer he probably fared better than average, but he had it rough. Fourth-grade rice twice a day, with a little salt. That did it, and there was no more.

Punishment for officers was usually to stand at attention for an incredible length of time—usually one, two, or three days . . . continuously. If the guard didn't like your expression, he slapped you hard. Two of their officers were beaten to death with bamboo sticks; two others whipped until they would be crippled for life, but they were taken away and never seen again.

Since they were given no medicine, when working in the jungle, the prisoners died like flies. From what little pay they were able to get out of the Japs, they shared in the expense of buying what drugs they could find to purchase. I believe the officer said that he had had malaria 36 times in three years. Still, he looked fairly healthy when I first saw him.

One of the sabotage tricks used by the British while building the railroad for the Japs was to carry the queen white ant and several others wrapped in mud to the pilings of the trestles, plant them near the uprights so the termites could eat.

But as harshly as the Japs treated the prisoners, in a sense they treated their own soldiers worse. A Japanese officer or noncom thought nothing of knocking another soldier down, beating him with anything he had in his hand. In Japanese hospitals the Japanese patients were given few drugs, little medication, two-thirds of an ordinary food ration, permitted to talk only occasionally at stated times, and not permitted to read or write at all.

Since they were no longer of use to the army, they were not worth wasting much time on.

This applied to the honorably wounded as well as to others who sickened from malaria, dysentery, etc.

The Lt. told of seeing trains of wounded Japs with ugly, dirty, bloody dressings; unkempt, unfed. One man with an arm-and-leg amputation had two bloody bandaged stumps, clutched a handful of raw rice in his remaining hand (his ration for a five-day trip), begged a cigarette from the hated enemy prisoner of war. He got it.

I am amazed at the equanimity which not only the British but our own American POW's show toward the Japanese when discussing the hardships they underwent while in a Japanese camp. I do not think that they consider the Japanese quite human. I am sure that they pity him.

I finished a book this evening before dressing. Talked with Pilgrim and Dols for awhile in the former's room. Axtmeyer, Hines, McKinley, and Fischer came along on their way to the club. I joined them for a rather careless late evening but left before they did. Gus had returned from the Chinese consul's party at which he had met a Red Cross girl. While we were talking, the gang mentioned above came roaring along headed by Dols, who was more than three sheets to the wind. We got them out of our room, and then they went down to serenade Whit, ended by squirting the fire extinguisher on both Whit and Napper, which made both boys exceedingly angry. Everyone thought it funny but they. By 2 a.m. all had quieted down.

> So much in love with you,
> Dick

September 5, 1945

Dearest:

Well, for the first time in two years, I played golf. My score was 6, 6, 6, 5, 5, 5, 5, 5, 4 for 47 on the first nine. Since it was getting dark, we just practiced on the tenth coming in to the club house. My drives and second shots were as good as ever, but my approaches were weak.

The Tolleygongo Club is a beautiful oriental group of buildings in a gorgeous setting of tropical gardens. The fairways are luxuriant and the native caddies move your ball to an advantageous position, so that in all justice, you had to kick it off the clump of grass. There are bars not only at the club house but scattered out on the club. Furthermore, the course is no pushover, though I ought to play those nine in 42-44 after a little practice. There are several wicked water holes. The traps are jokes after playing Ohio State.

Four of us made the trip out: Clare, Ellen, Howard Gerber (Pilgrim's new assistant who replaces J.J. Weger), and myself. As I recall, aside from a time or two with you and me on a par 3 with Jean Lindsay, I never played golf with a girl. Of course, it was necessary this time, for only Clare had any golf balls.

The clubs which we were provided with were rather rickety, but I used only four and made out fairly well. I was the only one who kept score as the others were pretty bad, including Howard, who complained that I was never satisfied, no matter how close I came to the cup. We got back about 8 p.m. Howard and I dropped the girls off and came on down to our mess to eat.

I'm seated in my easy chair writing, and Gus won't talk to me. I can't tell whether he's angry because he thinks I neglected him or not—but I asked him to go out to the golf course with us and he said he hated golf. His jaw isn't healing properly after his dental work—It is quite swollen, so that might account for it. At any rate, I hate to see him acting like that.

Latest rumor is that the whole theater will be cleared by February '46 at the latest.

I'm living in anticipation of seeing you, precious girl, soon.

> Ever in love,
> Dick

September 7, 1945

Dearest Ritter:

Your letters of August 25, 28, and 29 came today and very welcome they were, but it will mean a famine for me for the next few days, I know. Nevertheless, it is such a thrill to look at your beloved handwriting that I hunger for it and gulp down the life-giving spirit you infuse me with.

Today it proved to be a little cooler than before with the first cool breezes that I have felt since coming to Calcutta. They have held until tonight . . . and sleeping should be good.

(At the moment, Rosenthal is in here trying to talk with me while I keep on typing in his face.) Gus hasn't showed up since this noon, when he wouldn't talk again . . . he wouldn't talk this morning either. If he is sick, I wish he would admit it; this business of acting as though he were angry is getting me down. When he does not talk, I don't, and it makes for a [Later handwritten note in the margin: "He came in drunk a few moments ago."]

Rosenthal finally left, crying about the personnel situation, which he says is all snafued because no one tells him anything.

There seem to be a lot of new officers running around, so I presume that some of the up-country outfits are beginning to shut down. I just heard the announcement of points for officers over the radio. All I need is 85. Well, I have half that many. That rather tickles me . . . the brass is holding on for dear life. Incidentally, at the moment I am not so much concerned with getting out of the army as I am in getting home. Why the hell don't they devote a little energy to getting us back, then worry about the other while we are on the high seas? Of course, that would be the sensible way of doing a thing, and the god damned army has never given any reason yet, so probably will not begin to at this late hour.

Once again I got little accomplished today, but have long since quit worrying about it, for the Col. simply won't see my patients and that is all there is to it. He has a stack of charts on his desk that have been there for over a week. His nurse told me that he comes in, looks at them idly, then walks out again. So be it.

This morning Gerber and I went to the Col.'s famous N-P class for the new nurses.

There were about 15 nurses there, Gerber, Pilgrim, and myself. The Col. did a good job of teaching, but he didn't try any demonstration of hypnotism, which is the reason we went.

We now learn that Pilgrim is sold on it and wished to see it for ourselves. So Monday morning will find me Johnny on the spot. Gerber and Ellen Diemer apparently hit it off well, for they are having dinner together tonight. They came around to ask Clare and me to go, but she and I decided against it. Golf, yes, but the other, no. Besides, I thought you would prefer it that way, not that one is apt to fall for Clare, who is not very pretty . . . her fair, blond face is angular, and she inclines to a sharp tongue with a shrill voice. I am sorry for her. She is 32, single, and a Catholic.

It is now approaching 11:00 and no Gus. Rosy suggested that maybe he had turned in to the hospital. More likely he is out on a bender.

One year ago today, we set out from Bombay for Calcutta.

> Goodnight, precious little wife,
> Dick

September 8, 1945

My Darling,

I didn't do many of the things I'd planned to, today. It was so very warm. As you know, it makes it that much harder for a person to get their rest. You know about that in India!

I picked up Mary Ellen and we went downtown to eat. We got caught in the rain which makes it a little colder outside. But we needed the rain badly. We ate at the Phoenix and had a pretty good dinner.

Since Uhlman's is next door, we stopped in there and I came out with a new coat. It is a black chesterfield (that is a straight line, tailored coat, you know) made of material similar to what we call camel's hair. I paid less that I thought I'd have to—$35. I hope I like it as well as I think I will.

Then we went down to Lynn Lion's store to see Helen, who was helping them out today. Frank was meeting her after work, so we stayed a party of two.

We went to see "Murder, He Says," with Fred McMurray. I don't believe it impressed me as much as it did you, but we got in, in the middle, which wasn't so good.

After the show, we went to Mary E's for coffee and rolls. She has a grumpy landlady who asked us to turn the radio down when we were listening to the news. Mary Ellen thinks she is trying to get her out so a friend can move in. We were very polite to her, although Mary E was upset over it, and we both said we'd like to turn our husbands loose on her.

I plan to sleep in the morning. If I can't, it will be a good time to do school work. I made some newspaper clippings this afternoon and mailed them to you tonight.

It is time to go to bed.

> *A great big Hug and*
> *All My Love,*
> *Ritter*

September 10, 1945

Dearest Ritter:

I was almost calamitous, today, when at noon I learned to my dismay that we had Vienna sausages for the main course. I cannot eat those embalmed earthworms, stewed in their own grease, but I consoled myself with the thought that tonight I will eat, indeed I will, double portion of whatever it may be, even C-rations.

Tonight we had to wait for our plates, all except the commanding officer who came in and was seated although he is the one who ordered that we stand in line for our food in the first place. (And if you ask me, which you didn't, I would say that is what is wrong with this damned army in the first place . . . someone gets the bellyache and he sends through an order which ends in everyone getting a belly-ache only for a different reason, no doubt. Also, maybe it isn't exactly a bellyache we get, after all, but it is an ache.)

Getting back to the waiting, the cook handed me two magnificent looking, oh the shame of it, lamb chops. Now I am back in my room, disconsolate and on the edge of starving to death. This is a bitter way to finish all these months overseas. If it were not for your lovely portrait staring straight at me, I would be tempted to settle the matter once and for all. How? Well, I have two quarts of good whiskey in the closet. But never worry, sweet, I could not drink alone with your steady eyes set on me. With you, now that is another matter.

As you can see from that long-winded first paragraph, maybe I am not as weak as I first thought. Your very nice August 30 letter rolled into camp today. Your idea of meeting me after I leave India is good. We could meet in some eastern city for a day or so, then travel home. Prefer-ably by train, for I wouldn't want you driving that far.

Don't count on that wonderful experience before next spring, my sweet, for the damned fools are moving as though it will break their stupid hearts to give up their cute little war, which the brass was fighting so comfortably from headquarters.

Besides, this is probably the first time in years that the top men, who are nearing 50 in most instances, have managed to get away from mama, and they are enjoying squiring around anything that wears a skirt and dabs Tojour L'Amour [*sic*] behind her ears. The old billy goats. On the other hand, if all the women who were behind at home were as lovely as my attractive girl, we would get to hell out of here in a hurry.

I cannot recall (what has happened to my memory?) whether I have said anything recently about sending things through to me. I am reconciled to passing another Christmas abroad, so do as you like about sending things, but do get a package or two off, so that I will have something to open on that festive occasion.

What happened here today? Well, I finally got in to see the Col. with five men today, this afternoon. This morning I attended the Col.'s class and enjoyed hearing him talk about the sexual cases to the nurses. He told me later that he was embarrassed, but I think he was enjoying himself.

The weather is threatening and has been all day. Hard rain, misty rain, and clouds.

Just now it is thundering and lightning.

It has been fun talking with you, pet, but I imagine that I ought to bring this to a close.

> Forever yours,
> Love and kisses,
> Dick

Calcutta street scene: traffic in Calcutta is a nightmare tangle of street cars, rickshaws, buses, oxcarts, and army vehicles.

Gharries, Old Dobbins Last Stand.

September 13, 1945

Dearest One:

Five letters this afternoon and not a single one from you. Imagine, if you can, my disappointment, especially since I have gotten no September letters from you and the one from the Pattons, I heard from the folks, Alice Jarvis, Tom and Jane, and Harry Baill.

Mother wrote that you are as "beautiful as ever." When a mother-in-law as matter-of-fact as my mom says that of a daughter-in-law, what a wife the son (that's me) must have! I'm properly thankful, precious child, indeed I am. Fate compensated for some double-dealing to me when it gave me you with your marvelous faith, love, and generosity.

Today has been a beastly, hot, sultry day—one that I was glad to write off forever. I was tired, worn out, and

had a tummy-ache. But tonight I feel better and look forward to the morrow. It would have helped if I had seen
your beloved handwriting!

Example of my life on the ward:

4:45 p.m.—Pause for several minutes after two
neuro-psychological consultations to talk over last night
with the Col.

4:50—Pause again at Ward 46 to see Pilgrim about a
patient and he's not there so chat with Howard a second.

4:52—Take Lancaster, one of the n-p
[neuro-psychiatric] conferences, to one side to tell him of
our decision to Section IX (separate from service) him.

4:55—Jim Beasley wants to see me for a minute. He
wishes to borrow 10 rupees to pay off a boy leaving tomorrow. I take him into the office to ship him the pages.

5:00—Little Miss Howe peeks in (she was to be married tonight) to say she hadn't yet heard from her fiancé,
who went to Delhi yesterday. She has unpacked—is
unhappy—very. I take her hand (I'm 14 years older) and
tell her of us—7 long years. She's known her sweetheart
for 90 days. She smiles through unshed tears and says wist-
fully that maybe it is for the best.

5:05—A patient who leaves tomorrow wants my view
of his case, and insists that he will respect my opinion. I
doubt it, but tell him frankly that I think his trouble is
deeper-seated than he thinks, warn him to learn from
experience.

5:14—(I'm so tired. I want to go home. That's why
I'm watching the watch. Now the late afternoon sun breaks
through the clouds, shines in the office.)

5:18—Close my appointment book. Stand up with a
sigh of relief.

5:24—As I walk out of the office, my hands loaded
with papers, big Buddy Brees (235th) bars my way. He has
written some song lyrics. Will I listen? I stand by, while he
half croons them to me. They aren't bad.

5:29—Goodbye to Woody and Dotty (Miss Howe) and walk through the door to be joined outside by Howard Gerber, who is just leaving 46.

Tonight Gus and I walked to the show area which has been doubled in seating capacity now that the POW's are here in number. There must have been 500 or more people seated under tonight's new moon. The movie was Humphrey Bogart and Lauren Bacall in "The Big Sleep." No one ever learned what the big sleep was but there was no doubt that the picture was well received. The lines were ultra-clever and the characterization good. I rather thought they overdid Humphrey's fatal fascination with women, but maybe not.

We stopped at the club where I refused Gus' invitation to drink and instead watched the Bingo game for a moment. Then I caught our taxi to the area—am now busy writing you this letter.

And so, think it time for me to draw this to a close—not that I want to stop writing to you, or thinking of you, or loving you, but so that I can dream of our reunion.

> Ever yours,
> Dick

September 18, 1945

Dearest:

Such a pleasure to receive your September 6, 7, and 8 letters today—and good to see that you are settling into a routine. At the close of summer, you had become entirely too preoccupied with your thoughts, which tended to become morbid and introspective. Now I agree with you in everything that you were thinking, but it does us little mental and spiritual good to grieve about such matters—It is much better that we look to the glorious future with joy and thanksgiving that things were no worse—that our capacities for fulfilling the lives of one another are so great, so faithfully sure.

As I have written, more often to the folks than to you, the end of the war reinforced my will to continue putting up a fight against despondency. But the mood soon passed, but not until I had struggled to regain my power to rationalize, to go from there to an acceptance of seeing reality. Yet, this period of futile waiting will come to an end, and from it each man and woman will have received his or her just deserts.

I am writing this from the Adjutant's desk, where I am on duty as AOD [Assistant Officer of the Day] during the noon hour. The ugly little Anglo-Indian girl blocks me from the typewriter, smokes cigarettes endlessly and ignores me, barely responding to my forced "How do you do?" Hers must be an unhappy life though some of her kind appear to have made a good adjustment.

The heat is most oppressive—weighs down like a slab of rock on the body, like a dark veil on the mind. It refuses to rain, and that is merciful.

This morning passed in a haze of interviews and dictation. One was for the purpose of getting my views on a POW from the *Houston,* sunk March 1, 1942, and in a Japanese prison camp for 3 1/2 years. He became temporarily deranged about August 4 after being brought to the 142nd. I declared him normal but there are instances that smell fishy. He was only mistreated once by the Japs, claims the Australian Medical Officer declared him unfit for hard labor such as working in the jungles.

He came to us weighing 227 pounds. When his condition is contrasted with that of Wainwright and countless others, the implications are pretty ugly. Nevertheless, indicative evidence doesn't count. He is rational enough now.

As usual, Woody Flanagan and I started for the EM [enlisted men] mess to check it and eat there, when Ruth decided she wanted to go along. Needless to say, she created quite a commotion, but the treat to the boys was well-deserved, no doubt.

This afternoon passed almost as rapidly as the morning. About 4:00 a terrific downpour started, the heaviest of the summer. Howard and I actually waded a time or two when we went to quarters at 5:15. I drank beer with Gus and cursed the army with him, then took a nap.

At 7:00, I picked up Riley (39, gray-haired nurse on closed Ward 52, well on her way to being a neurotic or chronic alcoholic) and Spranger and went to the nurse's mess for dinner, where we had huge steaks. I just got a phone call, so will pick this up from here tomorrow.

> Goodnight, darling girl,
> Love,
> Dick

September 20, 1945

My Darling,

I have a lot to write about today's activities. They were so humorous, but consequently I'm too tired and will just hit the high spots instead of describing some of the persons I met tonight.

First of all, your September 10 letter came today. You were burned up and discouraged too, I think, and spoke of the possibility of not getting home before spring. But in a later letter you were more optimistic, so here's hoping.

I rushed home at 5 o'clock to be ready for our school show by 5:30. As one of the new teachers, I was initiated. We as the newest were the program, our stunt being "an old-fashioned school." The committee provided us with a few articles of clothing, dinner bucket etc. Only two of the four men teachers (the other two are coaches) were there. We had a little time for preparation. One of the men was the teacher, the other was Elmer (my brother in the skit), and I was his crying sister Daisy Mae. The other girls were our mother and father who came to visit. Some of the others recited poetry and answered questions incorrectly. We worked out a few clever lines but could have used more wit. Everyone was kind and said they enjoyed our horseplay.

Ruth Stuart invited me to join her, Mildred Masters (the music teacher at Donnell) and Golda Fox (our first grade teacher) at Golda's for a bridge game. Golda is older but is awfully nice and by the way has a boyfriend. I had already had a long day but accepted. I had forgotten all I knew about contract bridge and Mildred and Golda are just learning, so Ruth is the patient teacher. I invited them here next week. I like them, and I am anxious to learn a little contract. I've always played in the dark.

That is a brief resume of the day, Sweetheart, and now I must get to sleep.

All my love, Dearest,
Your Ritter

September 20, 1945

Dearest Ritter:

Unfortunately, no mail from you today, sweetheart, but that only means that we will get some tomorrow, maybe.

Today, the following:

Worked fairly hard all morning on interviewing and dictating. This afternoon was in conference with the Col. and Major until 5:30. Dottie Howe showed up with her husband-to-be and introduced him to us. He is a nice fellow.

Gus went to the movie tonight while I joined the Col. and others at a sort of farewell party for Clare Sprangers who finished her work at the 142nd Neuro-Psychological section tonight at 7:30. She will sail within a week.

Our table was outside under the moon, stars and palms. How nice it would have been to have had lovely you there, sweetheart. There are times when Calcutta isn't so bad, if it just weren't for our loved ones not being with us. The rains have made it cooler, so that it is much pleasanter sleeping lately—so much so that I use a sheet.

Have I told you that I now have 41 patients on the ward, 16 of whom are boarded casuals from up the line? The casuals cost little or no work, but the remaining patients are all very difficult cases. Anyone with any gumption at all will not come to the hospital now. So that means that practically every case we have is a primary behavior disorder, emotional immaturity, a psychopathic personality, or a chronic or psychopathic alcoholic. Actually, nothing, positively nothing, can be done to remedy the condition of these men.

I have a particularly bad case or two which I'll write up on the typewriter for you in a day or so.

We received two bottles of jungle ration this month—Old Crow rye whiskey and Dixie Bell gin. I still have last month's whiskey left, as I rarely touch it here in the room.

Everyone got two cases of beer this month, too.

Sweet, hope school is going better.

> Forever in love,
> Dick

September 21, 1945

Dearest Ritter:

Another day nearer you, my dearest, and from all that I can gather, I feel that I shall surely be on my way home by January. The gossip has this hospital losing its general status as of one month from today, when it will become a station hospital. I am not sure that will happen within a month, but it is sure to occur soon, for the character of a hospital is determined by the number of beds. The latest information which we have from Delhi seems to indicate that evacuation is to be from Karachi because of the difficulty of getting ships into the Calcutta harbor. Someone was telling me that the clearance is often only a few inches. No matter how that turns out, we are optimistic for a rapid shifting of troops in the theater.

Mrs. Wale and I worked like beavers all morning, got large quantities of work out of the way. Gus and I went to a meeting of the Officers' club at 4:45 at which Col. Pete presided. I guess we had no conferences this afternoon, but plan to have one in the morning. The Officers' club meeting was interesting, for one faction wanted the excess club fund thrown to the Officers' mess, while the other group wanted it used to reduce the price of drinks. We now have about 15,000 rupees profit. At any rate, I voted with those, of whom Pilgrim and the Col. were two, who wanted the fund retained at the discretion of the club council. We won by a vote of 39-36. I bought Clare's jungle ration, but gave the gin to Gus to give to his boys.

We took it easy until the middle of the evening last night, then went to the club for awhile. The night was magnificent, with a full moon in a star-studded sky. It is cooler in the evenings, too, and makes for wonderful sleeping. At any rate, it makes me ache pretty badly for you, darling, and I cannot wait to arrive home. Keep the home hearth burning brightly, darling girl, and I'll be there before you know it.

> Ever in love,
> Dick

September 22, 1945

Dearest Ritter:

Today is Saturday, and even as you welcome the weekend, so do we, for our two half days off are precious to us. Not that we work so hard, but rather the idea of freedom to do as one likes makes the half-days memorable. Unfortunately, I gained no half-day this afternoon, but instead conscientiously returned early at noon to check a patient whom we consider sending to the locked ward—51.

This boy was born in Germany, came to America at the age of 3 1/2 with his parents. He is now 22. When he arrived on my ward, he was quiet but cooperative, seemed to be holding something back. His complaint was a tight-scary sensation in the chest in the region of the heart, which sent his pulse rate up. Under psychotherapeutic treatment, he began to exhibit anxiety symptoms. Soon he was calling to nurses and ward men to hold his hand, to feel his pulse, to check if his heart were still beating.

He told me that he had stopped masturbating because he thought it gave him a headache (his original complaint). When he tried to start three months later, he couldn't get an erection. He became frightened. For several days now, he has reported little or no sleep at night. However, his eyes are not bloodshot, he has no circles under his eyes, and his face is placid and doesn't show signs of strain. He often gives the wrong answers, psychiatrically speaking, to questions asked him. He tells us what he thinks we want to hear, not what the usual sick person would say!

The Col. agreed with me that the boy is faking, and so I came back to observe him.

He did go out to play ball, came back in looking much better, but worried because he hadn't been tired out by the exertion, was certain that that was abnormal. But I re-assured him and got away about 4:15 p.m. with instruction to the nurse to watch him.

Gus and I fooled around the room when I finally got back in the afternoon, slept an hour or so. Then to Karnami for dinner. We got to the club rather late. Col. Pegg, head of dental service, and Col. McShane were also at Peterson's table. He had Lt. Fagler, who was on my ward for awhile, with him. The moonlight was pretty. They turned off the lights, and nurses and officers danced under the moon!

Tiring of watching, I returned to the area and joined Pilgrim and Weiger till a late hour, in talk and a little whiskey.

> I'd like my arms about you, my darling,
> Dick

September 23, 1945

My Darling,

    The folks were out so I stayed around the house all day except for a trip to the post office to mail you two envelopes of clippings. Regler had an article last week on the labor situation and claims the administration underestimates the work hours lost by strike during the war. He also comments on people receiving unemployment benefits while out on strike.

    I decided to drive over to Birdwhistells this evening and asked Mother to go along.

    As I made the stop on Lincoln approaching Blanchard, a car from the north turned into Lincoln. A car was coming from the south and I started to pull behind it when it started to turn in. I immediately stopped and was not yet out into Blanchard but probably had more than my share of Lincoln Street. At any rate, the driver (she) made too big an arc and larger than necessary and ran over the curbing on the northeast corner. We all had to get out of our cars.

    The man in the car was quite bullish at first but when I didn't say I'd take the blame, he tried to appeal to me, that it wouldn't cost me anything if I'd say it were my fault. Some woman came out from her porch and said, "Why don't you just drive on, it was all their own making." He wanted me to take the blame without calling the police, but I said he better call them. The policeman was very nice and said I had nothing to worry about. He said you just call your insurance agent and forget about it. He said he'd have the record of it and the agent can look at it if necessary. So I stopped and told Dad about it. The point was they were driving too fast to be going to turn but naturally I was glad they hit the curb instead of us. I didn't care if the insurance company pays but I hated to admit that it was my fault when they were at least four fifths in the wrong.

    Mrs. Birdwhistell said she heard over the radio last week that the boys from India and Burma will be the first home since England will take over there. And if enough ships are available, some

*will be home by Thanksgiving and many by Christmas. That
sounded good to me!*

*I have playground duty this week, which will make a little ex-
tra pull on me, so I guess I'd better say goodnight, as it is 12
o'clock. I feel rested after this weekend. I couldn't say that last
Sunday night.*

> *Lots of Love, lots of hugs, and*
> *Lots of Kisses,*
> *Your Ritter*

October 12, 1945

Dearest Ritter:

I am sure to be acting officer on duty this coming
Monday and probably next Sunday, for I notice that Milner
draws it this Sunday. It will be just as well, then I can get
the task over with. We have so many new people on the
lineup that I have gone much longer than usual as it is,
which is all to the good.

This morning I tried to send the man who ran over the
Hindu child back to duty, taking him to the Col. for a conference. Imagine my consternation when he broke down
and cried like a baby to the Col.'s questioning because he
was afraid that he would never be able to explain to his religious mother why he had taken a life. As I have already
written you, it was not the driver's fault. The Biblical in-
junction "Thou shalt not kill" doesn't apply in his case because he did everything possible to save the reckless boy.
The Col. had an excellent idea—send the chap to the
chaplain. We will see what Colbern reports.

While sitting there talking with the Col., he called
transportation for a jeep, so I asked him if I could invert
tomorrow, taking the morning off and working the afternoon. He asked me to go along with him this afternoon,
said that Ann was taking him on a walking tour of the
shops. I did not need a walking tour, but I did need a
chance to shop, so after some persuasion, I promised to

go. We spent the entire afternoon walking down Park
Street, through the shops across from Newmarket, New
Market itself, and on Chowringhee.

I almost bought you an inexpensive star sapphire, but
every American has sent one home, so I hated to do that.

One of the dealers talked us into going into an adjoining building to see his warehouse, which turned out to be a
room on the second floor of a building. He had inlaid coffee tables of atrocious taste which he assured us he could
pack to be sent to the States.

There was nothing there I would have put in a chicken
coop—except a beautiful vase of simple pattern, but alack
and alas, he knew it was his best piece. Rubbing his hands
together, Mr. B.R., as he called himself, said, very oily,
"Very expensive, very nice Chinese bronze, 40 rupees." So
we left.

I did pick up a final Christmas present or two for you
and for your friend Barbara, a white formal scarf with gold
and silver overlay and a throw scarf for a davenport or
grand piano or what have you. The latter is of fine Kashmir
weave, wool, and pattern. Speaking of Kashmir, we saw
some stuff in a window, which we liked, I think it must
have been some bedspreads. Heaven help me. The cheap-
est of the lot was 522 rupees, the most expensive 2200.
One fine, brown, exquisitely soft woolen spread was 1300
and there was just the cloth, no embroidered, brocaded
pattern. Whew! The dealer remarked that it was an unusually long piece, and Peterson retorted that it ought to be at
$400, that indeed, one ought to be able to wrap the whole
house in it at that price. Ah me!! Have you any idea how
much they want for a tiger skin? We priced several today.
They begin at 350 rupees for one with the head; without
the head, 100 rupees cheaper.

I was pretty tired when we taxied back at 6:00 but the
Col. insisted that I stay and watch Ann and him play a little

badminton, which I did, and then the Col. got us some beer and we sat in the gathering darkness drinking it.

Ellen and Howard have insisted that I go along with them to play golf tomorrow afternoon which I have agreed to, though that will make it a threesome. That little blonde, Betty Bratt, had said she wanted to play, had even called me after she left the ward, but I wasn't at all interested. You must believe me, I am not interested in anything she has to offer. As a matter of fact, the more I see of other women, the more I grow in appreciation of you, sweetheart!

Well, honey, I had best say goodnight. You are a darling.

> Love me, eh?
> Dick

October 12, 1945

My Dearest Dick,

I am looking at fifteen beautiful red rose buds from you. You do the sweetest things!

They are lovely, and most precious is the sentiment they convey. I cherish all of your love and return mine.

I shall take some of them to school and enjoy them there. It is nice that I have them for my bridge party Thursday night too. Mildred, Golda, and Ruth (the same three) will be here, and Ruth will continue to teach us.

During my weekly free period today, I was in the rest room and Mrs. Collins stopped to visit—So I decided to tell her that I stood up with her at the faculty meeting. She had pretended she hasn't recognized me. She proceeded to tell me that she and Carl are separated and twice broke into tears. I felt so sorry for her and almost sorry that I'd brought up the subject. She said she hadn't told anyone around here. Of course I said I wouldn't mention it, but I know that Carl makes no bones.

She didn't lay all the blame on him but tried to blame the Army for his behavior. She said their sense of values is so different—things that she values highly he has little regard for. Besides my flowers I had another nice surprise tonight, your letters of September 14, 18, 21, 22, and 23. Yesterday and today have really been big letter days.

I'm so hoping you get home by Christmas, but if you are on your way by January, as you suggest, at least I'll know it won't be long.

Tomorrow morning I take the car to have the rust spots taken care of, which will complicate my getting to and from school for a couple days. It turned cold today, so I suppose rain has stopped. Sweetheart, a kiss for each rose and —

An awful lot of love,
Your Ritter

October 12, 1945

My Darling,

Don't take too seriously anything I say tonight because my spirits are at rock bottom.

Your September 28, 29, 30, and October 1 letters came today and of course included the news Colonel McConkie gave you.

I was definitely counting on your at least being on your way home by Christmas. With a cold nagging, I was in no mood to receive such discouraging news. Now that I've had my weep, I can start readjusting my thinking. To make me feel worse, practically everyone I know here in town has her husband on the way home or about to start.

We have P.T.A. Monday night and I have two art exhibits to put up, so I stayed until 5:30 and got things pretty much under control tonight. But grade cards are yet to be made out this weekend.

I went over to your folks for awhile this evening, but didn't stay as long as I would have if my stopped up head didn't make me feel so miserable—and I bought those expensive vitamins too. I really don't feel bad otherwise though. It's just that I can't breathe through my nose.

I'm glad you understand my shorter letters since school started. I certainly want to talk and talk with you but you know how fatigued I can get at the end of the day. I'm doing much better than the first couple of weeks but it will never be an easy job.

And there are times when I think only a fool would put wear and tear on her nervous system that teaching does, particularly on a rainy day when I'd like to glue all 36 to their seats and tape each mouth shut. Of course part of that is my own fault for not being strict enough. We teachers agreed one noon that teaching makes the years show on the teacher. Then I remember other kinds of work and wonder if I am lazy. But of course all I really want is a normal life. The life we've looked forward to for so very long!

I know if there is any way of getting here sooner, you will. I am so impatient! Hold me tight, Dearest!

> *All My Love,*
> *Ritter*

October 13, 1945

Dearest Ritter:

Recapitulation: August 7, 1944, arrived Bombay
September 4, 1944, left Bombay
September 11, 1944, arrived Calcutta
September 20, 1944, left Camp Kanchrapara for Ledo as train guard
September 1, 1944, arrived in Calcutta with Turner
September 4, 1944, left Calcutta
Either 6th or 7th arrived Tenth at Dinjan, Assam
September 13, 1944, arrived Calcutta by plane.

Which surely brings us up-to-date, right on the nose. One year ago today, I was in this town, and how happy I am that that year is behind us, with both the ETO and CBI and Japanese war brought to a tactical close. If we have luck and leave as a general hospital soon, then I may be home in three to four months, otherwise it may well go into spring of 1946. You know that I incline to the former view, but I have no reason for being sure that I would go with the 142nd or even of knowing that fate might not send the 142nd to some other theater.

After I wrote you last night, I expected to get to bed in reasonable time, but that was not to be. No indeed. Gus came in in a disgusting state of inebriation, and was so argumentative that I finally had to tell him off . . . after which he rather sullenly went to bed, lay there looking and sounding greatly like a dully animated porcine structure. I was about ready to turn the lights off when Captain Parsons entered, awakened Gus, and both of them indulged in drunken horseplay. Then they decided to have some more drinks, and to satisfy them, I had a bottle of beer with them. They talked about everything, with Parsons rather rational, Gus clever enough, but belching hoggishly every few moments. Not an inspiring sight, I assure you.

If my previous description of him sounded unflattering, it was because I was so impressed with the pig-like characteristics that his nose, mouth, and receding chin, with that crew cut lend his features at such moments. Shove an apple in his mouth and you might be very surprised indeed. If sound effects oinked, that would do it, and you could never tell the difference.

At any rate, Parsons wanted me to go outside to talk to him privately. He wanted to tell me something in my professional capacity. It was largely to the effect that he was drinking too much, realized it, and wanted to know what was wrong with him. From what he said, it seems that he feels inferior because he has only a fifth grade education; has been overseas before but this time he had to leave a wife and the only home security he ever knew. He hates his own people, and dislikes his present job of utilities officer very much.

He kept me up until 3:30, and of course I did him no good. I understand now why he stresses that item of rank so much . . . it is the only thing he can pull.

After only several hours' sleep, I decided to try to get out of playing golf this afternoon, but it was no go. If I went it helped them get transportation (a damned hot ambulance from the motor pool). I cannot understand why they would want my company. I napped for an hour, then Howard and I were driven around in our ambulance to pick up Ellen. It was a short trip to the Royal Calcutta Golf Club, which is right across from Tolleygongo, where we previously played.

On my way back, I had them drop me off at the ward to see if I had any mail. In addition to other things, your October 4 letter was waiting. While we were there, a patient brought Ruth a gift: an Indian recording, in English, of "Lily Marlene." Vince hunted up a phonograph that would work and we began playing it, continuing for some time. It had gotten dark and I didn't realize that a big rain storm was coming.

At 6:20, one of those tropical cloudbursts smashed down on us, kept right on crashing until 8:30. About 7:45, Ruth and I decided that rain or no rain, we were going to get something to eat. So we started for our mess hall. The area at the back of the ward, through which we had to go, was completely covered in water. I know it fairly well, but Ruth doesn't, and despite my guidance, she fell in a ditch. But it wouldn't have made much difference, for we were completely wet through when we reached the Mess Hall. A group of officers were waiting, in raincoats, for the rain to let up, when we approached. Uninhibited Ruth yelled at them, "Sissies!" The Col. and Ann were inside and we dripped to their table, where the Col. blandly introduced me to one and all with, "All of you know drowned-rat Beard?"

One thing led to another, and it was spontaneously decided that we would make a party of four to go to the dance. I changed first, joined them at Ann's quarters, from which we got transportation to Ruth's, where she had been for us. Southern Avenue was flooded from curb to curb. After a crazy evening at the club, Ruth played drums in the orchestra and the Col. drank too much, and I presume that I did, and then the Col. decided that we should eat. We went back to the big general mess for coffee and sandwiches. I finally got back about 2:30, rather tired.

And so, love me, dearest,

Dick

October 14, 1945

Dearest Ritter:

Yesterday's letter was a description of a full day. Such days do help pass the hours, true, but the letdown is even greater the next day. My longing for you becomes physical, darling wife, and I would not turn from it if I could, yet I realize that if I am to stay reasonably well adjusted that I must not dwell on our separation and its hardships too often. If I seem to be heartlessly racing around Calcutta, my own, you must realize that it is not for lack of devotion to you, but because I do love you so and miss you dreadfully.

This morning was busy, but I took time out to hear Rev. MacFarland, a Methodist educational advisor, talk. He did such a poor job that I doodled the hour away. (His 20 minutes!) Tonight I had dinner with Chaplain Colburn (Major) and heard about MacFarland's work. According to the Chaplain, the only good colleges in India are the Christian Church schools.

Of course, I slept this afternoon—a deep, sound sleep. Refused an invitation to go downtown for Chinese food, instead ate poorly of salmon at our Mess. Our Sunday dinner was ham, but salty.

Tonight I saw Betty Hutton in "Incendiary Blonde" in Technicolor and plenty of Betty. I thought it a good picture though wondered how true to a Texas gunman's actual career it came. Rather a tragic affair, considering all the foolishness that entered in it.

More and more officers pour into our compound, but no one leaves, except an occasional one, like Weger. It will break someday!

> Goodnight, my ever loving darling.
> Dick

October 17, 1945

Dearest:

Today saw me break a swell resolution and go out for a little exercise. Ruth had wanted to get up a picnic, but you know my dislike for those; fortunately Col. Pete came through with the idea of all of us playing badminton, so we did just that this afternoon. Pete, Ann, Ruth, Pilgrim, Cols. Fowler, Schinther, Thiesseu (from Cleveland) and myself. Col. McConkie, whose room is next to the court, looked on for awhile. I hadn't played the darn game for 8 years but picked it up soon. Jones and I teamed up against Pete and Ruth, lost the first game. Then, with various partners, I succeeded in winning the next two, one against Peterson!

Food has been bad recently, so Ruth and I tried to talk the Col. and Ann to go down to the Cathay Restaurant, but no luck so we went alone via taxi. The meal was very good, the usual egg and vegetable soup, sweet and sour fish, etc., though Ruth insisted on eating chow mein, too. We were seated at the only table overlooking the main floor, at the balcony's edge. She was dressed in her cream beige uniform, which is trimmed in maroon, with a white shirt and maroon tie. There were only four women in the restaurant, at least 75 men, most of them in uniform. Needless to say, they were all sneaking looks Ruth's way.

Fortunately Ruth had a date for the dance and so I didn't have to suffer through that agony. I dropped her off at quarters and then came to my quarters where I have been reading through a swath of *Republican-Couriers.* I noticed a J. Clark Moore was listed as a casualty. Could that be the Clark I went to school with?

Mrs. Wale was very upset this morning, having had her head knocked against a support in the bus by a careless GI driver. She protests bitterly to me, but there is nothing I can do. She is darn close to being neurotic herself.

I was talking with an ATC flier this afternoon who told me that most of their installations up the valley were closed and that the pilots were just lying around, with nothing to do. He was of the opinion that we would have to get out soon. The hospital equipment has all been sold to the British, we learned recently.

In Neuro-Psychology conferences this morning, I presented 5 patients: 2 were sectioned for chronic alcoholism; 2 sectioned as primary behavior disorders; and one, poor chap, was returned to duty!

So tired, but so much in love with my precious wife. (The more women I know, the more I appreciate you!)

> Devotedly,
> Dick

October 20, 1945

My Darling,

It has been a beautiful day and would have been an ideal one to go the Ohio Purdue game except that when I last heard the score, it was Purdue 22, Ohio 0.

I went to Dr. Biggs this afternoon. He said my throat didn't look very bad, that my trouble was in my larynx. Of course, laryngitis is always hard to get at, since the main cure is resting ones voice. Another day's rest should help a lot. If it doesn't, I may stay home Monday. I just can't teach without talking.

After repeated trips to Walgreen's, I finally managed to get one roll of film for you.

Each time I had to ask the manager personally and when I got it, he brought it out wrapped up. I think that is the first film I've bought since the war started. I mailed the film and tobacco to you today.

Mother complained about never getting outside of Findlay. Knowing she'd like to go to Florida, I told her this might be the ideal time and we could get along here. Mr. Crawfis would probably fire the furnace and do that kind of work for us. Then she decided that she wouldn't want to go with Daddy not well and that the car isn't in good enough shape.

Of course Mother doesn't have the money that she had on the farm, and she doesn't like the dole, but as I remember there was usually some complaint there too. I realize it costs quite a bit to board me and have often offered her something but she always refuses.

In fact, she never lets me take her out to eat, she always takes me. This winter I'm spending 50 cents at noon for what we at the coffee shop charged 25 cents.

Well, I expect Mother will be as glad to have me in my own home as I will be to be there. I've no doubt been a problem for her and I know I've meant more work for her.

All My Love,
Ritter

October 22, 1945

Dearest Ritter, my sweetheart:

Imagine if you can, the hardest kind of downpour, such as we have occasionally in Ohio for 15 minutes during severe storms. Imagine that, then presume to think what the situation is here. There have been literally sheets of rain glassing the sky for 96 hours, with only short intervals of respite. At the moment, 9:45 p.m., it has been raining so hard that conversation could not be conducted for 45 minutes. And it has been raining like that all day.

Last night, while I tried to carry on as AOD (acting officer on duty), it rained desperately in spurts which came every 15 minutes and lasted about five or ten.

Synonymous with the ringing of the phone for me to go out on a call would be the start of another downpour. Tonight we have lightning and thunder with the rain. It looks outside now as it did in the opening scenes of Bromfield's "The Rains Came."

This noon the water was over six inches deep behind the ward and over the road.

Col. Peterson telephoned for transportation and an ambulance came for us. This afternoon I hit upon the idea of riding my bike through it, for the storm had let up a little. But coming back at 5:00, I had to splash through about four inches, came out of it safely. The thin-tired bike makes it easily through the oozy mud of the lawns, which is something that our heavier ones would not do.

Today your letters of October 11 and 12 arrived. In the Columbus Day letter, you are very despondent for several reasons, one being McConkie's estimate of how long we will be here. The only thing that will make his guess true is the fact that we don't have the transportation. We have officers stacked up here in huge numbers, so that it is frustrating to try to do anything because of the crowd.

Since I have been living a retired life recently, that hasn't bothered me except in the mess hall. I try not to let how unhappy I am creep into my letters . . . but in truth, darling Reva, I get desperate with sadness and have to fight myself as I have never fought before. Since it will neither get me home sooner nor help either of us in any way, I simply must not let down.

Nor must you.

Even if our hearts are breaking for one another, we must wear smiles on our faces, a laugh on our lips. I am looking at the thin gold band I wear on my left hand's third finger. It symbolizes us, the beginning and the end, the complete cycle, a lifetime of love, kindness, and joy.

I completed my rounds and undressed wearily at two this morning. I had been in bed five minutes when a call came for me from Ward 4. An officer, a Captain Pfandler, was causing trouble, would not go to bed, was cursing the night nurse and the ward man etc. By the time I got there, he had quieted down. I talked with him awhile. Overseas two years. A pilot. Jeep accident. Dizzy spells, sufficient to board him. Investigation over some unmentioned matters in Burma. Ordered held by the authorities at the base section. The Capt. was taking his anger out on us here at the hospital. Tsk. Back at three to the Receiving Room. Finally to bed by 3:30, asleep by 4:00.

We boarded two patients this morning, decided to scratch from Saturday's shipment the fellow who accidentally killed the Hindu boy because I caught him reading his chart last night. He failed to tell me the truth, and I thought that if his religious scruples, which he has been so highly tooting, permitted him such leeway, then as far as I was concerned, he could go back to duty. That caused a painful interview between him and me later in the day, because he was already listed on the shipment and had been called to get his baggage in order. I went into my song and dance about accepting the consequences of our acts. I don't think he liked it. I don't give a damn whether he did or not. I am tired of dealing with weak minded, sanctimonious hypocrites.

The Col. knew that I was tired, suggested that I take as much of the day off as I liked, then insisted that I have coffee with him in his office. Gerber and others showed up . . . one thing led to another, and I didn't get away in the morning. Since those boarded charts had to be in today, I had to return this afternoon. Mrs. Wale, who has been disgusted with the weather, and who didn't go home to lunch because of the rain, was not only difficult but made many mistakes (and she got that raise that I put in for her, to Pilgrim's disgust, for his man didn't).

The boys kept stringing in, with one complaint and another. We have no regular afternoon nurse, now that Ruth is on nights, and so that demanded extra attention. Tsk. One thing and another kept me there until 5:00. When I got back to quarters, I went to sleep immediately, awakened at 7:30.

I am tired. The weather is gloomy. I am alone, for Gus is at the club. Your letters were so disheartening. I am afraid that I am guilty of pitying myself . . . and that will never do. I assure you, light of my life and the loveliest woman I have ever seen, that even as I write these lines, I stiffen my back and look straight ahead again! Circumstance cannot beat us down. I will be home and our love will be a wonderful thing. Let me see you smile, honey, just for me? That's a good girl!

> Yours ever,
> Dick

October 22, 1945

My Darling,

I never realized how much easier it would be to teach school and have silent reading and all written lessons. That is what I did today, and consequently my voice was in pretty good shape tonight. In fact, I did more talking out of school than in.

After school we had our deck tennis tournament. Our first team won so they go back tomorrow night. Our second team won its first game and lost the second, which served the purpose of holding us there until the last ones.

Eleanor Curtis had a nine-pound baby boy yesterday. That reminds me, Mother read somewhere that a lot of adoption agencies are being crowded with children of wives of servicemen who have had children by someone other than their husbands.

I surely would like to hear some good news from you on your coming home. In tonight's Blade *they say by mid-winter they'll be discharging all enlisted men with two years' service. And as I stated before, the point system will be down to 50 by December 1 for enlisted men.*

Darling, it is time for busy little Ritter to get her sleep. So goodnight, my Sweetheart.

> *All my Love,*
> *Ritter*

Calcutta, India
October 23, 1945

Dearest Ritter:

This letter is being written the morning of October 24. I wrote you a short note last evening, but just did not seem up to trying to write out a description of all that happened yesterday. I think that all in all I had my worst day of psychiatric experience the 23rd.

Here's the way the day started out. Cloudy. Tassio came in to tell me that the patient who figured in the accident that killed the Hindu boy and whom I had taken off the Friday shipment, was on the warpath. He had gone to see Col. McConkie, and he had Col. Powers' assurance that he could leave today. Hmmm.

I noticed the chap, named Warren, in front of Col. Peterson's office, Ward 47, dressed in fatigues and looking very desperate and determined. Nonetheless, the Col. didn't show up until after ten. In the meantime, Warren came back to the ward (55). I went out to tell him that we would go to see the Col. at the earliest possible moment. He was sitting on one side of the bed while I sat just next to him on the adjoining bed. Suddenly he opened up on me, as it were, with the comment that "You are no psychologist, I wouldn't let you analyze my hogs."

I was somewhat taken aback, but I agreed that he wouldn't have to keep me from it, I wouldn't take the job in the first place, having my hands full of the owner. But Warren kept right on talking, despite my efforts to placate him. He wanted me to take my insignia off, so that he could beat me. He worked himself into such a rage that he started for me, his wicked little eyes bloodshot and blazing.

For the first time since I have been here I felt a delicious little thrill shoot through me, as though a pressure had been released, and finally I was to be permitted to let off a little steam, too. I was sure that I was dealing with a madman, and prepared myself to give him the surprise of his life. I sat quite still, looked him in the eye, and said, simply enough, "Sit down." Just like that. For one long moment he wavered . . . then a lifetime of retreating dropped him back on the bed. He continued to vilify me. At the outset, he had asked me if I were a Jew. He condemned the Jews for keeping him in the hospital, charged that I was allied with them. Of course, he could name no Jews. (He didn't know about Gerber.)

Finally, he went into a paranoid state completely, threatening to kill me if he had the chance, and to kill anyone else who interfered with his plans to get out of the hospital. It did absolutely no good to argue with him or try to explain. He accepted what he liked, rejected every shred of information that didn't suit his plans. He dropped his cloak of Christianity completely. (It is interesting to note that the most devoted follower of the church whom it has been my misfortune to have on the ward turned out to be the most vicious personality whom I have encountered.)

I got his promise to not do anything drastic until he had seen Col. Peterson. Just then Col. Pete and Major Pilgrim came in. We called Warren in, and he began sobbing out his imprecations against the Jews, the army, and intimated that he had been persecuted as much as he intended to take. He wildly threatened to kill, to commit suicide, etc. He claimed that he did not care about the death of the Hindu boy, but that it was just another jab at him by fate which permitted others to make fun of his misfortune. It was pretty obvious that he had lost his mind, so we decided to send him to 51. That was it.

In the meantime, I got a phone call from 51, from Berger, who is replacing Battista, to the effect that a patient we had discharged just a week ago had been brought in during the night, dying. I hurried down, but they were just taking him out to another ward. He had been unconscious —still is as of the morning of the 24th—and all the doctors who had been called in thought that he would die, did not know whether he was a suicide or not.

While I was down there Milner took me in to see another of the patients we had on the ward two weeks ago. He was a pitiful looking object: naked, sitting on the cement floor of an isolation ward. He recognized me, smiled, then refused to do anymore than grin enigmatically. Schizophrenic.

But, also in the meantime, Pilgrim and Gerber had gotten their orders returning them home, Ellen Diemer had not shown up, was instead in the hospital with a case of GI's, and there was no nurse at all on 55 during the day. Hmmmmm.

Everything considered, the 23rd could not be described as one of my better days.

This afternoon, though, Piscatelli sort of made up for some of it by making a fine Italian dish, serving me a generous helping. This evening, Gus and I saw Laughton in "Captain Kidd," enjoyed Laughton's part very much. Dropped in at the club for drinks with Pilgrim.

The rain held off most of the day, misted during the movie. Back to quarters and fairly early to bed.

Who do you think I love? Right, sweetest girl!

Dick

October 24, 1945

Dearest Ritter—

No news tonight, just the old, old story—I love you, honey girl, I love you, love you, love you.

Don't you know, darling Reva that I see your lovely face in everything beautiful? The dawn, the palms' graceful tops, the blue of the sky, the moon, the stars?

May 16, 1930—the day we first met—was the most momentous day in history.

July 3, 1937, was the most thrilling.

May 29, 1938, the most soul-satisfying.*

That you and I are permitted to be entwined—that is all the riches I need—all the heaven I ask for.

You must not doubt, divine wife, my love for you—these months away from you are fasting periods, in which I grow more devoted, more consecrated.

All of me, everything, my dearest girl, goes out to you—without you, the world is void—with you, the universe is a blinding flash of happiness.

With you,
Dick

*[Editor's Note: Because teachers at Reva's school were not supposed to be married, the Beards' first wedding was a private civil service in July 1937. Their "official" marriage took place in May of 1938.]

Calcutta, India
October 26, 1945

Dearest Reva:

I have just been out for a walk around the hospital area. All was quiet among the wards, with most night ward men nodding over their desks, no nurses in evidence, probably all to late dinner. Occasionally, patients would be grouped in the office, having rested all day, unable to sleep at night. One Indian guard had a coughing spasm as I passed—consumptive. The waning moon is a halved orange, not too bright to obscure the stars, light enough to make clear the paths. It is midnight, sweetheart, and my thoughts naturally turn to you. I am holding you tightly—very.

We shipped over 400 patients today. Our total census is down to 1200, in our section. We shipped 106, have 107 left. The lowest ever. There are 7 men in Ward 55, only 3 of them active cases.

I was simply lazy today. Yesterday we got 6 or 7 large packages of magazines given to the ward. With so few patients on hand, I felt justified in taking *Life, New Yorker,* and other magazines for my own use. So I stayed up late reading. Tired; but no work to do.

Dictated briefly to Mrs. Wale, let her go at 12:00 today. Spent almost the entire afternoon writing personal letters.

Tonight Whit, Gus, Chan (a Chinese 2nd Lt. who has recently joined the outfit) and I played anna poker. I lost 1 rupee, 2 annas in two hours of play.

Gus and 3 others were turned in for being noisy (drunken) and had to report to the Executive Officer. That was hardly fair to Gus, who makes comparatively little noise when drunken.

Pilgrim, Jones, Thorsen, Peterson and I played badminton tonight. I was with Jones and we got licked. I played poorly.

That just about concludes it, sweet, and maybe I'll have more to tell tomorrow.

Ever yours in faith, love, and devotion,
            Dick

                    Calcutta, India
                    October 30, 1945
Dearest:

This is one of these nights when I am struck with a paucity of material to write. So I presume I could mention that:

1. Pilgrim left for Kanchrapara without saying goodbye.

2. Lt. Hale, nurse from Texas, who spent one afternoon on 55 (this ward), received her orders to return to the States about 4:30 p.m.

3. Two nights ago an inch-long lizard crawled over my sheet, blinked his miniature eyes at me, almost came to my hand—some atavistic impulse led him to retreat.

4. Tomorrow is pay day.

5. Why does our Mess Hall always have gravy without potatoes, or potatoes when there is no gravy? Deliberate? Or just the army way of always doing the wrong thing if it is possible to avoid the right?

6. Why did Major Blumenthal, who was cursed as a "damned Jew" by our drunken neighbors, sit at the dining table last night and sneer at Lt. Col. McShane's big, blond nurse friend?

7. Why do rumors persist that our CO will be relieved? (Wishful thinking, no doubt. Jim Haden said he knew it wasn't true.)

8. Why is my temper so short these days? Perhaps I lack sleep from reading so late—or maybe I just want to go home!

Today was gorgeous and the sky at 5:00 was as lovely as only an Indian fall sky can be.

Lt. Col. Pleasants sat in on some of our Neuro-Psychiatric conferences this morning. We disposed of all my active cases. This afternoon I got a case from Leeds, one he considers hopeless, and one from 46. Incidentally, Capt. Bradenkoff, who replaced Pilgrim, went into the hospital for dysentery yesterday. Major Levin, who is practically worthless in that capacity, is trying to take over. He doesn't know anything about it and refuses to learn.

I think tonight I'll try to get some sleep. Remember that I love you deeply—you are my wife.

Devotedly,
Dick

October 31, 1945

My Darling,

Your letter of October 20th and your very sweet letter of October 23 came today.

Your sweet sentiments do me much good.

We had our big Halloween party today from about 1:15 to 3:15. Need I say I was glad when the party was over? An hour isn't bad, but two is too long, especially when food is involved. The children seemed to have a good time though. The hard part is to keep them under control and of course the principal would show up. He always does at inopportune times. I have decided from what I've heard that he preaches progressive education but practices or wants practiced or should I say wants results of the old fashioned methods. Frankly, he bothers me. I think he is a high-strung grandmother pushing his teachers.

Tonight Mildred, Golda and I met at Ruth's for bridge and had a nice evening. I really haven't learned much yet about contract, but several interesting points came up tonight. We each won a rubber and stopped at ten o'clock. Then we spent almost two hours in the kitchen eating and drinking. We started out with coffee, then Ruth brought out some blackberry liqueur (similar to a brandy), which tasted like a sweet wine. We all drank enough to warm ourselves up and had a nice chatty evening. Ruth and Mildred are rather lively people and the stimulant made me talk up, which amused them.

I am bubbling with secrets. Mr. Miller, who is in his forties and one of the two new teachers and a bachelor, is interested in Ruth. She said she won't consider dating for awhile, but give her time. According to her, she and Jim were very happy together and from the picture she has painted, I doubt that Miller will measure up.

Sentimental Ritter wants to know. Will you always keep first place reserved for me?

Dearest, it must be nearly one o'clock and I have a shower to attend for Edith Edwards tomorrow night. So me thinks I better say goodnight to my husband, the Best One I know.

So much Love,
Your Ritter

October 31, 1945

Dearest Ritter:

Happy Halloween, my darling Reva, and may you and I pass all our future 31st together.

While I hinted that I had little to write about last night, this evening really finds me plunged into despair, because my activities have been so lethargic in nature that I cannot hope even to arouse your interest.

Let's see what I can find. At work this morning I spent much of the morning dictating to Mrs. Wale—those cases that were presented to the N-P conference yesterday. At dinner last night, and while the Col. was having coffee in our ward kitchen this morning, I intimated that I was greatly dissatisfied with one of the decisions made yesterday. It concerned a young Italian who had apparently gotten along fairly well in the army, though poorly vocationally in civilian life, until he arrived in Karachi several months ago. He had been stationed in Oran, met a girl there, liked his work, and didn't want to leave. It seems that he had an understanding with the girl, who couldn't speak English very well, and who couldn't write at all. At any rate, they planned to be married when he was suddenly sent on to India.

Once here the letters all went one way, for she couldn't or didn't answer him. He lost all appetite, dropped 40 pounds, developed a wheezy voice, and in general looked pretty bad. The Col. had decided to section him, which requires considerable time in a unit, in an administrative matter. I couldn't see sending a man in that condition to duty, not only because of the censure which we would get, but because of him, too. He simply cannot eat.

A bite or two only at any one meal. I managed to talk the Col. into letting me board him to the States.

I am losing Tassio in a few days, and I don't mind it, for he has a bad habit of standing around when I have visitors, apparently thinking we like to talk to him . . . he comes from the ratty part of San Francisco (boasts of stealing bikes when a kid), will soon be returning there. He does not have the advantage of being an interesting character.

In his place I have a new ward master who is long, lank, and scrawny, and belies his last name of King. Eunice Brinkman, who is one of the few nurses who ever cleaned my desk and had your picture cleaned off for me each morning, was transferred to 45 and I had lumpy, though small, Miss Malaneux in her place today.

We were paid this morning. Howie showed up from Kanchrapara, had lunch with me, and then chatted for an hour or so in my room this afternoon. He left to go downtown to buy a pillow. Good old broken down, poorly run Kanchrapara—not even furnishing captains with pillows. I shudder to think of how they must treat their second lieutenants.

The remainder of the afternoon I spent in delicious sleep, and though I regretted slumbering away such a delightful day, I profited by the rest.

While looking out of my window before slumber, I noticed something that I hadn't observed before. Those awkward looking robin-like birds were paired off; seemed to be frolicking together. One would ruffle his feathers, squawk, then with open beak, run affectionately against the breast of the other. Not to be outdone, the mate, whose voice was a little more melodious, would nudge her slightly larger partner. Oh, it was very coy and domestic. Perhaps they were celebrating the official closing of the nesting season?

Just before I drifted off to sleep, two crows plunked down on the lawn, had fun scaring one another with a crumpled sheet of paper which they would take turns throwing in the air. But they are very suspicious birds, spent much of their time nervously gawking around. They are smart there, for Major Anderson often steps to his back door, shoots at anything that moves with his air rifle. If the birds only knew, they are quite safe as long as they remain still. What a shot.

Well, I have been wandering on for several paragraphs, and probably have bored you as much as I ought for any one night. It will not bore you to read how much I miss you, dearest Reva. It has gotten to the point that I hardly dare think of the sweetness of holding you in my arms as I so often used to, sharing the "knocker" joke which made you blush, and the lovely aroma of your slight, tender body. But it will be nice to come home to. Yes, my Reva, very nice to come home to.

Hopelessly in love with you,
Dick

Richard sent this photograph to Reva in November 1945. On the back he wrote, "This is Dick as you probably prefer to think of him."

November 1, 1945

Dearest Ritter:

You are doing right well by me, sweetheart, on the matter of tobacco, for your October 24 package came today. Thanks, immensely. Clippings postmarked October 21 arrived, and your airmails of October 20, 21, and 22 piled on my desk in a heap of love and devotion.

How unfortunate when one must stand helplessly by and watch a loved one perversely make everyone miserable. Who can know what thwarted ambitions, what fading dreams, what unrealized desires, are struggling under the blanket of repression. Too late we appreciate what we were once too blind to see. Life is not what we thought, and we feel frustrated, irked, and desperately unhappy. The simplest way to let off steam and still remain sane is to take it out on the other fellow. No real satisfaction comes from this, but we have at least expressed ourselves even though poorly. Sympathy and understanding may help, but I doubt it. You, Ritter are a brave girl. Keep your head high yet a little while and soon we will stand side by side, arm in arm. Then, no matter what life offers, it will be a little easier to take.

Today was such a day as the poet dreams of, too bad it couldn't have been lived that way. Instead, because General Terry was visiting us, we had to go back early. Actually, he never got near our section this noon, but one can never be too sure. I have several new cases, so am kept fairly busy.

About 4:00 p.m. the phone rang and it proved to be Bill Seeger, down from the 12th with Capt. Kurns and Lt. Enrich. I met them in the Great Eastern Hotel lobby at 7:00, then we went to the Cathay for an excellent Chinese dinner, then to Karnami for drinks, though Seeger and I went to Ernrich's room, did not drink. Kurns was in the process of really hanging one on. We stood around in the main bar room, then they brought me, in the Provost

Marshall Ernrich's jeep, to the 142nd Club. There we
spent an hour or so and I managed to check with Ann
Fazler about dates for the fellows for tomorrow night. She
had arranged it, then they began to get worried, which
amused me. We have a lot of new girls, but of course I
hadn't seen them, since I have been staying away from the
club. Peterson came by and I introduced him. They left
about 10:30 and I came home via 55, for we have been
having some noise recently and I wanted to check on it.
Everything was OK.

Ellen Dierner was back on duty to my relief this morning. This afternoon Miss O'Hara stood in. Both girls are
popular with the fellows and it helps keep matters going.

It is about 12:00 now. Oh yes, I got another Nagasaki
letter from Tom. He is finding his way around. I'll send on
the geisha girls' picture. Jack Pochrass mentions "Reva", is
now a Captain.

> Much love, darling,
> Dick

November 9, 1945

Dearest Ritter:

I am none too happy over today, but it did bring me
one ray of light. The October letter of both you and the
folks arrived. My uniform money was in the folks' letter
and you might telephone them that it came at an oppor-
tune time. I still had sufficient funds for my ordinary ex-
penses but didn't have any extra in case of an emergency
or in the event that Gus and I go see the Taj Mahal.

I haven't liked today because I seemed tired and out of
sorts. Further, our boys haven't been behaving in the ward
at night. I am beginning to get very, very tired of it. Someone will get drastically scorched if it doesn't change, of
that you may be sure.

Otherwise, work moved pretty much as usual, with one
conference or interview following another.

This evening Gus and I defeated Chan and Whittaker in horseshoes, though I failed to acquit myself with honor in the second game.

About 8:30, Gus and I wandered to the club where we joined the Colonel's gang in charades. The best of the lot was my guessing, within 20 seconds, of the Col's portrayal of "Goosey, Goosey Gander." I haven't the slightest idea of why that nonsense popped into my head, but it did. Gus doing "Lady Godiva" was funny, too. He got the darn thing across by giving them the time element and the idea it was a woman, then made the second syllable "dive," and damned if they didn't guess it.

It's late, so my blessings, sweet,

Dick

November 10, 1945

My Darling,

I spent this evening calling. I went to Eleanor's. I took the baby a rattle. Eleanor tells me that she is expecting a telephone call from Phil very soon. He is on his way home. From there, I went to Mary Weitz's. Mary still has her ankle in a cast and will have for some time yet.

Next week being National Education Week, the Superintendent suggested each school have an exhibit in a downtown window. I was on the Washington committee, so we decorated the Myers Dry Cleaning window. We put in a homemade library set (bookcase, table and chair), a toy train of match boxes, an easel and bulletin board of art along with books and writing paper. We were quite pleased with it when we were finished.

Mr. Corbin paid me a rather nice compliment the other day. I'm sure that it isn't true, but it made me feel that I'm not doing too poorly in art. He said, "You do just as nice work as Miss Little with half the fuss." Miss Little had a reputation established (she taught art last year) and I'm certainly not establishing one, but at any rate it was encouraging.

Every once in a while, I reach the end of my string and don't know what I'm going to do next. We have been drawing, mainly cartoons, in India ink and though I dread it, I guess the next step is to do some lettering. I purchased a few bottles of colored ink, which we pass around to touch up the children's work.

This week I found myself approaching the next P.T.A. without anything very showy to put up, so I decided to do some paper collage. I suggested Thanksgiving scenes to the children and gave them bright, black or white mounting paper. They cut mostly in silhouette, mounting such scenes as a church, pilgrims, possibly including some woods. We had several "Mayflowers" too. I had white India ink for them to outline windows, doors etc. Of course it made showy work and I feel more pleased with it than anything I did the last six weeks.

For Christmas, I think we'll make plaster of paris plaques. I've never done it before, so here's hoping. You can see teacher is experimenting and learning. As you know, I've met new demands but am learning not to worry so much about them.

I run myself ragged and have more work than I like, I find disciplining the students in two art classes tiring, but of course there are some things about this job I do enjoy. And I rather like the added social life, which we had none of at Mt. Blanchard and when I feel like mooning, it helps when I think how much luckier I am than those around me (teachers, I mean) and that you will soon be home. Make it soon, Sweetheart.

All my Love,
Ritter

November 10, 1945

Dearest Ritter:

This is AOD day.

AOD day is never a good day; today it is even worse than usual. It has been worse than I ever want it to be in the future. (Even as I write this, the phone rings, and Receiving Officer says that a man has just been killed by knifing, that I must come to the office at once to see him, get

240

the details, etc. That is the way it has been all day, and I shall be happy when this day dies forever.)

Now the following night: I did not get this letter finished!!!

Insofar as I can see, yesterday should not have happened, but since it did, I might as well record the grim facts here. Now that I look back on it, there was a certain element of humor in the whole panoramic tragi-farce.

Just as I was getting started in my morning's work, we were notified that a man from Mt. Clemens, who had missed Wednesday's assignment and therefore listed as AWOL had been discovered hanging in the latrine of Ward 53 which was closed a week ago. Lt. Griffin made the grisly discovery when he was inventorying and searching for what was presumed to be a dead rat, as several complaints had been made about the odor emanating from that region the last day or so. As AOD, there were several details which I had to take care of, and since he had been transferred to my ward, that had to be considered too.

I braved the pungently sweet odor of putrefaction and pushed into the latrine, then slowly edged open the door behind which he hanged. I was alone and not prepared for what I saw. It was pretty bad. Gus got pictures. I did not get sick at the stomach, as some did, though I had to spend the next two hours outside until he was finally taken away.

Not much lunch (as is understandable), then to sweat out (literally) two hours in the Adjutant's office. At that moment, I was at my lowest physically and mentally. About one o'clock I gave myself a good talking to and immediately felt better.

Thank goodness my talks do someone some good. I planned to take it easy during the afternoon, as the AOD ordinarily does not officially have much to do until after five, but it wasn't to be today. I was called from my quarters to the phone regularly and finally back to the Adjutant's office. It seems that the suicide's body had been unceremoniously dumped into a grave at the American cemetery without benefit of autopsy and without authorization and some dope said that I had authorized it . . . Lt. Col Powers was beside himself until it was finally straightened out. They decided to leave the body there, it being so far gone that Major Blumenthal felt nothing could be learned from an examination of it . . . besides, there was no question but that it was suicide.

Then, on top of everything else, Ladd Laughbon showed up and I had to entertain him in my room and at dinner. It was more fun than I thought, and he followed it by his usual bent, arguing deliberately and naggingly with Gus and me, which we don't mind, as we do it with one another. He, like everyone else, is confused and doesn't know whether he wishes to go back to Spokane as a teacher or not.

On Ward 55, where we have been having so much trouble, I called all the patients together this morning and asked that we have their cooperation and pointed out that their conduct would have to change. Jarett, a bearded patient who is a lawyer from New York, proved such a fascinating conversationalist that I spent a half hour talking with him, then this call on a murder came through and I had to hurry to the Receiving Room.

The boys in the Receiving Room took me to the morgue, where they were laying the 20-year-old boy, packed in ice, away forever in a plain, varnished pine coffin. I learned that the ordinary seaman, a Negro, was captured on the spot. The essential tragedy in all this was that the boy (who died from a severed jugular vein) had not even been involved in the original dispute but was merely trying to help a group of white seamen take the knife away from the crazed and drunken sailor. His life-long friend, John Smith of Milwaukee, was unable to realize that his classmate and friend was dead, but he gave me all the essential information and took back to the ship all but the blood-stained trousers.

At any rate, I got to bed a little after four, went into a dreamless sleep at once.

The sun was shining Sunday morning when I awakened. It always shines when I think of you. My love to you, sweet,

Dick

November 16, 1945

My Darling,

We got our November 11th holiday today and I suppose the hunters got their pheasants.

Your November 7th letter came today and I was very glad to hear that your thumb was better. I repeat, don't neglect anything like that.

A box also came from you. I like the black evening hanky very much. It is a pretty thing. I'm afraid we're going to have to learn to dance, yet. Won't my evening bag and hanky be elegant to-gether? There were two more brass bowls, the shopping bag (that was a good idea), your pipes and pencil, the gong, and your folks' lace tablecloth. I like the gong—It really is oriental with an oriental sound. We're going to have to find a house to fit our brass. Did I tell you I would like a small brass dish with a lid to use for a candy dish, something like that little incense bowl?

Mary Ellen had Helen and me over for dinner tonight. Naturally I enjoyed it. Helen had received a long letter from her sister Ruth, who told her she had more to lose than to gain in the en-gagement she's considering. She asked Helen some pertinent ques-tions, such as: Is he always considerate? Do your friends like him when first meeting him? Is he an intelligent conversationalist?

We have two reading tests a year, one at the beginning and one near the end. It tests for word recognition, comprehension, etc. Most of my children ranked as I thought they would, but a few surprised me.

Darling, I love you! I love you!

Hugs and kisses,

Reva

Toronto
November 23, 1945

My Darling,

I am so worried tonight that I'm afraid this won't be much of a letter. I've been following the news reports closely but can't get any additional information since Lowell Thomas. He reported the riots in Calcutta and said an American Hospital has been barricaded, which must mean yours. It sounds so very serious that I won't have any peace of mind until I've heard from you as of this date.

I had a good cry. Mim cried with me, then she and Ray talked me into believing that if things are really serious you will be evacuated. I'm trying to tell myself that maybe there is a bright side, that even if the trouble in Calcutta subside, which I surely hope it does, it may speed evacuation.

We just heard a newscast from a Toronto station. The commentator said that things have quieted down in Calcutta. The riots of three days have subsided. Either it just got in the news or by our traveling and pretty much lack of news, we missed it. At any rate, that latest report is better for me to go to bed on.

> Goodnight, My Beloved,
> Your Devoted Wife
> Ritter

Toronto
November 25, 1945

My Darling,

I haven't heard any late news. Saturday evening is a poor news night. But this morning's reporter said the British army quieted the disturbance in Calcutta and that no American lives have been lost. I feel easier about it, but I surely wish they'd send you home soon.

The family is all remarking about how Jill has taken to me. It is just that I've spent quite a bit of time entertaining her. I came with the purpose of getting acquainted with her and seeing her parents. And so, I've spent the time right here.

*I don't have much to report. Right now, Mim and I are get-
ting a going over from Mother about not going to church. As a
matter of fact, I have gone some lately, but I kept still. Mim took
up the ball and is getting in deeper. She is being too frank. I
should have kept my big mouth shut. I had to chime in.*

*Children ought to learn young to always agree with their par-
ents, or should they? The whole discussion started over Jill being
taken to church at an early age, then a sly rub about my going to
a show on Sunday night but not to church on Sunday morning. It
is just that there is too much temptation to be in bed early.*

*It is after eleven and 7:30 a.m. will come soon, so Goodnight,
My Sweetheart. I will write a longer letter tomorrow night.*

> *Take care of yourself. So much love,*
> *And lots of hugs and kisses,*
> *Ritter*

December 1, 1945

My Darling,

*I was awfully disappointed not to get any mail from you today,
but I did get something very lovely, your red roses. I wore one in
my hair tonight too. The teachers' Christmas party is Tuesday
night. I will inquire if they wear hats. If not, I'll be able to have
one yet for then, too. You're a wonderful Sweetheart. I wish I
could tell you that with my arms around you.*

*Alleda Hall and I had dinner together tonight and she was
very complimentary of my purse. She said, comparing it with theirs
in the store, she would set its value at $35. She, Mary E and
Helen have recently complimented me on my coat (last year's) so I
don't feel so disgruntled about it. I hear fur coats are coming up
in price, so I intend to forget about one.*

I did buy a hat at Elida tonight.

*I'm counting on a letter by Monday. The roses smell good,
Darling, and are beautiful.*

> *You are my love, My Husband, My Life.*
> *Lots of kisses,*
> *Ritter*

Agra, India
4 December 1945

Dearest Ritter:

What can one write who has seen Taj Mahal? We approached it with fear and misgivings, for its countless reproductions on brass and ivory had led us to scorn it as the symbol of the tourist. Jouncing along in the tonga, we saw its dome, gleaming in the afternoon sun, rising above the tree tops. The road led into a valley, and then into a large courtyard in front of the main entrance. The front building is a masterpiece itself, and could be so considered here, if it weren't for the magnificent Taj. As it is, one doesn't see the Taj at all until he walks through the entrance, then the "dream in marble" is outlined against the blue sky through the vaulted archway. We need not have worried—anyone with love in his heart, with any conception of beauty, with any appreciation for sheer loveliness, will catch his breath and murmur, "Ah."

Perhaps the word 'purity,' associated so often with gleaming white, is the first thought that occurs to one. It is closely followed by a concept of beauty that will never fade: simple, yet complex—one's idea of friendship, family, youthful love crystallized for eternity.

I need not describe the Taj Mahal to you, for you know what it looks like in a picture. I may add that if you don't, you will when I get our prints, which we are taking, to you. We are literally taking hundreds of pictures—many in color, which won't be available for some time.

Perhaps I had better recapitulate the events of the day for you. [Gus and I] were awakened about 8:00 by a bearer bringing us tea and toast . . . At 4:00 we set out for the Taj with Siddons accompanying us. We left late to get the benefit of late rays of the sun on the white marble. One of the thrills of the excursion was to wander to the top of the southeast minaret. We were in complete darkness most of the 100 ft. (?) trip, in a stairway so narrow as to accommodate only one person at a time. At the top there was no protection from falling, but everyone strolled nonchalantly about—except for me, and I hung on for grim life! . . .

A big, big day it [has] been—but one filled to the overflow with a magnificent experience, one which you and I must share sometime.

Ever thinking of you,
Dick

December 9, 1945

My Darling,

In another hour, or rather now in India, is your birthday. I hope you have some nice birthday presents. You don't seem to be looking any older according to your pictures, even though thinner and I want you to gain that weight back. My Dearest—here is a very big bundle of love for your birthday. It is tied with longing for you.

It may be Christmas or after before you receive this so I'll send along my Christmas wishes too. It will really be Christmas, birthday and all the holidays rolled into one when you get home. Mother reminded me today that I have your last year's Christmas and birthday gift from them and that she will give me this year's. I believe you'll have enough for that portable typewriter you mentioned and the golf clubs from me (all to be purchased yet).

They say one reason nothing is on the market yet is that the manufacturers are holding back until after the first of the year. I'm having an awful time with hose (there wasn't a pair in the Findlay stores yesterday) and looking forward to the return of nylon.

Wish I could crawl in this letter and come along. But you already know how much I long to be near you.

All my Love,
Your Ritter

December 15, 1945

My Darling,

I was elated to get your December 4 letter today. I wish that I could have seen the Taj Mahal with you. Your enthusiasm makes me feel very pleased that you got to go. And how fortunate too that Gus is along with all his cameras. The hotel luxuries sound like a bolster to the ego. It would be nice to be waited on like that. In the U.S.A. that is something that would be hard to get even if you paid for it. Clerks, taxi drivers etc. still haven't come down off their high horse.

This is a miserable night. It is starting out like last winter, with several inches of snow on the ground. The thermometer is down to at least zero, and a wind is blowing. I suppose the county schools will be closed.

When I got in the car to come home after playing bridge today, I held my breath, but even though the starter sounded weak, it caught right away. The gears were so stiff, but I'm telling you, we were stiff too. At any rate, by the time I got home the car was limbered up.

But I decided even if it were late I had better put it away, that no one would be out to frighten me on a night like this—so the Chrysler is in the garage. I was glad that even though the alcohol registered for two above yesterday, I told the station to add a quart.

I bought a little Christmas tree today for school. It isn't as full as I'd like, but I didn't see any that were, and I won't go to shop around in the cold.

Reverend Muir is taking over the pulpit at church the first of the year. Helen wanted to hear Dr. Broady (Muir's substitute) tomorrow and I planned to go too but called it off tonight when I realized how cold it will probably be. Besides, I have work to do since I didn't do any today. We plan to hear the "Messiah" tomorrow night.

Darling, I wish you could warm me tonight. My fortune reads "Happy News." How much I want that special news!

So much love,

Your Ritter

December 24, 1945

My Darling,

Christmas Eve without you is very empty but no one could do a better job filling the gap with thoughtfulness than you do. The pajamas are exquisite—and you will surely like their softness too. Mother said she temporarily forgot about having the scarf made, but there is enough material and I shall do that. So many lovely things make me feel bad that you had only triflings.

Thanks for everything—the flowers too. I did a peculiar thing today but I thought you would want me to. Gladiolas came from you and I remarked to Mother when I opened them that they didn't seem like you. She said that you had replied that she thought roses were my favorite flower. As you know, I'm very sentimental about the flowers that you send and think of them fondly as a part of you. And you would never send me anything but a dainty (perhaps that isn't the best description) flower—Of course there might be exceptions for a particular occasion. So I telephoned Sinks and asked if they didn't have roses. They said they did and I said I knew that was what my husband wanted me to have, so an exchange was made and I have your roses! This morning it seemed awfully important to me that I have your roses and tonight too—at this hour, my spirit is very weak.

This is a terrible night. It rained and the streets are icy. Ruth and I were going to church but we called it off. When Daddy went to drive the car for me, he pumped it a bit which flooded it and apparently the battery is too weak to turn it fast enough to catch the pedal to the floor. I tried several times and finally gave up. So it has to set out tonight.

Thanks, my Darling, for all the nice things. I shall slip into my pj's before I go to bed.

Take care of yourself and come home soon!

An extra big hug and All My Love,
Your Ritter

Christmas, 1945. After the Taj Mahal in Agra, the Jain Temple in Calcutta was Richard's favorite Indian building. He spent as much time as his schedule allowed seeing various parts of the city.

Together at last.

Part Three
1946: Return to Home, Wife, and Love

Officially, World War II ended on September 2, 1945. However, for many soldiers, it lasted months longer. Along with thousands of officers, enlisted men, armed forces reserves, and civilians working in the war effort, my father was detained overseas until spring of 1946. Carriers had to be provided to ship the troops home, and disassembling support units in the CBI theater was a gradual process. It seemed to Richard that America's men and women in Calcutta were at the bottom of the "return home" list. Despite earlier ships leaving for the home front with incomplete passenger loads, he was not able to ship out until March. Richard's 1946 letters poured out a yearning for home, an intense longing for Reva, and the details of quitting India.

On New Year's Day January 1, 1946, the *New York Times* reports,

> The noisiest throng since the advent of 1941 —1,000,000 frenzied horn-blowers, cow-bell swingers and clapper-manipulators—brought in 1946 in Times Square last night. Packed solidly from Forty-second Street to a point just north of Forty-seventh, their hoarse shouting and mechanical noise-makers created a din that all but flattened the ears.

On the other side of the world in the rapidly downsizing of 142nd General Hospital, Richard faced a second Christmas without Reva. He was more than ready to leave India. On January 2, 1945, Reva's thirty-first birthday, his letter again laments the inactivity of the hospital, yet reflects his optimism of learning a release date for himself to go home. Just a few days later, he learns of a postponement and his letters seethe with impatience at the wait. His commanding officers will tell him nothing about going home, instead hinting that his departure might be a very long time away.

Most of the 1944 and 1945 letters are handwritten on onionskin pages, but many of the 1946 letters are typed. Richard contrasts the lack of personality of typewritten letters versus the poetic quality of handwritten letters. He continues efforts to strengthen Reva's spirit by urging her to look forward to their future reunion. He writes to Reva of his hope that by January of 1947 their lives will fall back into place. The fact that he and Reva will be together in starting a new life in postwar America cheers him greatly.

The 1946 letters frequently include descriptions of the moon. For Richard it seemed to provide a magical bond, shining (though not at the same time) on both Findlay, Ohio, and Calcutta, India. The moon over Calcutta inspires Richard to many passionate reassurances. He imagines future moonlit drives with Reva. The enchantment of Indian sky and nature, the pockets of loveliness amid Calcutta's dirt and poverty: these are pegs upon which Richard maintains a barely optimistic outlook.

On February 6, 1946, Richard's displeasure reaches a new peak. Reva's letters are not getting through, and he vows never to forget how much he hates the Army. His letters reflect bitterness for what he sees as the ineffectiveness and hypocrisy of the Army mismanagers. He asks Reva to help him remember how much he detests the Army. (Editor's note: Time erased some of Richard's anger. In later life, he would speak with pleasure about his Calcutta sojourn, entertaining his college classes with tales of India.)

In earlier letters, Richard wrote of his desire to explore an India other than the bars and brothels frequented by many of the men. On February 22, while visiting Delhi, he is able to indulge this urge. He describes for Reva the temples and ruins discovered through his meandering exploration.

On March 27, 1946, Richard is at last on the way home in what he describes as a "slow boat." On April 1, 1946, still en route, he describes crowded conditions on ship—fifty men sleeping on the floor of the lounge—and reports learning gin

255

rummy from a mouselike boy named "Rous." Sleep is difficult on board, and the resulting discomfort and fatigue lead
Richard to view his colleagues with disdain.

The letters of April 5 through 16, 1946 chronicle the
journey home. Unlike the sea letters of 1944, which were
heavily censored, these epistles include specific places. We
read that Richard's ship is sailing through the Philippines
and San Bernardino Straits. It circles Luzon, where the men
detect signs of war's ravages. In addition to spotting whales
and playing gin rummy, Richard passes the time with books.
For Reva's benefit, he comments on an author's style and
worth. (Editor's note: This habit he will continue for the rest
of his life. Instead of voicing his observations to Reva, he
writes in the books themselves—reader comments in the
margins and evaluation paragraphs in the front pages.)

After the ship moved to higher latitudes, writes Richard
on April 8, the weather turned cool. He speculates on their
route—through Guam, the Marianas, Wake, and Midway. As
may have been the case with many on board, the sea journey
wreaks havoc on his gastrointestinal system. He looks forward to buying decent brands of tobacco and of not having to
trust the Army with anything.

By April 12, the ship is above Wake Island, and Richard's
letters exclaim his excitement at viewing a school of whales at
very close range. Overhead, gulls are sure harbingers of nearing shore. America is in sight. In his emotional last letter of
overseas duty, penned on April 19, Richard anticipates his
reunion with Reva. Sleep escapes him, and he remains awake
for first sight of the "lovely California landscape" and "the
encircling arms of land that have been called—appropriately
for us—the Golden Gate." The morning is clear and springlike, the hills green, and an army boat with a WAC band sere-
nades the returning soldiers.

Seeing the "clean, landlocked city of San Francisco"
thrills him, as does passing under the Oakland Bay Bridge.
It matters little at this jubilant time that the vaunted steak

dinner, intended as a welcome-home treat, is tough. Profoundly more comforting than drinking milk for the first time in eighteen months is Richard's first postwar telephone conversation with Reva. Although letters served well for eighteen months, they lacked the intimacy of living, breathing voices. In his April 19th letter to Reva, Richard concludes, "So closes the story of my first partial day on American soil . . . made memorable really only by the sound of your voice."

Calcutta, India
January 2, 1946

Dearest Ritter Mine:

It must be a very cool evening, for I am chilled to the bone. "To the marrow," as Gus put it upon his and my return from the movie "Too Young to Know." The show aroused considerable comment, not because it was very good, but because its opening scene was in Bombay, according to the script. Since coming back, we have been reading, drinking tea, and listening to the radio. I spent a few minutes with Archie Hooper, who now lives in Quarter #7. Captain Hooper is a very big, 29-year-old music teacher from California. He's the assigned Special Services officer. We are becoming good friends, and I find him an interesting person.

Some changes are taking place. For instance, Gus's Museum and Medical Arts Detachment was formally deactivated December 31, 1945, and Gus is now assigned to the 14th 2nd. The Pink Palace and Qtrs 4 have been vacated and nurses are again living in the China area in Quarters 1 and 3, which doesn't please the men at all.

Though I didn't have to, I returned to the office this afternoon, spent most of it writing letters, though I did have a conference or two. Upon coming to the area, I decided to join the fellows in volleyball, which leaves me with a sore arm and some strained muscles, but ought to be good for me. Gus reneged on his exercise program after the first day, just as I knew he would.

A headache I'd had earlier was practically gone this morning, but I didn't do much work. Ellen and Phyl dropped in for a half hour chat to talk over how absurdly everyone had behaved Monday night. My linguist, Corporal Maurer, left for 15 days in Agra and Delhi. I heard that Ruth left by the midnight plane tonight, but haven't seen her for several days to talk. The scene is surely changing. I hope I'm missing (from here) soon.

The hospital census is now 444, and very few people have any work to do. Many make no pretense of working, yet the closed hospitals up the line each have one officer and several GI's guarding them. The army just won't let go! Further, our census is due to drop again when a shipment goes out the 6th. Of course, Karachi closes this month, and I suppose they will use that as an excuse to remain at full strength this month. Just as a guess, unless something happens, I would say that my chances look better for March than for February. But maybe I am too cold tonight—not in my heart, though.

Happy Birthday, sweet wife!

Many, many returns of the day, and every one of them with us closely together—I love you, darling, and think you sweeter, lovelier, and more charming as each year passes.

Goodnight, my own precious, goodnight.

Dick

P.S. I forgot to mention that we took our last trip today noon in Gus's command car, for tomorrow he turns it in. Jim, Dottie, Gus and I ate well at the Cathay, then while Jim and Dottie were in New Market, Gus and I watched an Indian magician do a levitation trick, in which a helper, covered by a dirty shirt, lay down on the ground, was apparently raised 4 feet by magic, and lowered. This trick was done three times. Of more interest to me was the

balancing goat act, in which a large speckled goat stood on
a 3-inch hour-glass block of wood, and, still balancing, got
on a two-inch piece placed on the other, without falling
during the operation.

January 2, 1946

My Darling,

*You really are spoiling me, so many nice things for my birth-
day. The roses are lovely (a brighter red than usual) and the pictures are very nice. They are pretty and our only watercolors. They
will make a nice grouping too. Should I go ahead and have them
framed, if so any definite ideas?*

*Your letters of December 14 and 15 came today. I enjoyed the
pictures. I would like to see the Taj Mahal. It certainly must be
breathtaking. Your Agra shopping sounds mighty interesting and
I'm looking forward to my gifts but I do hope you can present
them in person.*

*I didn't mind today as much as I thought I would. This
morning the children looked sleepy and were, which at least made
them quiet.*

*Thanks Dearest for making my birthday the nicest possible
without your being here.*

My Darling, you are so very sweet and I know how lucky I am.
   All my Love,
   Ritter

Calcutta, India
January 6, 1946

Dearest Wife:

It has just occurred to me that I have written that date
line to you for over 250 times. I hope it doesn't go over
300! Tomorrow we go to Personnel to sign as to the length
of our stay in the army, for the second or third time. Once
again I'll indicate that I want out as soon as I am eligible.
This stalemate must break reasonably soon, and some indication given us of when we will be sent home. The utter

folly of holding us in India merely because we are not eligible to be discharged seems to have occurred to no one except the victims themselves!

Gus and I are spending a quiet evening at "home." At dinner tonight Pete and Ann talked me into going to the movie with them: "Mexicana." We walked out on a pretty shabby affair, and I turned down their invitation to have a drink at the club. It often seems to me that the walk alone which I often take through the hospital grounds is one of the happiest periods of any day for me. It is then that I think of that which concerns me most—my wife, myself, my home, and my work. But I am not alone, really, you are always with me.

So impatient I get, my sweetheart. You don't mind, do you, Ritter? For it shows how much I think of you and how I long for you, my pretty. Though your letters reflect the same impatience, and fine mind, I need your words to keep me going. As you note from my letters of the last several days, we have again had no mail. I am half afraid that this situation will continue to exist from now on, on our end of the line. I only hope that you are getting my letters regularly. I think probably it is easier for me to wait than for you—though it is getting harder.

My stint as Acting Officer on Duty wasn't very exciting last night, and I am grateful for that. Nonetheless, it became cold, and I made a pretty fast round at 2:00 a.m. I didn't argue with any love makers, though I surely saw a lot of it. Maybe it is the cold that makes them sit and stand so closely? Captain Bob Jaedache (Detroit) did three appendicitis operations, finishing at 11:45. Jaedache, Erger (Medical Officer on Duty) and I had midnight lunch together—mainly consisting of three fried eggs.

The 4th, I think it was, I mailed you the "surprise" package which you are to open as soon as it arrives. It contains a gift for just you, two for us, and one for you to keep for me. I am anxious to get your reaction to the "your" gift.

Well, darling lady, while I am feeling much better today, I think it well to go to bed early—so, I love and kiss you.

Ever mine,
Dick

January 6, 1946

My Darling,

The weather has been like spring today but I've been lazy. I slept until nearly noon.

Then this afternoon I did a few odd jobs and some more. I'm not sick but I haven't felt quite up to par so I thought I'd take this opportunity to get in some rest.

I doubt that you and I realize how much the cost of living has risen and will be surprised when we rent a house. Helen Avery says one family just couldn't live in Detroit on $200 a month. Of course, rent in the city is the big item and one can realize why Mim [Miriam, Reva's sister] and Ray are so cramped when you know they pay $60 a month rent.

The "Hour of Charm" is on the radio now. I wish My Charmer were here to listen with me. Each day it seems I get more impatient. I'm impatient now for mail too. The winter is going fairly fast with only two more weeks in the first semester but it is regrettable to wish away time. So many things will take on meaning when you are home, but right now most of all I just want to cuddle up and feel your arms about me.

Darling, Sweet Dreams, Love Me!
Your Devoted Ritter

January 8, 1946

Dearest Ritter:

Today has been another of the endlessly pretty, cool, and invigorating days which distinguish the Indian winter in Bengal. Gus and I were late to breakfast, unaccountably

so, but did take our time anyway. We simply sit until we
have absorbed all the eggs, toast, and coffee we care for.
This nicely dulls our mental apparatus, but since we have
no need for it, it makes no difference. After drinking coffee until we are quite rotund, we waddle back to our quarters, and emerge about 8:30 to stroll to our respective of-
fices. Gus has set up headquarters in his old building, by
the way. I think the cold is letting up a little, for I don't
freeze as much as I used to. And my cold has dropped to
my throat, where it chokes me up on occasion, otherwise
not bothering me very much.

My classes were small this morning, so I invited the
men into my southern office, where we get a little sun, and
I ran through a brittle assembly of remarks culled from
their test papers and commented upon how lucky they
were to be comfortably assigned to the 142nd instead of
being released to a port battalion, or something like that.
However, I don't believe what I say particularly, for if they
were in some other outfit, perhaps their leaders would be
interested in getting home, and I know that our CO [com-
manding officer] is not. Nothing makes him so happy as an
opportunity to say, "My boss tells me that I'll be here for
quite awhile" . . . and similar remarks calculated to drive
men who love their wives and their homes to madness. He
seems to ignore the fact that others, who are not professional army men, might look upon this squatting in India
with considerable disfavor.

At 2:00, the administrative men trooped into the CO's
office like a trained group of martinets, whereupon, like
the gentle rain from heaven, there dribbled upon them
comments initiated by quick glimpses into assorted note-
books. This method of reporting and handing down directions so fascinated me that I missed a great deal of the
import in favor of the technique. Besides, I was forced to
sit in the front row, and was afraid that if I were asked for
a report that I might give one: a factual one, with vivid

impressions neatly labeled which would cause the bald one
to suffer apoplexy.

There is not much doubt left in anyone's mind but that
the RA (Royal Air Force) boys love the idea of taking their
time to clear the theater, but there is not much doubt left
in my mind but that they are going to have trouble if they
don't get the lead out of . . . I have been trying to get my
sights leveled, but I am about ready to quit talking and
start acting any day now, if I don't get good news to report
to you.

More and more boys are coming in for advice, once
they learn that I am a college teacher, and willing to talk
over education, careers, etc. Four or five were in today,
and we continue to sell USAFI[1] courses rapidly. At ten in
the morning, a big, big nurse titled Lt. Ondisko, came in
for an hour's chat. She used to be an assistant historian
and wrote a history of the nurses' share in the activities of
the 142nd. Her bovine features lighted with interest when
I remarked "what rare individuals nurses are," but soon
dulled when she learned that I was interested scientifically.

At 5:00, I trudged to the 1700 club, where Mookerjee
Boone ("El Capitan") was holding forth with a stiff-necked
Jimmy Haden. There also were Phyl, Ellen, Dottie, and
assoted (I meant "assorted," but I like "assoted," too)
glancing uncoyly over their shoulders at officers intent on
an early evening drink. Ellen brought me a villainous mix-
ture of gin and coke which had the effect of a pine-tar cold
syrup. Ruth had called in that afternoon, saying that a
Cathay party was in the making. By 6:00, Gus, Boone, Jim,
Dottie, Ruth, Ellen and I were on our way downtown, and
once again we gorged something terrific. Ellen has no business going, for she had an eight o'clock dinner date with a
Major. Ruth was teed off because Pete hadn't come. But
we had a good time, and how I like that food!

Back at the hospital, Gus and I dropped in at the movie
outdoor emporium to see a horrible creation called "She

Went to the Races." I stuck it out, but Gus had better sense, and he went back to quarters a half hour ahead of me. Once again I walked slowly home, thinking of you, dearest one, and of the fact that no one could much longer keep us apart.

I love you, darling Ritter, always and always.

Ever yours,
Dick

January 9, 1946

Dearest Wife:

Because I suspect that you like to see my handwriting whether you can read it or not, more than my typing, I'll undertake to write by pen again. It is my personal conviction that I do much better on the typewriter, but it does lose personality, I believe. Can you read the charge of love for you that should flow through my fingertips to the paper? Can one imagine sweet Elizabeth Barrett writing her Portuguese sonnets on a portable?

When I pore over the details of each day for you, you must pretend that it is my song of love and adoration to you, darling. It is the only way that I can bring you to my side—at the moment. Writing has always been a trial (whether I do it well is beside the point), but it is not when I am writing to you. I love these hours put aside to talk to my beloved girl.

Human beings are rarely ever satisfied. It just occurred to me that a year ago many of my letters were complaining bitterly about the bugs, particularly those low-cruising "B-29s" but also about the general discomfort of my surroundings. Now look at me: a first lieutenant instead of a corporal, in Calcutta instead of Feni, comparatively luxurious quarters instead of a bamboo basha, reportedly at peace instead of at war, BUT still away from my sweetheart.

Perhaps we should take heart from the question "What will January 1947 bring?"

Among other things—you will be with me. Hold this thought tightly to your heart, my darling, and don't let it go for a moment. If I can't be with you, I don't want to be.

What happened today? What did happen is hardly worth recording (except for this hour!) A small class at 10:00, with much of the morning taken out for personal interviews—more and more men are streaming in. It must be refreshing to talk to an officer who doesn't think the sun rises and falls so that his brass can glitter!

There is a big dance at the club tonight following the Colonel's dinner, which dinner I wasn't invited to—and so had a wonderful reason for not attending said dance—and didn't.

Poor Gus is club officer tonight, to his usual disgust.

As you can surmise, yet another day with no mail. However, we had a lot delivered January 3—so maybe tomorrow will be a lucky day!

In the meantime, I know I can depend on your keeping your pretty chin up.

I am in love with you, girl of 16 years (I regret not having shared your first sixteen).

> Your adoring husband,
> Dick

January 13, 1946

Dearest:

I don't have much to report for today, now that I sit here thinking it over. There was another two o'clock mass meeting today of GI's downtown, in which our India-Burma mission was stated as "Getting out of India." Cards were distributed to the men to send to their congressmen and friends. I was shown two of them, but they were poorly written and poorly stated the India-Burma situation. They should have had someone like myself help them.

There is no other subject of conversation anymore, and it looks as though the authorities will have to quit stalling.

In my own case, I tried to get Pete and Powers to give me an approximate date, but this they wouldn't do, or couldn't. I'll put continuous pressure on Powers, he's the key man from now on. I doubt if much can be done for 30 days, though, until they ship out what is called the "Immediate Division"—about 8,000 enlisted men and 2,000 officers. Once they have cleared out about 16,000 men and officers already at Kanchrapara plus the Intermediate 10,000, they will be ready to move. But, we have just one more ship coming in this month—isn't that a shame? And there positively can't be much done until the ships arrive in February. I suspect that "good" General Terry has ordered a few more than he expected since this rumpus started.

A quiet, leisurely morning. Pete called to ask me to take pictures with him, but I had already promised Jack Rosenberg that I would take his place this afternoon at the Adjutant's office as AOD. I had an early turkey dinner, then spent the afternoon writing letters and talking with the enlisted men who dropped in.

Tonight a group of us went to the movie, Claudette Colbert and Don Ameche in a farcical comedy, "Guest Wife," which we considered pretty bad.

I've been reading the comics and thinking of you, sweet. I stayed up late to finish "January Thaw"—one of your Christmas gifts to me—last night, and so am quite tired tonight. So, at 11:30, to bed.

I love you, darling,
Dick

January 14, 1946

Dearest Ritter:

Another week has begun in a somewhat more cheerful attitude than before on the part of many of us. There is still a great deal of complaining because the front office acts like a scared rabbit on the subject of manpower, talking of possible epidemics, etc. as an excuse for keeping from two to three times the number of men they need. With a little over four hundred patient census, for instance, we have one hundred nurses, or one nurse for every four patients. This is patently nonsense, but I believe that proportionately speaking, the administrative officers are as overstaffed. Now that we have gone down to a 750-bed operation, we will keep only 70 nurses, and presumably will let some of our administrative officers go too. But if all organizations are as overstaffed as we, it is easy to understand how they drag this business out.

There is no question but that Colonel Peterson is returning to the states. Again there is murmuring on the part of Reserve officers, especially those who have heard his hard comments on civilians who think only of going home. He has about ten months overseas duty. He leaves Wednesday. I have had an excellent opportunity to really needle him and couldn't resist. Friend or no friend, the fact remains that the regular army seemingly has never stayed in this theater very long . . . but always find some good excuse for getting to hell out, though they talk in the godamnedest terms about serving their country and performing their mission. Once I hear a commanding officer begin with that preamble, I know that is his swan song, that he is leaving the dirty end of the stick to his men while he wings homeward.

I spent most of the day reading current events, trying to line up some information for the week's lectures, then decided to call Leeds, who is our hospital representative on the GI mass meeting committee, to talk to the men. Just after I had made that decision, a phone call came from McConkie ordering me to report to the front office, where he wanted to know the temper of the men . . . sort of asking me to be his stool pigeon. I replied, respectfully enough, that the men would be all right if they could be sure that action would be forthcoming.

Gus and I entertained Mookerjee Haden with a game of darts, which Jim won over me by scores of one and two more in each game. I would start out like a house afire, then dampen down in the last frames. Fine business. It made me a little homesick, reflecting upon the fun we had the winter of 1943–44 with darts.

I have nothing specific toward going home. I wrote that I planned to explain in the folks' Sunday letter about the shipping situation, then I forgot to do so. Here it is: Originally seven ships were scheduled for January—from the Calcutta port. Then, no one knows why, four of them were canceled. Then, and we know why this was done, they were reordered. In the meantime they had been deflected to China, though one of the four had been kicked around so that it went into dry-dock. That was *General McRae,* I think.

Orders were sent that the ships were to go to their original destination, Calcutta, but three ships had already reached China, and thus had several extra thousand miles to travel to make it. The fourth ship, the replacement for the *McRae,* was sent directly here. However, so much time had been lost that none of the four will make it in January.

The shipping situation looks like this: there are 41,000 troops still in India, with 15,000 at replacement depots, and 10,000 from the Intermediate section slated to ship to the depots. There is at least one ship yet to go out of Karachi this month.

An optimistic estimate would range up to 25,000 troops that will go out on these ships, but at least 21,000 will be shipped, leaving about 20,000 here the middle of February. Now, everything depends on getting enough ships in here the last of February. If they do, most of us will get out then; if not, we should make it the first part of March. The damned mail situation is stymied again.

Apparently they are shipping mail only once or twice a week. What can one do? Only remember that I love you very much, and always will. Forever in devotion,

      Love and kisses,

      Dick

                        January 16, 1946

Dearest Ritter:

I think I'll write this by pen tonight, honey, and as always, my love goes forth! I think you are wonderful.

What is there to say about today? Well, for one thing, it warmed up amazingly—and was so hot at noon that I regretted having on woolens, for the first time in a month. It is still moderate this evening, and the almost full moon shines brightly. How glorious if it could shine through the elm, as you and I sat, close together, whispering. Let's drive out that way soon after my return, shall we? And while we are on the subject, how many nights are you prepared to go to bed early? Indefinitely, I hope. This has been a long, long wait, my dearest wife—it should be the sweeter for the waiting. It will be a grand and noble sensation to return to you as I left, because you want it that way and what you want is an eternal principle with me. You need never fear, dear Reva, you need not fear.

This noon there was a gathering of the Mookerjees at the Cathay—Jim, Gus, Ellen, Phyl and I ate, leisurely, for an hour or so. [The "Mookerjees" were apparently members of an informal social club.] Then Gus and Jim went out to take movies of the Calcutta crowd, while Ellen, Phyl and I returned to the hospital. Phyl and Ellen leave tonight (9:30 by plane) for Agra for a week.

We have a hilarious group that usually eat together now, something like the McGraw-Kenyon-Beard combination at Feni. It includes Jack R., Jim H., Gus and myself as a nucleus with Boone and Munson and Hooper sometimes joining. We make a lot of noise, but we have fun.

After our usual hi-jinks, we went to see Jinx Falkenberg in "The Gay Senorita," which was pretty sad. It was nice in the moonlight, and Gus, the dope, went to sleep. We paused at the club for a moment only, then back to Room Ten, where Gus and I picked up the game of darts where we had left off before dinner.

Well, precious gal, my love to you, and now goodnight, my one and all.

Your husband, Dick

January 23, 1946

Dearest Ritter:

My love, the passage of each day means that we are that much nearer, no matter what my release date over here may be. Despite my talks with McConkie, he still insisted on listing my release date as April 30, when the report went in today noon. That is in contradiction to a memo that points out that "50 plus" point men are to be moved by April 1. A fortunate circumstance took place today, however, when Roy Bryan became Assistant Executive Officer. He will do everything he can for me. Incidentally, I am the high point unreleased man in the organization. If it shrinks by even one man, they will have to let me go.

On May 27, I will have had three years service, and I am sure that I can get out on that, if nothing else. Then almost two years overseas service won't hurt. Further, National Welfare can be invoked, once I hit the country. To utilize that means that I must sign a contract with a school, and get their sworn affidavit that I am needed, so you can see why I don't want to do that. I don't want to be committed to an institution such as State during my first year back.

At the moment, here is my idea of what we should do. I will get back (this may change) sometime in May or early June. If you haven't acted on my suggestion to quit teaching, you will have taught practically a full year, so you will have a vacation coming, and I think I may have earned one. At any rate, I will want to enjoy yours with you. We will spend a week or so at home, seeing the folks whom we should see, then we will take off for the east, going to Toronto for a few days, then on to New York, where we will stay in a big hotel (To hell with that dollar-a-day joint), eat in big restaurants, sit in the park, visit the famous spots, look up a few friends, go to plays and musicals, and stay in our room.

Fine! After that, back to Ohio and the task of getting a contract signed for 1946–1947 school year. That may take a little while, and a number of visits to various Midwestern universities. During that time, I can be collecting books, pamphlets, etc. on the latest in education for study during the summer at my leisure. Then, darling mine, what do you say to a summer spent in Florida? It may be that one or both of our parents will go with us, or they may exchange—with one couple going down with us, the other coming back.

At the moment, I am intrigued with the possibilities of what we did in 1940, but you may have some refinements to suggest. When it looked as though I might get home within 60 days, I thought about taking a teaching job during the summer, but I believe now that that would have been unfair to you, and would not have meant too much to me. It surely is fun to be writing about prospective plans that do not seem too far in the future. Since I have thus made up my mind, I am going ahead with my various letters to educators, the first of which will go out this weekend. I think I will try to feel out the Toledo situation, just in case.

Such a garrulous chap, for I have talked for over a page and haven't said anything about the events of the day. Not much to report, really. The Indians are celebrating the birthday of Subhas Bose, the chappy who headed the INA[2] and whom most of us consider a traitor, and so American personnel have remained near the hospital. There have been only a few disturbances so far. They awakened us this morning with a parade that started out at five. How these folks love parades. On the other hand, they haven't much else to do.

> My sweetheart, how much I love you.
> Hugs and kisses, darling,
> Dick

January 25, 1946

My Darling,

It was so nice to find letters from you when I got home although they weren't any more recent than the January 6th letter I received Tuesday. The mail is still very slow and according to the paper the telegraph company is still out on strike at least in N.Y.

Your letter sounded optimistic, but I am quite worried about the unrest in India.

Lowell Thomas told of the trouble in Bombay and added that riots might spread throughout India.[3] A later commentator said that fighting in Bombay has waned. Just as I had gotten reconciled to the fact that the mail will probably be slow then these disturbances come along to worry about. I surely hope you can come home soon.

Your Kawoodie[4] pipe sounds like a wonderful buy. I am seeing a few better pipes in the stores now but nothing outstanding. In fact, I keep putting off sending things, thinking you'll soon be out of India. I've procrastinated sending you "Ohio Schools" until then. I may as well just save them for you.

I was going to a show but with no one to urge me, didn't go. Ruth isn't home yet, and I don't know what Milly was doing. She may have gone home.

I tried to telephone your Mother several times and couldn't get through, so Mother and I drove over. She was making candy so we stayed for some of it.

The weatherman says it will be much colder tomorrow, which won't make it so nice for Mother to shop in Lima. I really don't expect to look for anything but shoes.

I was sorry to learn that you had a cold. I hope you don't have any more and that you have some warm clothing to wear home. My voice is much better. I guess that medicine is really helping.

My Dearest, do take care of yourself and hurry home. I love you! I love you!

Your Devoted Ritter

Calcutta, India
February 3, 1946

Dearest Ritter:

I have been thinking, when I last heard from you, your letter of January 16 which arrived January 30, you had not received anything later than my December 28 letter. That means that as of this date, we are 37 days separated (add one more for each day that I don't hear from you) in our contact-communication. It makes me a little sad to think that instead of getting closer to you, the end of the war and the closing of the theater has pushed you farther away. It makes me bitter, too, but I must try to keep that out of my mind as much as possible. When will men of goodwill escape the pernicious influence of hierarchies which deny them their natural heritage? I see little of goodwill about me, instead the authoritarians are making it as rough as possible for those of us who have a right to think that we should be encouraged in our desire to get home soon. To men who have been away from home for two years continued absence from loved ones is not a joking matter . . . and it is a peculiar sense of humor which thinks that it is.

But to get back to the movie. It was Roz Russell and Lee Bowman in "She Wouldn't Say Yes." I presume that it was witty and clever, but I doubt if I were in the mood, for I still felt let down at its conclusion. Gus and Jim insisted that I go to the club for a beer, but I soon excused myself

273

and walked home alone, thinking. Gus returned shortly, and then Jack came in. It is amusing, now that I look back on it, but Jack must have made Gus very angry. When the latter loses his temper, he takes on the appearance of a Chester White shoat, with about the same amount of expression. The whole affair was about Jack's desire to have a party for our own personnel, and he wanted to hold it in the Mess Hall. Until yesterday, when he became Club Officer, Gus had been in favor of it, but he had changed his mind suddenly. It is grim that people working toward the same end have to work at cross purposes because one feels that his prestige is being singed. It's that sort of thing in the army, even more than in civilian life, which sets a stupid tone for the whole enterprise.

While I thought it chillier this evening again, there can be no question but what our spring is just around the corner. The doves are back, with their beautiful haunting call. And other singing birds have put in an appearance, and the crows are busy building nests, silly things. Someone met a certain colonel the other day. He was carrying a sun helmet in his hand, and felt it necessary to say, with a giggle, "I'm getting prepared for the monsoons." Since they won't start until late May you can imagine the enthusiasm with which his statement was greeted.

Well, sweetheart, the underground has it that I may see you before either of us has thought possible, in view of the middle of January developments. Let's hope so. It has gotten so bad with me that I take no pleasure in anything but a great desire to love you with you in my arms.

Forever in devotion,
Dick

February 6, 1946

My Darling,

I was certainly surprised to get letters for the third day in a row, and so many. The only trouble with that is there can't help

but be a famine for a while now. I like your long typewritten letters, but I do love to see your handwriting.

I'm afraid you will find my patience of early January (when I
was actually thinking you'd be sailing in February) all gone. May
is just too far away. Keep after them, Dearest. It is awfully hard
for me to give up the February idea.

It was nice of you to give me that special reassurance. I recently remembered that you hadn't lately, which leads me to believe
you are a good morale officer.

There is almost a blizzard tonight, a light snow with a very
strong wind. That is one point for waiting a few weeks. The storms
should be over—but not later than the first of March.

Dearest—let's do take a ride out to the Old Elm—And love
me! Love me so hard, Sweetheart!

> Night Dearest Darling,
> All My Love,
> Ritter Yours

Calcutta, India
February 6, 1946

Dearest Ritter:

I dropped into the office by chance this evening and
found that I had the grand total of three letters from you,
that and no more. But how wonderful, how very wonderful
to see your dear handwriting again. And yet, my rage was
great, in fact I am so angry that I cannot really type coher-
ently, to think that the stupidest outfit the world has ever
seen, would be so unthoughtful, so downright, damned
criminal, as to let our loved ones at home sit there with
bitterness in their hearts wondering what has happened.
You will hear all kinds of excuses for that. Airplanes are
flying everywhere, many of them with all kinds of civilian
freight and civilians, and the least that could be done
would be to hire civilian pilots and mechanics to get the
mail through. I want to be sure to write it again, and again,
and again, so that I may never, when I incline to forgive in

later years, forget how much I hate the army and the hierarchy that mismanages it. They never needed more than half of us in the first place, and there is no point in their denying it, for every PFC knows better. It only makes certain bigwigs sound like damned fools to get to their feet and act as though they don't know better.

Your January 15, 17, and 18 letters tell the sad story of no mail, and the last explains why I have not received a cable, which must have been the final straw. I assume that you did get mail Saturday the 19th? I have already written concerning cables; we hear that despite promises, they move slowly. For instance, they take three or four days to go from here to Bombay by civilian mail. I will check into it, though. The whole world is f—— up, and I have only one desire, to get back to you. I grow incoherent just thinking about the situation. I do not know exactly how I stand anymore, and neither do the people downtown, for all our names have to be submitted to the China authorities, and they can take any of us they like. Three of our doctors went on orders yesterday. Please don't worry about that happening to me, for I doubt if even an unfeeling fate would deal us a cruel blow like that. Please do not get too upset; it doesn't seem that these clouds can possibly dodge our footsteps indefinitely. But my enthusiasm over the chance of getting on a ship this month has been dimmed, and I presume that April 15 looms up again. All the other men declared surplus are at Kanchrapara; I shall not forget that McConkie could have done that for me, and I would never have been missed. When I write and talk after the war, I see manifold opportunities to avenge myself. Pray God that my tongue remains bitter and my wit a razor's edge of scorn. When they had me in their power they gave no quarter; now they need expect none from me.

I probably should not send you the first page of this letter, but I shall, regardless, for I want you to know that, with you, I am most bitter about the situation. I see so much of smug hypocrisy and damnable inefficiency about me that my rage rises in a screaming crescendo, and I refuse to keep my mouth shut or my fingers still.

Now, enough of that.

This letter has been briefly interrupted while I listened to Walter Hampden in bits from "Cyrano de Bergerac," even now coming over VU2ZU.[5]

So, perhaps I should say goodnight, having by now written myself into a good humor, for what man, in all the world, has so much awaiting him when he returns home from the wars? What man indeed deserves such of the world's largesse? Better that I should thank God on my bended knees for the grace of the years which I have had with you, than to rail at him because I am now denied that breath of life. Ah, Reva, my beloved!

> With me, knowing that you are,
> All things are bearable,
> Dick

February 12, 1946

My Darling,

I am very nervous now (11:30 p.m.). Your Mother called me and said Gay had heard that there is trouble in Calcutta. I just got in on the last of a broadcast which said something about Britain's trouble with India. Now I have to wait 1/2 hour before another newscast. Many times the last couple of months I've felt all caved in. At this minute I am so upset I know I'm incoherent. If I could only think that you are on your way home. Dearest, you must get home soon!

I had dinner at the Phoenix with Mary Rice and Ruth Brickman and went to see "Spellbound" with Gregory Peck and Ingrid Bergman. It was, I thought, a good psychological study.

Then I came home to read the paper and some of the letters which I received today. My Darling, the news I hear shortly will determine how well I sleep tonight. Beloved, there is only one thing

on my mind now and that is your safety. What heaven it will be to
have you by my side. I love you so much. I miss you so much.
> Night, My Darling Husband,
> All My Love,
> Your Ritter

P.S. The report only mentioned that some U. S. Army men
were injured by stoning in Calcutta and they will use their guns if
necessary. Some business! My main consolation is that I know
you'll try to stay away from the trouble. Surely they'll move fast in
evacuation.

February 14, 1946

My Darling,

Thanks for the lovely Valentine. The bright red roses whisper
your love. Early this evening I thought the mail had probably
cheated me out of my Valentine but at about 11:10 tonight, the
roses were at the door.

I picked up Milly and we went to hear Schlagle, President of
the National Education Association. His two-hour talk was good,
although he is just an average speaker who says "jist" instead of
"just." He told of his experiences at the San Francisco and London
conferences. He is pro-British and pro-Russian. He believes we
should help the British get back on their feet and believe in the
Russians. Among the American delegates to the San Francisco conference were Statinian (sp?), Gildersleeve and Stassen. He mentioned the first and latter several times in very favorable tones. He
spoke about how much more other countries' diplomats know about
us than we know about them.

After the program, Milly, Ruth, and I went to the Phoenix for
coffee. Three ex-GIs sitting near us tried to attract our attention
but we made ourselves safe when we invited Florence and Rosa
Hudral to join us. I came home in a blizzard, parked out in front
and came in to find Daddy ready for bed, so I put on my overshoes
and took the car around to the garage.

The only Calcutta report today was that the British are patrol-ling the streets. There won't be any peace of mind for me until you get out of there. Tomorrow is Friday, and I am glad for another weekend. I want to be in my Valentine's arms. Hurry home! So much love, my Sweetheart!

> *Kiss me Goodnight,*
> *Ritter*

Calcutta, India
February 16, 1946

My Darling Ritter:

Glorious news from you—letters: Heaps of letters—and all is forgiven. Isn't that just like us? Our snarl turns to tail wagging when we are pleased. Here's the list: January 21, 22, 23, 28, 29, 30, February 1, and 4 airmails; and January 22 and 31 clippings. Two valentines arrived from the folks, 4 in envelopes, and a dozen letters from friends. This influx of mail would come on a busy day, and I didn't get all the mail read until after 11:00 p.m.

Today has been rugged. First, I stayed up half the night, expecting to take this afternoon off, then learned that Ben Berger couldn't be at the Board meeting, and so had to sub for him. We met at 8:00, knocked off at 10:00 to handle 16 more applicants, reconvened at 1:00 (which meant that I couldn't join Gus and Jim in Chinese food this noon!) and that meeting lasted until 6:15 p.m. Fine stuff! And I just wrote Mim a letter extolling army official loafing. I should eat that letter!

The ban on leaving the pool was lifted at noon today—and so the Hospital was pretty well deserted tonight with everyone taking off for Karmain and downtown spots! Except me. I expected to stay in my room, but Jack per-suaded me to go to the movie with him. It was a farce, poorly timed but fairly well done, entitled "Janie Gets Married" with Joan Leslie and Robert Hutton. They had her whining during the entire show and the scenes with the WAC were ridiculed openly and loudly, as were those in which references were made to the ex-soldier's sacrifices and heroics. Robert Benchley was very good.

The moon is full—and the air springlike, but not springlike either, because it is too soft and caressing. The night is a moving frame in which one walks. How sorry, since I must go, that we aren't going tonight. It must be nice up there! [Apparently Richard was observing planes overhead and imagining his own departure from Calcutta.] Hilliard and I got quite a shock this afternoon when we overheard a telephone conversation between Col. McCorkie and General Evans. It sounded as though we were to leave for Delhi within a half hour. No time to bathe, dress, or pack! But the General took only Col. Sloan and Ben Berger in his (the Gen's) personal plane. They had to hurry, but they saw the moon, I am sure. Hilliard, Rudford, and I are leaving for the airport at 5:30 a.m., but we don't emplane until 7:45. The flight takes 4 or 5 hours, depending on the headwinds. As I have mentioned in several other letters, upon our return I will cable, letting you know that we are back in Calcutta. Please don't worry: but since I know that you can't help yourself, I will get off a cable upon my return Friday or Saturday. If luck is with us, I can also give you word that my orders are in!

The afternoon session was prolonged but amusing in spots. McCork stops to inquire into generalities, while Powers muses over his charts like a bewildered child. Col. Smith, the AC flight surgeon, and Lt. Col. Sloan had a hot exchange which pleased everyone.

My next letter will be from Delhi, my darling girl. I love you.

In devotion,
Dick

New Delhi, India
February 18, 1946

Dearest Ritter:

I knew that I was omitting something important from my two letters of the 17th. At 5:00 Sunday afternoon, Ben Berger left for the States, accompanying Gen. Terry as his physician in charge! The Berger saga is something to write home about. Several days ago the Gen. was hurt in a jeep accident, and from what I learn here, no one in this theater wanted to take the responsibility for treating him. When Sloan and Berger arrived, it was a question as to which should go with him. Of course both wanted to make the trip, even though he would have to return to India. Col. Van Auchen (theater surgeon) told me tonight that his decision was an easy one to make. He knew that I was coming to Delhi, consequently he could do without Berger, but Sloan, as president of the board, had to stay.

Today's activities were manifold. Breakfast at 8:00, followed by a general organization board meeting at 10:00. As I suspected, Sloan was coherent, to the point, and efficient in his administration, a wonderful, though scathing, contrast to what had happened last week in Calcutta. By 10:30 everything was in order. I spent the interviewing hours in my room, where a cheery fire kept me warm, writing my letters to you. At 1:00, we were to start, and the officers (38 of them) came in in droves. The bulk of the psychiatric interviews fell to me, a job for which I am embarrassingly prepared. There were no neurologists available in Delhi, but one of the internists (a youthful M.D. with no specialty) did the nervous system for me. I'll send you a mimeographed copy of the interview, to give you an idea of what we covered.

None of the candidates reached me until 3:00, since I was at the end of the line. From then until 7:15 I worked pretty hard, trying to estimate personality, stability, and lack of adjustment characteristics. The task is made more difficult, for these men all minimized variations or covered them up entirely. After the evening meal the board assembled—Capt. Brinkley's quarters, where Col. Van Auchen joined us. Here again, Sloan's smooth administration made the work a genuine pleasure. We had covered all 38 cases by 10:30, though about half will be recalled for further checking. Four had been accepted, while 15 had been definitely rejected. We had a good time during the session, with my comments of the goings-on in the psychiatric interview affording the most amusement. For instance, a flashy Major of 47 with waxed mustaches, which he persistently twisted, told me that he went to high school. "To high school?" I queried, "How many years did you complete?" "None," was the astounding answer, "None! I just went to it!" This Major, by the way, is one of the staff Inspector Generals, among the most intricate, delicate, and difficult tasks in the Army. A sad commentary indeed!

After the session, we all adjourned to the Club, where a little party in honor of the three visiting nurses was in process. I had just entered the room with Rod when I heard someone yell "Dick" in no uncertain tones. There was handsome, blond Joe Mims, one of Ellen's heart-throbs, fairly gone in his cups, hurrying toward me. Nothing to do but accompany him to the bar, where, over a couple of Tom Collins, he poured out his story of his relations with Ellen. Because I am a kindly fellow, I "yessed" and "noed" for an hour, after which Van Auchen approached and rescued me. Van Auchen and I talked for an hour. He was kind enough to say that he thought I had done a good job—which indicates that he doesn't know much about psychology, but is a very good fellow despite the lack. Incidentally, that brings up an interesting point. None of these doctors know much about it. Remember my comments on the Officer Candidate Board at Myitkyina?

Line officers are equally ignorant. Most of them have a healthy respect tinged with dislike for anything labeled "psychological" however. But, if I have any success in the field, and despite my own candid opinion of myself, I seem to have, it may be because I refuse to use technical language (damned if I can think in it) but instead discuss subjects in terms common to all. Instead of saying a man is an esthemic type, I say he is slender, unsure of himself, youthful in appearance, and acts immaturely. Then everyone gets a good picture of what I mean.

Do you know, darling, that it has taken me an hour to compose the first three pages of this letter? I believe that my brain is atrophying—what I need is about 50 years of your company.

Then to bed, after looking into the fire for awhile, but not seeing the flames, instead, big brown eyes in a heavenly frame that think I am a pretty nice fellow. At the moment, Reva, or in any other moment of eternity, I can imagine no more worthwhile goal in life.

> I love you, dear wife,
> Dick

February 19, 1946

My Darling,

Your letters of February 5 and 6 came today. Need I say that I am most discouraged? I feel so depressed. I could easily become a psychiatric case. Sometimes my moods change to anger and I'd like to tell someone off.

I am sure that my endurance is being taxed no more than yours, but I feel so miserably old under the strain. As you say, enough of crying on your shoulder. It will do no good. But please do horrible work; apparently doing your best is very foolish.

Mother heard the preacher who has attended all of the peace conferences and acted as interpreter. He says Russia has organized her communistic campaign and will soon without a war have the world communistic. He says Roosevelt was a tool and Truman, who does nothing, a better leader at this stage. Of course he ties this all in with Bible prophesy.

The strike situation is quite alarming. You know at one time last week, New York, Philadelphia, and Pittsburgh were all tied up. Now a telephone strike (nationwide) is threatened.

I was sorry to learn from your letter today that cables are so slow. I can't give up hoping that you will leave this month for home and not China. They surely will send you home and soon. Keep me informed by letter since there is always the possibility of a telegraph strike.

Dearest, you know how much I love you, how much I long to be in your arms.

Take care of yourself. Love me?
Your devoted Ritter

New Delhi, India
February 19, 1946

Darling Ritter:

There was little work done today by the board other than for a few rechecks. I was held up by one Lt. Col. who never showed up. Not that it made much difference for I wasn't too anxious to go anywhere. I called Joe Mims at 10:00 to explain that I would be held up for the day—which may mean that I won't see him, for he plans to leave by plane for Madras in a day or two. My canvas bag, bought for the Agra trip, got badly ripped in two places—probably by rubbing up against a steel trunk or nail—and simply isn't serviceable any longer. 27 rupees wasted.

We got up about 7:45; I had a luxurious shower before going to breakfast. As with all places except the 142nd, table bearers take orders and bring the food. An excellent feature, for breakfast, is the use of a toaster placed on the tables, where one can get hot toast as desired.

The weather is perfect. The hottest was 78 degrees, the coldest 50 degrees for the 18th, I noticed in the local paper. The sky is the deepest blue imaginable, and since everywhere one looks there are yellow buildings, you can appreciate the lovely, almost startling, contrast.

Temple and burial or tomb ruins are everywhere. We located one village within what had been an old fortress. The natives get in and out by using holes which they have knocked at irregular intervals in the wall. (I am writing this with the board perched on my knee, while supervising typing of forms.) Living conditions within were hideous, from what we could see. On a sloping hill outside the walled village, in the early evening air, women and children were squatted, answering the call of nature. Primitive sort of thing, for the slope drained into their supply of water. Every few yards, or so it seemed, there would be little reed lean-tos, not more than 3 to 5 feet high and only 4 or 5 feet square. Men, women, and children were crawling in and out of these improvised shelters. As far as the eye could see, no cultivation was underway. The land looked poor, and was covered with a scrub bush. I can't understand how these people live—what they eat. Whenever we stopped the jeep, a crowd would collect. The amazing thing about India is the incredible number of people everywhere!

After eating dinner, I had to attend a board meeting which lasted a very short time. Then Sloan, Van Auchin, Rudford, and several others and myself sat around the Club just talking. Rud and Van Auchin are regular army, and it amused me to listen to their recollection: many of their regular army friends in the 30's have been killed in the war.

By 10:00 I was tired enough to go to my room, where I read for awhile, then slept soundly until 8:00 a.m.

> My thoughts are of you, sweetheart,
> adoringly,
> Dick

New Delhi, India
February 22, 1946

Dearest Ritter:

I decided on a lazy day—made no effort to do anything—relaxed in my room until 4:00, when Joe Mims
showed up—his Madras trip having been called off. He
stayed just long enough to make plans for tonight. That
aroused me, and I took a walk in the field across from the
hospital. Oh yes, it rained during the morning and stayed
cloudy most of the day. Tonight a rather brilliant flash
lightning hit the sky, but no rain, just wind. But, as I was
writing, I took the walk through dust and weeds to a building that looks like this:

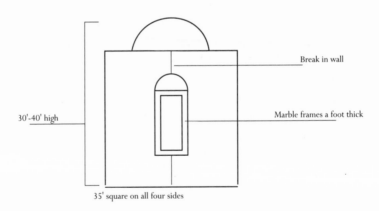

Break in wall

30'-40' high

Marble frames a foot thick

35' square on all four sides

It was once covered with an inch thick plaster, but only
darkened splotches of it remain. Though time and earth-
quakes have damaged the structure, it is a miracle that it
still stands, for apparently the rocks from which it has
been built were tossed in willy-nilly and surrounded with a
cement of unusual texture. The huge marble slabs which

make up the four entrances are in precarious balance—I walked gingerly, with lizards scooting out of sight as I approached. Nothing but rubble lay within the building. A mound of rock, that's what I thought it was, in front of the monument or tomb or temple turned out to be a deep well, at least 15 feet across, and 40 or 50 feet deep—or to the water level. There it lay, unmarked, unprotected—anyone could fall into it! Since this building is only one of 12 that I can see from here, you can imagine the multitude of such places, many of them constructed 500–800 years ago. Interesting, fascinating place, but unfortunately, my companions aren't the least interested, so I am not seeing as much as I should. I would go alone, but think it unwise, for the natives in the old section of town were demonstrating today.

Tonight I took the bus to Curyon, where I met Joe in his room 218. It turned out to be deluxe: deep carpets, expensive radio, record player, scotch whiskey, and a bearer who stayed to serve the drinks. Friends dropped in, particularly a lawyer named Tucker, and we talked until 8:00, then to the Curyon Bar room where free drinks were being served. Having had two scotch and sodas, I stayed clear of further drinks until after we had eaten. Rudford and Sloan were there. I met a number of people, including several women. These women are all of a type, regardless of their color. They want something to drink, and they stand too close to the end. We picked up a captain named Al Hockstetter, who stayed with our party. Al is an introvert, effeminate character. By 8:30 I was ravenously hungry and devoured roast beef, browned potatoes and gravy, and everything else brought to the table. Tony Cunningham yelled from across the hall, and joined us for coffee.

Al, Joe, Tony and I went to Tony's room where the drinking continued. By now Tony was drunk and amazingly funny, especially when he read us a letter he had written to O. D. Donnell. Reminiscing went on at a great pace until

11:00, then we went to Joe's room — another two hours, and finally they brought me out here. I was the only sober guy in the crowd!

My love,
Dick

I am posting this 11:00 a.m., February 23, 1946. We leave on the noon plane.

D.

February 23, 1946

My Dearest,

Happy Day! Your letters of February 10, along with those of the 7th, 8th, and 9th came today. What a thrill to know you'll be leaving India not later than the middle of March!

You should be back from Delhi now. So I hope to be receiving a cablegram in a few days. The paper reports a lot of trouble still in Bombay (I wonder if that will affect the cable service?) It surely will be a relief to have you out of that place, and how wonderful to have you home—and me in your arms!

It will be nice to have you home for Easter. By now you should know that I know you are a first Lieutenant and proud of it. My Dearest Husband, how wonderful to have our reunion near!

All my love,
Ritter

March 1, 1946

Dearest Ritter:

A fine state of affairs. Here it is March and I am not on that boat for home. How exceedingly pleasant it is going to be when the grand time finally does arrive. I am wild over you, sweet.

Not only was Berger sent to the states, but Levy and Leeds were both transferred to the China theater. That took all of our remaining psychologists, although there is a cryptic looking and acting individual named Wright

working in Ward 13. At any rate, Captain Murphy called
on me to help him with a couple of cases today. One of the
men was running a fever, so I passed him up until tomorrow, but did talk with a Captain Beck, suspected of being a
chronic alcoholic. He has been a nomadic coach most of
his life, having coached the national women's champions, a
Tulsa basketball team, in the middle thirties. On this side,
he coached the winning CBI basketball teams from
Pangarh. He makes no excuses for drinking, but his wife
recently wrote for a divorce, having first cryptically asked if
it were all right for her to have an operation, not explaining what kind of operation. At any rate, he also had syphilis several years ago . . . he probably showed those girls
more than how to play basketball.

Ellen called about a project which we had planned for
taking movies. The day was perfect, but I had these psych
cases coming up so couldn't get away for that long. We did
go downtown for a last lunch at the Cathay (she leaves by
plane Tuesday) and because no taxi, rode the street car.
Polite Indians immediately gave us seats, which embarrassed me to take, but I had no alternative. A number of
street cars passed us flying the Congress flag, with kids and
older people carrying on. When they saw Ellen, they
yelled, but the people in our car were reserved and made
no noise. There were parades, too, but mostly of children.
I suspect that they enjoy it; the parading around, I mean.
After a leisurely lunch, we returned about 3:00, this time
by taxi.

I fooled the fellows by playing volleyball tonight, and
had a good time. The group is quite congenial, now that it
is smaller, and everyone has a pretty good time. Then, the
big poker game. I thought at long last that I had hit a hot
streak, for I won 200 rupees in just a half hour, at the beginning, but I went into a decline, at nine o'clock, and at
one, gave up. I knew that since I won last night, that I

might have that luck, for one can't win all the time. None-theless, I did win: four rupees!

That incorrigible Rosenberg, who is a gambler par lux, took four hours out for a date, won before and I think after. I gave him my seat at one, I know, and the game went until 4:30 this morning.

See you soon, I surely hope,
Love and kisses,
Dick

March 11, 1946

Dearest Ritter:

This has been a very busy day for me . . . too busy, and after about one more of these, I expect to take it easy from now on. Odds and ends at the office until about 10:30, then to Hindusthan with the Message Center boys. From Hindusthan I walked slowly along Chowringhee carefully looking over the motley scene that won't be a part of my life much longer. Down by the Lighthouse movie theater, seven coolies were carrying an upright piano on their heads. Irresistible. Well, not irresistible exactly, for I didn't do it, but I did have the impulse to trip one of them, say the corner one, to see what would have happened.

At Hogg's market, better known as New Market, but more apropos in its correct appellation, I paused for awhile in one of the shops that I have dealt with before, and lo and behold, I bought more and more, until I had completed my Indian buying right then and there. I now have your May 16, 29 and July 3rd gifts, as well as a variety of objects that the folks have expressed a desire for. Incidentally, dearest, don't open your July 3rd gift, though I hope to be there to keep a watchful eye on you. They are closing out some of their ivory, or say they are, so I ended by buying Mom and Dad a whole menagerie instead of the big ebony elephant that I originally had in mind.

After my shopping spree, I walked to the Cathay and had a quiet little lunch by myself, consisting of sherry, egg and vegetable soup, and egg foo yong. By taxi back to the hospital. The assistant driver had to get out and push to get it started and when we stopped at the entrance to the hospital (for taxis still are not permitted inside, for good and sufficient reason), I asked the driver if it would go. He looked around and grinned, his head wrapped in an absurdly long dishrag, his regular features stamping him a warlike Sikh (there are some races that look out of place in a taxi!), then bowed his head, placed his fingers together in an attitude of prayer, glancing my way to make sure I was enjoying the spectacle. But it was to no avail, for when he pressed the starter, there was only a whirrr. This afternoon was spent writing my report, a history for the month of January.

Casey, my bearer, and I packed most of my things, borrowed from AOD Munsen's jeep, and took them to Dahkuria, where Casey made my bed and deposited my huge new bag under the bed. Incidentally, I can just lift it, and that is all. Whereupon came a disappointment: Parrish and I did not find our names on the shipping list for the Jumper. Now don't get upset, for if we miss it, we will make the Cardinal. Nevertheless, after all the rushing around, it would be sort of like the army to not have meant it at all.

As I have said before, if you should not hear by cable from me again, you may be sure that I made the Jumper, otherwise I will cable you *exact* information as to what and when. But this time I will wait until I know for sure.

I hope that your next letter assures me that you are in excellent health, and that all is well.

Much love, darling. You will get all the attention you can bear one of these days, and there will be no letting my darling do without whatever her heart desires.

My kisses on your lips,
Dick

Bay of Bengal
March 27, 1946

Dearest Ritter:

I love you, precious, and wish that I could write more encouraging news, but we will have to take comfort in the fact that I am on my way home, even though I am stuck on a tub that is traveling only 10 miles an hour. If luck is with us, this letter should reach you by airmail from Singapore, but the mail situation is bad here, and there is a good chance that I may beat this particular message home. I am writing the folks, also, hoping that at least one letter will reach home in time to constitute news.

The way things have turned out, I have continued regularly to supply you with false information, but you must know that I believed it at the time. This ship never had a chance to get to San Francisco in 21 days. On its last trip, when its engines were functioning properly, it took twenty days to go from Singapore to Frisco. Here is the trouble. A bearing has been overheating, and they have cut out one engine, reducing our speed almost in half, so that we make out less than ten miles an hour, or only 250 miles a day. Since this is a ten thousand mile trip, it is easy to see how much time will be required unless the repairs, which are to be made in Singapore, are successful. No matter what, I doubt if I get home before the first of May.

Life for an officer aboard the ship is easy, by comparison with the enlisted men. I share a cabin with eight officers. Our beds are comfortable, mattressed, sheeted, pillowed, and we are supplied with free towels. We share a bathroom with another group of men from an adjoining cabin. The officers have the best space on deck reserved for them, and I have been doing a lot of sunbathing. My work is light, having been assigned as a compartment officer in C-3 hold (which is similar to the one I came over in).

The meals are out of this world. We are served by civilians on table-clothed surfaces, in plenty of dishes, with three courses usually constituting the meal. The food is very good, and I should fill out my cheeks a little. So far no poker, and I doubt very much if I play at all, since the only game going is financed by the merchant marines, and is crooked.

A number of 142nd enlisted men are aboard, as well as Just, Parrish, and eleven nurses. Of the 70 women on the ship, 42 are Red Cross, 16 war brides. I haven't seen any attractive ones yet . . . suspect that there is only one attractive woman in the world for me anymore, and you should know her very well. It is hard waiting to hold you in my arms, but with each day my ardor grows, and darling, that will be a wonderful moment . . . all moments will be wonderful from then on.

> Your loving husband,
> Dick

> Singapore
> April 1, 1946

Dearest Ritter:

They haven't said I couldn't, and since I had such a charming correspondent to write to, I'm giving in to my inclination. It is just a little after 12:00 midnight, or just barely the date I've written above. I'm on duty, and having tucked my unlovely charges into their stinking bunks, I turned out the lights and came to the Officer's Lounge, which isn't much better.

Green jade characterized the waters of Malacca Strait and assorted islands stand as milestones as one nears Singapore. Lowering clouds and rain greeted us as we first sighted the magnificent harbor. Occasional masts stick above the water and buoys marked "WRECK" are testimony to what war has done. Though just a degree above the equator, the weather has been cool—comparatively speaking.

We tied up at the refueling dock about 3:00 p.m., the 31st. Just a moment ago I noticed the fresh water boat pull away, and we presume that the engineers are hard at work on the "hot" bearing which has cut our speed in half and threatens to make our Pacific voyage a long one. It is thought that we leave tomorrow night. We hope these letters go to the States by airmail from here, but can't be sure.

Everyone is as contented as can be expected under the circumstances—for every minute this scow dawdles on the road home is one that I am not with you. Every conscious moment is lived in expectation of being with my sweetheart again. What a brave darling you have been, Ritter mine! I love you; I love you; I love you.

We had roast turkey again today (Sunday) noon. Our meals are superb and served to us under good circumstances. My bunkmates are all good fellows, though they don't play poker. I'm sharpening up on cribbage, having played six games tonight, but unfortunately lost one—bad cards!

Despite my impatience, my love, I cannot find it in my heart to do anything but sing for joy that I am finally on my way to your arms—Goodnight, precious, and move over, make room for me, will you?

Devotedly, my one and only,
Dick

En route to ZI
South China Sea
April 1, 1946

Dearest Ritter:

This day started early for me, since I had the midnight shift. We were tied up in Singapore, and I had hoped to locate the Southern Cross, which is visible from there, but it began raining about 12:30 and had been cloudy before that. I spent most of my time in the Officers Lounge, just occasionally checking in the compartment to make sure all was in order. I began an invasion, or permitted its beginning, when I told a couple of enlisted men that they could lie on the floor of the lounge, though actually the coolest weather of the trip has been enjoyed in Singapore. At any rate, by 2:00 a.m. the whole floor was covered with about 50 of them. I think they would be better off if they just got used to sleeping in the hold, but they cannot be convinced.

I wrote an earlier letter, while on duty, the second one which I hope will be mailed from Singapore and which I also hope will reach you by airmail.

Of course I spent the morning in bed, but was up when we set sail shortly after lunch.

Soon the old tub was shooting through the water in ways that amazed us, used to its fumbling progress of the last week. Our last look at Singapore harbor was a thorough one, which permitted us to see the waterfront of the city, against its background of hills and jungle. Colonel Stewart, theater officer and newspaper or sports writer from Memphis (I think), explained the present situation of Singapore to several of us.

Colonel Stewart had an article in one of the last *Roundups*[6] that I sent. Incidentally, the Colonel is a cadaverous looking death's head, in my estimation, who seems intent on going home looking healthy if it kills him. He sunbathes until the perspiration runs in rivulets from his baked body, and his light-complexioned face must be heavily creamed to keep it from peeling all the way.

While on duty, a mouse-like boy named Rous wandered in the club to get out of the rain, timidly insisted that he be permitted to teach me gin rummy. This he did so well that I eked out a win on the first game, but the second reverted to my usual rummy luck, which is rum. He scalded me.

I read in bed for awhile, then spent an hour trying to get to sleep. It was announced that for the second time in five days we would set our watches up a half hour at 4:00 a.m. the 2nd. About 10:30, I got up, went to the Officers Lounge, where I viewed my colleagues with a jaundiced eye. It seemed to me that they proved the genius of the American people for making something out of nothing. How else could such material have been transformed into officers of the United States Army? One specimen, a spidery-legged 1st who goes around in shorts and a flapping, unbuttoned shirt, was playing gin rummy with a bespectacled nurse whose tight slacks revealed a typically feminine series of bulges in more or less appropriate places.

I fell into conversation with a lanky, ineffective 1st (everybody is a first) from Charleston, West Virginia, who said he had written a book while overseas, but hadn't been interested enough in Indian life to take a railroad trip, concluding that he saw enough in Calcutta and Karachi. Maybe. By 1:30, I was ready to go to bed. Goodnight, darling,

Dick

En route to ZI
Pacific Ocean
Off Philippines
April 5, 1946

Dearest Ritter:

We got through the Philippines Islands by noon today
and sailed off into the blue Pacific. Ah Hem. We entered
late last evening, and occasionally could see lights, once a
whole city, through the darkness. This morning I awakened late, having missed breakfast, and heard that Luzon
was just off port. I hurried upstairs, tsk, I mean topside,
and remained for two hours and 15 minutes while we were
circling the south end of Luzon.

During that time the two mountains on the southeast
corner could be seen, but their tops were obscured by
clouds. We never saw the top of the taller, but did see the
volcanic nature of the second, a peculiar funnel, broken at
one end, and spreading in a five-mile slope to the sea . . .
very interesting, so much so that one would almost see the
lava flowing. Of course, it is old now, and green, and covered with what must be pine, though from several miles
out it was hard to tell.

Perhaps we saw signs of fighting. We know there were
battles in the San Bernardino Strait which we took. At one
point, one of the islands to the south was definitely pock-
marked with fire, and often remnants of barbed wire forti-
fications down on the beaches could be seen. The utter-
most southern tip of Luzon was pitted with caves,
evidently worn by the sea.

Last night I went on duty at midnight. I hadn't gotten
much sleep before, having been reading an Erskine
Caldwell story, "Tragic Ground." It seems that one must
send his mind to the laundry each time he picks up
Caldwell. I also read a psychological mystery story, which
made two books in one night, which is probably too many.
What with the two hours of strong sunlight and the nine

games of cribbage that I played this afternoon with Jack (winning five after a terrific struggle with the kid), and after missing breakfast, and having a no good fish lunch and little sleep, it is no wonder that my head began splitting late in the afternoon.

To make matters worse, the wind came in from the south for the first time, leaving our cabin drenched in humid heat. I stayed away from the movie, took a couple of aspirin, and slept for two hours. During that time I dreamed that you and I were celebrating a wedding, and I couldn't get my clothes together properly or get to the right hotel room. Silly, huh?

I love you, honey girl,
Dick

En route to ZI
Pacific Ocean
Above Guam
Monday, April 8, 1946

Dearest Ritter:

It has definitely turned cooler as we move into the higher latitudes. I find from "White Caps" (that paper is well received by everyone) that we were only 5,500 miles from Frisco last Saturday, and since we traveled 813 miles Saturday and Sunday, we now are 4,687 miles from the goal. You cannot be sure of just how the shortest distance can be arrived at from a flat map. On the map it is apparent that we should go to Guam, then the Marianas, Wake, Midway, etc., but if nothing happens to our engines, we will go way above all those groups.

Today has been a rough one with me. It is either the griddle cakes soaked in molasses which I eat almost every morning, the occasional piece of candy I taste, or the tobacco that has been cramping me for the last week. Today was the worst, and I have almost concluded that I had better give up smoking for the trip, though that seems silly on the face of it, and I doubt if that would upset my stomach, though it is true that the dopes have nothing in stock except Velvet and Model tobacco. How wonderful to be able to buy decent brands and not trust the army with anything.

My feeling toward the army is symbolized in an incredible dream which I entertained this afternoon. I dreamed that apparently the military personnel on this ship, were instead of being in a ship, in a very high building. The army decided to move the building out of town, with us in it. We weren't told, so that some of us were in the top at the time. Apparently it was placed on a truck and we started down the street. The rolling ship must have given emphasis to the character of the dream, for it was very real to me, and I expected it to topple over any moment. In some fashion, I got down beside the driver and we continued to swing around corners and flash over bridges. We came to a railroad culvert, and I shouted, "You can't go under that"; the driver grinned and drove right up the curbing and over the tracks. Finally we came to one where that wasn't possible, and the driver tried to get under an 18-foot clearance with a sky-scraper. I awakened while he was sweating . . . and so was I. I don't think I trust the army or its personnel. But I love you,

> Dick

P.S. There is a phenomenon that I think I have forgotten to mention that often is evident at night in the warm waters. That is the phosphorescent globules that slide past the bow. I understand the globes of firefly light are caused by creatures in the water exuding a phosphorous glow. The balls differ in size, though most range at least a foot through. Rather eerie looking, and around the Philippines, quite common.

En route to ZI
Pacific Ocean
Above Wake Island
April 12, 1946

Dearest Ritter:

Excitement! Excitement! Whales and ships.

Early this morning, I must have been awakened by a flashing that came in through the porthole, for I got up to see lights answering—the flashes upon the water apparently the reflection from our own signaling lights. Ships that pass in the night. This morning we encountered another . . . an interesting sight out here, for the ocean is so vast that one rarely ever sees anything except this big spot of mouthwash . . . saline solution. This morning's ship was an American freighter.

But the most interesting sight was our encounter with literally dozens of whales. We first noticed the mammals just after breakfast, when we saw a series of spouts off the port. Occasionally the back of one of the whales could be seen, as they sported with one another. But the real revelation came when the whales came closer to our starboard side . . . no more than 100 feet away.

I saw as much as 15 feet of the backs of the huge animals myself. They do not swim very high in the water, but undulate like the porpoises. We passed the school about 0930. In the afternoon, while I was sleeping, we came into another school of them, striking one big fellow—according to several unreliable witnesses.

Floyd McDonald and I played a number of games of gin rummy, this time correctly, for that Rous kid didn't know what he was talking about—with me edging over him just a trifle. I like that game, by the way.

We saw a movie in what is turning out to be rather cool weather for those of us with the watery blood of India in our veins. The movie was "Uncle Harry." Geraldine

Fitzgerald has several remarkable scenes, and shame on Ellen Raines for walking (slinking) into a room that way!

We have been kidding quite a bit about our second Saturday this week, and tomorrow is the day after, you know, and that sort of thing. Incidentally, no one seems sure as to whether those are gulls, terns, or albatross following the boat. I did a little checking on our situation, and we are quite a way to the east and north of Wake.

Love,
Dick

En route to ZI
Pacific Ocean
April 13, 1946
Saturday . . . again?

Dearest Ritter:

This will be a very short note, for I wish this day done with and forgotten. I managed to do my eight to 12 shift without much trouble, and even to eat my meals, but my cold was running terrifically, and when I tried to vary the monotony of lying in bed by reading, my rummy eyes began to ache.

Came night, and the evening brought cold with it. Although we closed the porthole, which helped, any attempt to go on deck cut through us, our Indian-ink, though red, still not good American blood. The ship rolled so badly that the boys made an improvised inclinator of a string and coke bottle to try to figure out the degree of our roll. No one got anything decided but they had a fine argument trying it. Benton spun us some yarns of his years in Arabia, Saud's cruel justice (hands cut off, men strung up like vines to die in the sun), and of his torpedoed ship in 1942.

My nose was still running, and my head was on fire. Just as I would get into a comfortable position, the ship would purposely roll or pitch; this made me sweat, and my

301

eyes were standing out like sore thumbs. Oh, I was miserable. I damned the army for not having a drug store so that
I could buy aspirins . . . and at two, I gave up the fight,
crawled lamb-like to the dispensary and got two
aspirins and a knockout drop, which laid me to rest until
7:00 a.m.

Needless to say, I did not go to the ship's movie, which
might be where I got my cold, by the way.

I need your arms around me, then let my head ache.
Dick

S. S. Marine *Cardinal*
Pacific Ocean
April 16, 1946

Dearest Ritter:

We are nearing San Francisco. At noon today we were
a thousand miles out, tossed about like a chip in a flood;
now to port; now to starboard, shuddering recovery, terrific vibration, as though the ghost of Henry Kaiser was
somewhere about, hammering his handiwork apart at its
welded seams.

So—my darling girl, it shouldn't be too long until I'll
be seeing you. We don't know what is happening when we
reach Frisco, though we do know that we are going to
Stoneman Field from the ship, which is about 40 miles
out, the Field, I mean. If we don't entrain at once, the officers will have an opportunity to go into Frisco, where I
expect to phone you. If we stay at the Field, or leave at
once, I understand that telephoning isn't permitted. I
know you will be disappointed if I don't get through to
you, so, I will do the best I can. As for information on the
trip, I've posted two airmail letters from Singapore, a radio
gram on April 3 from near the Philippines, and another radio gram on April 14, giving the 19th as one docking day.
There will be a routine telegram going out the 19th telling
of our safe arrival, I hope. If I get to telephone, I'll speak

with you before this reaches you, otherwise this will explain why I haven't phoned.

The trip has been routine, with the ship making over 400 miles daily since the bearing was repaired at Singapore. (The listing is terrific and my back muscles are sore from trying to maintain a balance.) I work four hours out of 32, which isn't any strain. We eat well, for the officers are nicely taken care of. My cabin is a little crowded, but my bed is broad and generous, and comfortable. The ship is a poor one, however, flipping about with every little shift of current.

So, I'll close this with the expectancy that I'll be able to hear your wonderful voice again soon. Our reunion means so much to me that words fail me, and I have recourse to the simple statement, I love you, wife of mine,

Dick

En route to ZI
Pacific Ocean
Tuesday, April 16, 1946

Dearest Ritter:

My duties began at midnight, and for awhile I had a good notion to ignore them and just sleep, but I didn't. The death's head Colonel, Stewart, was around, and some belated bridge players were still at it, and two or three officers on night duty kept lonely vigil with me in the lounge. About 12:30, Frances and an amber hued Captain flew in through the door and down the stairs. My cynical mind sought explanation, and found it in her desire to hurry to prevent impregnation, his to take a pro [prophylactic]. On the other hand, they may have been honestly cold, for it was a bleak night topside.

I slept most of the morning, talked most of the afternoon and evening. Our group—Zimmerman, McDonald, Benton, and myself spend most of our time in the cabin talking and reading, and kidding.

303

We had a boat drill today, about the fifth that we have had on the trip thus far. It has been a lowering, dull, gray, cloudy overcast day, with rain often lashing the turbulent waves. The ship has been pushed by a rear wind, and as proof made 432 miles yesterday, but we pay for it in the increased pitching and tossing which we are undergoing. The tablecloths are wet down, so that the utensils and plates won't slide, but catsup bottles rolled over merrily this evening during the meal.

However, it should soon be over, and we have had several meetings already on disembarking . . . sweet word. Holy Joe is having a field day in the officer's lounge with his female and male Hallelujah chorus, his Bible study, his evening vespers, for it is too cold to meet outside.

I believe that I had better bring this to a close, as my typewriter almost slid off the box when the ship canted twenty degrees to starboard. (We have a proper inclinator set up now.)

At the USA Camp Stoneman
Pittsburg, California
April 19, 1946

Dearest Ritter:

Darling wife, this is the letter that I have been waiting a year to write. Last year in April—and even before—I had fond hopes that my commission would see me returned to the US for rehabilitation work. It was quite a blow when I found myself assigned to the 142nd General Hospital, and after V-J [Victory over Japan] day, the realization that we would be separated indefinitely made me so unhappy that I took no comfort in the increased opulence of my own conditions, working and social. But finally, after so many endearing letters and such poignant dreams, I am again on American soil, and this reentry presages my reunion with you. It would be difficult to explain exactly how intense I am about you, Reva, but it is as though nothing would have any significance upon my return to "life" if you were not here to revitalize it.

Last night was a difficult one to get to sleep, even though we knew that we would have to arise early. I shaved, and then carefully bathed, for we didn't know how soon we would have another opportunity. After that I tried to sleep, but though our speed was reduced, the boat still rocked violently (a trick that it continued right up until they tied it to the dock) and my mind rocked along with it; largely of scenes which were to come of home and its meaning.

But I did sleep a little, being often awakened. By four o'clock, it was evident that sleep was gone, and by five I got up to stroll on deck. But this time, the deck wasn't deserted, for many of the boys had been up for hours. The officers were supposed to eat at 6:00, but it turned out to be a false alarm, or the merchant marine wouldn't cooperate, probably. When we did eat at the usual time, most of us left a tip, in my case two dollars, for the crusty little old man who waited on our table during the trip. He had been testy, inclined to scorn, ignored our requests, but he did have character; when I bid him good-by, he seemed touched by the sentiment, wished me luck.

At daybreak, some rugged, rocky islands had shown to port, and by daylight could be plainly seen. I had expected to have peculiar emotions upon first sight of the American mainland, but as on leaving the States, could find no particular reaction at all. I spent the hours from eight to ten on deck, watching the lovely California landscape unroll. Eventually we reached the encircling arms of land that have been called—appropriately for us—the Golden Gate.

They have flung a magnificent bridge across it, and we held our breath as the ship scraped under it with more clearance than we thought. The morning was clear, springlike, and the green hills particularly delightful to our jaundiced eyes. An army boat, with a WAC MC and a WAC band came tooting up, following us with a serenade. Ships blew hoarse salute, and from suburban and metropolitan San Francisco, innumerable signs announced that we were welcome, had done a fine job.

Alcatraz was a surprise, for it seemed minute, harmless, in the morning sun.

Nonetheless, it was evident that there were many buildings on the little rock, which wasn't the least forbidding. Tugs umphed us to Pier 13, and cheers broke out repeatedly as the boys saw American women (with shoes) who were waiting at the gate. The WAC musicians gathered on the pier to play, and the long waiting period set in, until our turn, at 12 noon, saw us treading the longest possible way through the ship to get off. This wouldn't have meant much, if it hadn't been for the huge bag that was burdening me. I had no more made the dock when, my fingers absolutely nerveless and my strength gone, I dropped the damned thing. The big shed looked endless, but I gritted my teeth, grabbed one end of the unwieldy object, and began dragging it across the cement. Some kind dock worker took pity on me, gave me a lift. USO women came to our relief, gave us coffee and doughnuts while we waited to board the ferry.

I made it to the ferry (under the watchful of an S/S WAC—there were a great many WACs on the job), and collapsed on the first floor of the ferry, thankful for the three hour respite that trip provided. As the ferry swung rapidly out and swung across the bay for Stoneman, we had an excellent view of the clean, landlocked city of San Francisco and the landlocked harbor.

We were almost under the Oakland Bay Bridge, which I think has the longest single span in the world. On the way we passed the graveyard of dead vessels which exhibited life not long ago. We also saw the aircraft carrier the Saratoga, which is to take part in the atomic bomb experiment. We used two ferries, the Ernie Pyle and the Maynard, to transport our 3,400 some personnel. We were fed a basket lunch en route. The California scenery continued to be impressive, and I believe you would enjoy a Western trip very much.

Another struggle with that damned bag when we disembarked, but an effeminate character named Gaines (Lt.) helped me, to my shame for not liking him, and I made it to the waiting truck. The bag and Beard have become quite a joke, and all the fellows offer free advice about what I can do with it. They hazard that I must have a "beebie" [girl] therein. McDonald helped me get the thing into the BOQ at Stoneman after our arrival there. Mac and I are rooming together and seem to hit it off well.

After brief orientation, we went for the vaunted steak dinner, but my steak was so tough, I divided it with Mac. The mess, to which enlisted men also go, is run by German PWs. As soon as we had eaten, Mac and I hurried to the telephones, were among the first to get there, and you know that I got my call in shortly after 6:00 p.m. Pacific time. Your voice was exactly what I thought it would be . . . low, pulsing, meaningful, lovely beyond description, the voice of Reva, my wife.

We visited the PX, many of the boys went to the club, but I decided to stay in. I should mention that we drank a lot of milk, the first for me in two years, at the evening meal. I was so beat up that I could hardly toddle. I crawled into bed, read for awhile, then Mac and Benton returned from the club with tales of milkshakes and hamburgers. Later Jack Hazen came in, talked until 10:30, then I was too sleepy to be denied . . . drifted off.

So closes the story of my first partial day on American soil . . . made memorable really only by the sound of your voice and the pleasant surprise of also hearing Ruth's voice, so very natural, once again. I believe I won't have any difficulty returning to my old way of life.

Just a few more days, precious—

I love you,

Dick

P.S. April 20: we expect to assemble at 2:30 this afternoon, probably leave within two hours on the train for the east.

Postwar reunion. Finally together again in spring 1946, Richard and Reva took an apartment in Findlay, Ohio. Shortly afterwards, Richard landed an assistant professorship in guidance and counseling at Iowa Teachers College in Cedar Falls, Iowa.

Epilogue

By now, gentle reader, you are acquainted with Richard and Reva Beard through the letters they wrote—from Calcutta, India, and Findlay, Ohio—during the last part of World War II. "But what," you may ask, "was the rest of the story? What happened to this couple after WWII ended and Richard sailed across the Pacific Ocean into San Francisco Bay?"

As he wrote to Reva in his letter of April 19,1946, Richard listened to exuberant WAC bands, drank milk for the first time in two years, and, along with the other returning GIs, was treated to a steak dinner. Although Reva was not waiting at the dock, she was certainly there in spirit. At her parents' home in Findlay, Ohio, she was thrilled to hear her husband's voice over the telephone. Even though Richard was still a country away, it seemed indeed that he was home.

Once again, my father traveled across a country by train. The ride from San Francisco to Fort Benjamin Harris, near Indianapolis, Indiana, went as smoothly as the ride across India had not. Along with the other soldiers, he waited in a debriefing building, emerging just in time to see Reva drive up in their ancient Plymouth coupe.

Findlay, Ohio, was just a few hours away, but a reunion with the families would have to wait a day. Every hotel was packed. "We drove and drove," my mother recalls, "before we found a vacancy." Just as they were about to give up, they finally got the last room in an old, decrepit hotel that offered a rope in lieu of a fire escape. It didn't matter. After the long wartime separation, the hundreds of letters, the yearning and homesickness, anywhere would have seemed like heaven.

In Findlay, Ohio, they rented an apartment for several months while Richard searched for a teaching position. Because of returning so late from the war, the job hunt was difficult. "Many positions had already been filled," Reva remembers. "Just as Dick was about to accept a government job in Wisconsin, he heard—through a friend at Ohio State, his alma mater—about a job at Iowa Teachers College (now the University of Northern Iowa)."

The young couple moved to Cedar Falls, Iowa, for that job. Richard advanced to the position of associate professor of guidance and counseling, the field that would be his life's work. The existence that Richard and Reva had written about and dreamed of during their eighteen-month correspondence was coming to pass: "home, wife, and love," as Richard put it; and of course, a teaching career. The only missing component was a family.

During WWII, all of Reva's querying at various Ohio adoption agencies had come to naught. Amazingly, the children they longed for came through a student at Iowa Teachers College.

I was five years old and my brother Johnny was seventeen months. Products of a short-lived wartime wedding, we lived in a series of foster homes. Our biological father had disappeared, and his wife—I'll call her Mae—was hard pressed to provide us with food and shelter. Seeking a teaching degree, Mae became a student at Iowa Teachers College about the same time Richard began his associate professorial position there. Mae heard a campus rumor that Professor Beard, the college counselor, and his wife were planning to adopt a baby. Acting, no doubt, on desperation, Mae asked the professor if he would accompany her to the foster home to meet my brother and me. This happened in 1947.

Fifty years later, I would have a conversation with my Dad that I will never forget. It took place in the Virginia apartment that he and Reva had moved to in order simplify life. Richard's health and mental outlook were failing badly. He was depressed. In fact, it was not long after our talk that my father lost his ability to speak or think clearly. At this point, however, he was lucid. He was trying to connect the five-year-old girl in braids with me, the middle-aged woman who'd come to call at the apartment. "I remember the first time I saw you." He smiled, his warm brown eyes crinkling. For a moment he looked like the father I had always known. "You were in pigtails," he mused. "You were running back and forth, swinging in a swing. You were a lively one."

In the spring of 1948, Richard and Reva became the legal parents of my brother and me. The four of us took a trip to Ohio to meet the grandparents, aunts, uncles, and cousins. We would not go back to Iowa except to pack up and move.

After two years of fierce Iowa winters, Richard and Reva craved a milder climate. Richard landed a summer school

The new family, circa 1950. (From left to right: Johnny, Dick, Reva, and Elaine).

Elaine, age four. Like many children born during World War II, she lived with just her mother and extended family during her earliest years.

teaching assignment at Marshall College in Huntington, West Virginia. So impressed was the college with him, he was soon hired as an associate professor. We spent four years in West Virginia, from 1949 to 1952.

In 1952, a move to Chapel Hill, North Carolina, and the University of North Carolina brought my father a full professorship. I remember our five years of living in Chapel Hill as the halcyon time of my childhood: far enough away from the loneliness and pain of my first five years, before the emotional storms of adolescence.

Children of a college professor and his kind, beautiful wife, my brother and I felt very special. We took family vacations to the beach or to visit the Ohio relatives. We had bikes, a dog, a turtle, and one of the first television sets in the neighborhood. Our lives abounded in love and cultural enrichment. Books and reading were central in the Beard household. When I was five years old, I recall my father reading to me every night. There must have been other bedtime stories, but my most vivid memory is of Lewis Carroll's *Alice in Wonderland* and *Through the Looking Glass.* No one had ever read me a story. I had never owned a book. I now fell asleep to my father's deep, rich baritone, imagining The White Rabbit, the Queen of Hearts, Tweedledum and Tweedledee, the Cheshire Cat, the Mad Hatter, and the Walrus and the Carpenter.

Richard was both a writer and a reader. All his life, my father read eclectically, enormously, exuberantly. He consumed mysteries, history, poetry, biography, science fiction, the classics of English and American literature, best sellers, humor, and cartoon collections. Although we didn't have a lot of money, I recall an abundance of books in our home.

When I was ten, my parents gave me a five-year diary, in which I dutifully chronicled the events of my life. This exercise inspired me to branch out into other writing, a venture in which I was greatly encouraged. Richard read my early plays, short stories, and poetry, and he urged me to continue.

We were a family who loved to converse. I recall discussing not only books with my Dad, but also current events, religion, philosophy, and, when I came home late from dates, the eccentricities of Reva and John. I recall that talking with Richard was often far more interesting than talking with most of the boys I dated.

Richard was both my role model and my best friend. I believe he would have approved of his letters being published for the world to read. Within his wartime letters, he mentioned folks telling him he should write a book on his experiences in India. In the classroom and everywhere else, Professor Beard loved having an audience.

During the mid 1950s, my Dad established an educational television program through the University of North Carolina. Neither Reva nor I can recall the exact name, but it must have been something like "Book Talk." Dad was the host and my friend Gloria and I were frequent guests. In the meantime, Dad's book collection continued to grow. In thirty years, it would top five thousand volumes.

Our Chapel Hill, North Carolina, home was nestled halfway up a spacious hillside on Roosevelt Avenue. One summer, my Dad and brother transformed a heap of stones into a stone wall bordering the back yard. More often than not, whenever they picked up a stone, a shiny black widow spider lurked underneath. As this preceded the age of "kindness to all living things," the spiders universally met the same fate: being smashed by the very rocks under which they were hiding. Looking back, I think the stone wall was perhaps a metaphor for the comfort and security of my life then, and maybe for all four of us. Reva was teaching kindergarten, a vocation she relished. When I think of North Carolina summers, I remember endless summer days of bicycling around Chapel Hill, babysitting jobs, and teaching swimming to tots at the Olympic-size swimming pool at the university. My parents, "Dick and Reva" to their peers, threw many parties and social events for students and friends. It was fun being in attendance, especially when Dad invited his Indian students, the women radiant in their elegant silk saris.

By the end of five years at the University of North Carolina, Richard was a full professor, achieving much recognition in his field of counseling. He was director of associations, guest speaker, consultant, expert. Nonetheless, the academic ladder was still to be climbed.

We moved to Charlottesville, Virginia, in 1957, where Richard would become head of Counselor Education. At a time when women students were not generally accepted, as a professor's daughter, I was admitted to the University of Virginia. I earned my undergraduate degree and teaching certification in secondary school education and a master's degree in English and American literature.

Richard taught at the University of Virginia at the Curry Memorial School of Education from 1957 until 1980. Reva taught kindergarten for twenty years. My brother became a craftsman, woodcarver, and antiquarian. In 1967, I moved to Santa Fe, New Mexico. For several decades, my Dad and I kept in touch with weekly letters. I still have every one.

After having perused the nine thousand pages of wartime correspondence between my parents, I thought I had finished. And yet, there was another body of correspondence I would need to review in order to conclude this celebration of a life. Bound in black leather and gold, engraved *Richard Leonard Beard,* was a volume I had yet to open. Presented to my Dad in 1980 upon his retirement from the University of Virginia, it comprised several hundred letters from students through the years—at Marshall College, the University of North Carolina, and the University of Virginia. The book had been presented to Richard during a night of tribute and his retirement banquet.

From the students' letters emerged recurring themes. My father, it seemed, had given his classes far more than the principles of guidance and counseling. The letters of these former pupils expressed gratitude for having obtained their doctorates, but also for their favorite professor's lessons about life. An Air Force colonel who had gone on to become a professor of air science was just one of many who named "Dr. B" as his most memorable professor, a real friend, a mentor and an inspiration. Others praised him for a warm, rich sense of humor, compassion, patience, keen perception, openness and honesty, enthusiasm, knowledge, courage and devotion. A career center director in Charleston, West Virginia, wrote, "Your kind words of support and enthusiasm often calmed my fears and buoyed my faltering spirit. You were an island of serenity in the midst of many storms."

A professor in Charlotte, North Carolina wrote,

> You have helped so many students in your tenure as an educator . . . that much of your enthusiasm, knowledge, courage and devotion will be perpetuated forever. There will be a time when you are no longer here, but you will never die, for each of us will transmit some part of you to the next generation, and they to the next. You listened to hundreds of students over the years.

"You shall always be our mentor and confidante," wrote another former protégé. And another: "As long as there are people, I'm sure that you will be engaged in lending a helping hand or assisting them as they engage a personal problem." And another: "I do not believe that all good things come to an end; I do believe that life will go on being good wherever Dick Beard is. And it will mean good fortune for those who are close to him."

As I read these glowing accolades, I realized how much Richard had taught me by his example. I especially related to the comment, made by a student who'd gone on to become a university director of counseling, "You always looked at what was possible, what could aid this person in distress." Voicing the same observation, another student wrote of the way my father faced life's day-to-day situations: "I learned from you an attitude of 'And this too shall pass' with regard to the unpleasant."

Others wrote of "Dr. B's" humanitarianism and respect for every person, no matter how high or low in status. An East Indian student related that she came to the United States in 1961 determined not to leave the portals of the University of Virginia without an Ed.D. (Doctorate in Education) in counseling. She referred to Richard as her friend, philosopher, and guide, responsible for all her accomplishments since 1961. "Your wisdom and foresight are a rich mine," she continued, "to guide me in my work in India as a teacher-counselor at Nagpur and Bombay Universities and student counselor with the US Education Foundation in India."

Although my father died in 1997, I keep coming across reminders of him. As I healed from the loss of such a wonderful parent, a memorable chapter was the arrival from Virginia of the last of his cardboard boxes. Inside crumpled pages of the Charlottesville, Virginia *Daily Progress* were leather-bound copies of *The Pickwick Papers, The Brothers Karamazov,* Maupassant's short stories, the works of Mark Twain, *A Tale of Two Cities, The Trial,* and the works of Poe.

Mark Twain was Richard's favorite author, and when I was earning my master's degree in American literature, I chose to do my thesis on Twain. Looking through the Twain volume, I saw on the inside cover his handwritten "7/28/32," the date he had acquired the book. There was also a listing of the pages in which he had underscored sections, a kind of index to his annotations. Turning to the first underscored section, located in *Tom Sawyer Abroad,* I read the following quote by Tom:

As near as I can make out, geniuses think they
know it all, and so they won't take people's advice,

but always go their own way, which makes everybody forsake them and despise them, and that is
perfectly natural. If they was humbler, and listened
and tried to learn, it would be better for them.

It was no accident that I'd opened *Tom Sawyer Abroad* at that
page. Tom's words perfectly reflected Richard's homespun,
down-to-earth attitude toward life. It was then I decided
that the World War II letters would be Richard's book, the
volume he ran out of time to write. At last he would have a
chance to speak for the little guy.

Elaine and Richard at the Beards' apartment in Charlottesville, Virginia. Although Elaine moved to Santa Fe, New Mexico in 1967, she
kept in touch with her parents through weekly letters. Richard wrote to
his daughter every Sunday until his death in 1997.

Appendix

Richard's Letter to Reva's 4th grade class

A letter sent by Richard to Reva for the benefit of her fourth grade students:

April 4, 1945
INDIA

Dear Boys and Girls:

It has been my pleasure to hear some fine things about the boys and girls of Mrs. Beard's fourth grade class. As she may have told you, I once lived near Mt. Blanchard, attended the M.P. Church, and often walked along the village streets. She has probably said that I am a teacher, also, and that I like to work with boys and girls, who usually teach me something new every day.

But how would you like to live in a land where most of the children do not have to go to school at all? On our way to headquarters in the morning, this is what we see: boys and girls and men of all ages down at the edges of the numerous rice paddy ponds that dot the landscape, washing their hands, faces and feet in the muddy water. They brush their teeth and gums by rubbing them vigorously with fingers soaked in the water. The men keep their breech clothes around them, but take off their shirts, which look just like the kitchen table cloth back home. The little kids are often completely naked, with only a charm suspended from a string that is tied around their tiny waists. They are quite black, with well formed bodies and attractive faces. Most of the people in this community are Mohammedans, though there are a few Hindus.

The ponds, which are about the size of a small quarry, are used for drinking water, for bathing, for cooking water and for laundry. If you wander through the countryside, you can see housewives (you must be very careful not to go too near, or they run and hide) busy washing clothes. They accomplish this by wading into the water, hitching up their skirts, dumping the clothes in the water, and then beating the life out of them against a log. The clothes are spread on the ground to dry, but tattle-tale gray whispers to all the world that dirty water and no soap won't clean.

The natives live in small clusters of bamboo huts, called bashas, built around a pond. There are various kinds of palms, banana trees, and shrubs for shade. Only the men work in the rice paddies and the women must stay at home. The kiddies dig grass for the undersized cows, whose ribs are always showing. Other children fish for minnows, stirring up the water until they come to the top. These little fish are dried and made into a kind of break-fast food. Everyone is barefooted and they usually walk to market, though occasionally they ride in diminutive ox carts which creak loudly.

More will have to wait until next time. Please study hard for your own sakes, and give a big smile to my favor-ite teacher, Mrs. Beard.

> Have a nice vacation!
> Richard L. Beard
> Sgt., Air Corps

Notes

Introduction

1. Some historians have said that the Hump airlift was a failure. Supplying the Chinese by air cost over six hundred aircraft and one thousand crew members. However, in addition to keeping China in the war, the army learned new methods of warfare. The United States learned to move troops and supplies quickly by air; the Berlin airlift was possible because of the Hump experience, and helicopters were first used in the CBI to evacuate the wounded from behind enemy lines.

The China-Burma India Theater and My Father Richard

1. Merrill's Marauders were infantry battalions formed for special duty in the China-Burma-India theater. Under the command of Brigadier General Frank D. Merrill, they fought to free northern Burma of Japanese so that the engineer battalions could build the Ledo Road. The engineers followed right behind the Marauders, often hearing the firing.

2. The Ledo Road was renamed the Stilwell Road by Chiang Kai-shek in February 1945, after he had fired Stilwell on October 18, 1944. The Ledo Road was also called Pick's Pike, after Brigadier General Lewis A. Pick, who engineered the road. One important reason for opening the Burma-Ledo Roads was to allow combat vehicles too large to be

flown over to be driven over and to allow some commercial traffic into China. The original Burma Road was from Rangoon to Lashio and over the mountains and deep gorges to China. When the Japanese captured all of Burma in the 1930s, the road could not be used until the Ledo Road (which had been called "impossible to build") was built to connect with the upper portion of the Burma Road. The new road—Ledo Road plus the northern part of the old Burma Road (named "Stilwell Road")—was used to haul munitions and supplies, which for the most part arrived in Bombay and then were transported by rail and truck to Ledo in Assam Province. For much of the war, Japanese submarines kept Calcutta from being used as a port; therefore, either Bombay or Karachi served as port of entry for most of the supplies. The total supply line from the United States to Assam Province, for transport by plane or truck convoy, was twelve thousand miles long, by far the longest supply road in military history.

Part One—Leaving Home

1. The perception within the CBI that the theater had no priority was based on fact. Actually, it was a Washington command decision that the United States was not to go all out in the CBI until the war in Europe was won. After V-E Day, the CBI had a high priority. Several theaters have named themselves "The Forgotten Theater," including Italy, Australia, and the CBI.

2. *Stilwell's Mission to China,* p. 81.

3. During his service in India, Richard Beard mailed money to his sister Gay in Findlay, Ohio, to buy flowers. Bouquets of roses arrived at Reva's door for birthdays, anniversaries, and holidays. These surprises did much to lift her spirits during the long wait for her husband to return home.

4. The L&W, on Main Street in Findlay, Ohio, was Richard and Reva's favorite restaurant. Most patrons sat at the

counter to eat, Reva recalls. Richard usually ordered veal cutlet or chile. The L&W was popular late at night, staying open until midnight or 1:00 a.m.

5. Army Post Office, c/o postmaster, New York. Richard's location was indicated by "390," but as he was not yet an officer, he was not allowed to divulge his exact location in India.

6. V-mail—Victory Mail reduced and photocopied letters. Richard rarely used V-mail, preferring to send letters of many pages. He often wrote a letter to Reva in the morning and another in the evening.

7. Rs 14—14 rupees. In 1944, one rupee equalled approximately thirty cents.

Part Two—Serving in India

1. Time-Life Books, *China-Burma-India, World War II*.

2. Mepracine was mandated for use by soldiers against malaria. Rather than curing the disease, it merely suppressed the symptoms. Atabrine was also used for malaria symptoms.

3. Time-Life Books, *China-Burma-India, World War II*.

4. Dengue fever was a debilitating tropical disease that often proved fatal.

5. Annas are Indian coins. In 1944, one anna was worth 1/16th of a rupee, approximately two cents.

6. Military personnel positions were indicated by numbers. The editor was unable to find out what "275" stood for.

7. Warrant officer was the lowest-ranking officer, being below second lieutenant. They performed various tasks. The rank probably began long before WWII, when all officers came from the "gentleman" strata in American society (a holdover from English society). The warrant officer position provided a rank for those from the lower society of such merit that they had to be promoted to an intermediate rank between gentlemen officers and enlisted men.

8. R.A.—Regular Army. During WWII, the army distinguished between men who were "regular army" (and therefore career soldiers) and those millions who were draftees or volunteers for the "duration of the war." Citizen (temporary) soldiers were members of the "Army of the United States," in contrast to career types, who were members of "United States Army."

9. APC's—brand of headache powder

10. Gurkhas were fierce Nepalese citizens who served in the British and Indian armies. They fought to the last man and thus were much feared by the Japanese.

Part Three—Return to Home, Wife, and Love

1. USAFI—U. S. Army Field Instruction (correspondence courses).

2. INA—Indian National Army (pursuing India's independence from England and in some cases helping Japan to win).

3. A political movement for independent government in India was growing during the last months of the war and beyond. The unrest that Reva writes about was the insistence of Indians that India be freed from its status as part of the British Empire; in fact, some Indians hoped that Japan would win the war. Since the U.S. was allied with England, American troops were stoned and harassed as soon as the war was over. Some Americans en route to the Calcutta dock were seriously injured. Reva read newspaper accounts of the Calcutta riots with great concern. Though near danger, Richard managed to leave India unscathed. Mohandas ("Mahatma") Gandhi, leader of the Indian nationalist movement, mediated with the British in August 1947 for an autonomous Indian state.

4. Kawoodie was one of Richard's favorite brands of pipe. He enjoyed smoking a pipe both during the war and afterwards as a college professor.

5. VU2ZU—radio station

6. *Roundup*—Army newspaper

Glossary

AC—Air Corps

Adj.—Adjutant (officer who carries out orders of commanding officer)

AOD—Acting officer on duty

APO—Army Post Office (number after "APO" tells the location)

ATC—Army Transport Command (planes delivering supplies and troops)

AWOL—Absent Without Leave—missing

Bashas—huts of bamboo with thatched roofs (Assam and Burma)

Beebies—prostitutes or "loose women"

BOQ—Bachelor Officers Quarters

Brks—Barracks

CID—Central Investigation Division (investigated corruption and abuses)

CO—Commanding Officer

CQ—Change of Quarters

CQing—changing quarters

C-rations—canned field rations

EM—Enlisted men

ETO—European Theater of Operations

K.P.—Kitchen police. This assignment included mess duties such as peeling potatoes and mopping the mess hall floor.

K-ration—Emergency field ration (one meal per box)

lst—First Lieutenant

MOD—Medical officer on duty

MP—Military Police

N.E.A.—National Education Association

Non-coms—Non-commissioned officers (corporals, sergeants)

N-P—Neuropsychiatric

O.E.A.—Ohio Education Association

OCS—Officer Candidate School

OD—Officer of the Day

PFC—Private First Class

Position "502"—clerk/typist

PRO—Public Relations Officer

PX—Post Exchange (sold snacks, drinks, and sundries)

R.C.—Red Cross

RTO—Law enforcement officer for the British forces

S/Sgts., T/Sgts., F/Sgts., M/Sgts.—Staff Sergeants, Technical Sergeants, First Sergeants, Master Sergeants

SOD—Surgical officer on duty

Spc.—Special

Suntans—U.S. Army summer uniform

USO—United Service Organization, through which civilians such as Bob Hope put on shows for GIs

V-E—Victory in Europe (the day that Germany surrendered)

V-J—Victory over Japan (the day the Japanese surrendered)

WAC—Women's Army Corps

ZI—Zone of the Interior

For Further Reading

Anders, Leslie. *The Ledo Road.* Norman: University of Oklahoma Press, 1965.

Belden, Jack. *Retreat with Stilwell.* New York: Knopf, 1943.

Bradley, James, with Ron Powers. *Flags of Our Fathers.* New York: Bantam Books, 2000.

Brokaw, Tom. *The Greatest Generation.* New York: Random House, 1998.

———. *The Greatest Generation Speaks: Letters and Reflections.* New York: Random House, 1999.

Chennault, Claire Lee. *Way of a Fighter: The Memoirs of Claire Lee Chennault.* New York: Putnam, 1949.

Christian, John L. *Burma and the Japanese Invader.* Bombay: Thacker, 1945.

Coe, Douglas. *The Burma Road.* New York: Messner, 1946.

Collis, Maurice. *Last and First in Burma (1941–1948).* New York: Macmillan, 1956.

Craven, Wesley Frank, and James Lea Cate, eds. *Services Around the World,* Vol. 7. The Army Air Forces in World War II. Chicago: University of Chicago Press, 1958.

Dorn, Frank. *Walkout with Stilwell in Burma.* New York: Crowell, 1971.

Dunn, James W. "The Ledo Road." In *Builders and Fighters,* edited by Barry W. Fowle. Fort Belvoir: History Office, Virginia, 1992. 327–346.

Fairbank, John K. *The United States and China.* Cambridge: Harvard University Press, 1948.

Finney, Charles G. *The Old China Hands*. New York: Doubleday, 1961.

Fischer, Edward. *The Chancy War: Winning in China, Burma, and India in World War II*. New York: Orion Books, 1991.

Fisher, Frank. "Vinegar Joe's Problems." *Harper's* (December, 1944): 66.

U.S. Department of State. *Foreign Relations of the United States,* Vol. 1. The Far East. Washington, D.C.: Government Printing Office, 1956.

————. *Foreign Relations of the United States,* Vol. 6. China. Washington, D.C.: Government Printing Office, 1967.

Gabbett, Michael. *The Bastards of Burma: Merrill's Marauders and the MARS Task Force Revisited*. Albuquerque, NM: Desert Dreams, 1989.

Green, Anne Bosanko. *One Woman's War—Letters Home from the Women's Army Corps 1944–1946*. St. Paul: Minnesota Historical Society Press, 1989.

Isaacs, Harold R. *Scratches on our Minds: American Images of China and India*. New York: Capricorn Books, 1958.

James, Bill. *They Sent Me an Invitation, So I Went to World War II*. Houston: Emerald Ink Publishing, 1998.

Kirby, S. Woodburn. *The War against Japan: India's Most Dangerous Hour*. The Official History of the Second World War, vol. 2. London: Her Majesty's Stationery Office, 1961.

————. *The Decisive Battles*. The Official History of the Second World War, Vol. 3. London: Her Majesty's Stationery Office, 1961.

————. *The Reconquest of Burma*. The Official History of the Second World War, Vol. 4. London: Her Majesty's Stationery Office, 1965.

Miles, Milton E. *A Different Kind of War: The Little-Known Story of the Combined Guerrilla Forces Created in China by the U.S. Navy and the Chinese during World War II*. New York: Doubleday, 1967.

Millett, John D. *The Organization and Role of the Army Service Forces.* Washington D.C.: Office of Military History, Dept. of the Army, 1954.

Moorhouse, Geoffrey. *Calcutta.* New York: Harcourt Brace Jovanovich, 1971.

Moser, Don, and the Editors of Time-Life Books. *China-Burma-India.* Alexandria, VA: Time-Life Books, 1978.

Mullins, Colonel William S., ed. *Neuropsychiatry in World War II,* vol. 2, Overseas Theaters. Washington, D.C.: Office of the Surgeon General, Dept. of the Army, 1973.

Newell, Clayton R. *Burma, 1942.* Brochure, U.S. Army Center of Military History, 1994.

Norwalk, Rosemary. *Dearest Ones—A True World War II Love Story.* New York: John Wiley and Sons, 1999.

Ogburn, Charlton, Jr. *The Marauders.* New York: Harper, 1959.

Peers, William R., and Dean Brelis. *Behind the Burma Road: The Story of America's Most Successful Guerilla Force.* Boston: Little, Brown, 1963.

Ravdin, Isidor. *The Reminiscences of Isadore Ravden.* New York: Columbia University, East Asian Institute, Chinese Oral History Project.

Reagan, Nancy. *I Love You, Ronnie.* New York: Random House, 2000.

Robins, Fred. *Overseas Diary: India and Burma, World War II.* Gainsville, MO: Rumaro Press, 1990.

Romanus, Charles, and Riley Sunderland. *Stilwell's Mission to China.* Washington, D.C.: Office of the Chief of Military History, Dept. of the Army, 1953.

———. *Stilwell's Command Problems.* Washington, D.C.: Dept. of the Army, Historical Division, 1959.

———. *Time Runs Out in CBI.* Washington, D.C.: Dept. of the Army, Historical Division, 1959.

Scott, Robert Lee, Jr. *God Is My Co-Pilot.* New York: Scribners, 1943.

———. *Flying Tiger: Chennault of China.* New York: Doubleday, 1959.

Seagrave, Gordon. *Burma Surgeon.* New York: Norton, 1943.

———. *Burma Surgeon Returns.* New York: Norton, 1946.

Shalett, Sidney. "Burma Gains Spur Hope of Getting Aid to China." *The New York Times.* 21 May 1944, 6B.

Sinclair, William. *Confusion Beyond Imagination,* 10 volumes. Coeur d'Alene, ID: Whitley, 1986–1991.

Slim, Viscount William. *Defeat into Victory, Battling Japan in Burma and India 1942–1945.* (New introduction by David W. Hogan, Jr.) New York: Cooper Square Press, 2000.

Smith, Robert Moody. *With Chennault in China: A Flying Tiger's Diary.* Atglen, PA: Schiffer Military Aviation History, 1997.

Stilwell, Joseph. *The Stilwell Papers.* Edited by Theodore White. New York: William Sloane Associates, 1948.

Sugarman, Tracy. *My War.* New York: Random House, 2000.

Tuchman, Barbara W. *Stilwell and the American Experience in China, 1911–45.* New York: Macmillan, 1970.

U.S. War and Navy Departments. *A Pocket Guide to Burma,* Washington, DC: GPO, 1943.

Villard, Henry S., and James Nagel, eds. *Hemingway in Love and War: The Lost Diary of Agnes Von Kurowsky, Her Letters and Correspondence of Ernest Hemingway.* New York: Hyperion, 1989.

Wedemeyer, General Albert C. *Wedemeyer Reports.* New York: Holt, 1958.

Wells, Ann Harwell. *Always in My Heart.* Franklin, TN: Hillsboro Press, 2000.

White, Theodore H., and Annalee Jacoby. *Thunder Out of China.* 1946. Reprint, New York: William Sloane Associates, 1961.

Young, Peter, ed. *Atlas of the Second World War.* New York: Putnam's Sons, 1974.

Index

Page numbers in boldface type indicate illustrations.

A

Acting Officer on Duty (AOD)
  for Adjutant's office, 266
  and Anglo-Indian girl, 206
  duties of, 164
  making the rounds, 260
  man hanging in the latrine,
    126, 241-2
  rape of Indian girl by GIs,
    190-1
  schedule for, 213
  stabbing incident, 126, 240-1,
    242-3
actors/actresses
  Allen, Fred, 182
  Allyson, June, 158
  Ameche, Don, 183, 266
  Bacall, Lauren, 205
  Benny, Jack, 183
  Bergman, Ingrid, 277
  Bogart, Humphrey, 205
  Bowman, Lee, 273
  Canova, Judy, 133
  Colbert, Claudette, 266
  Durante, Jimmy, 158
  Durbin, Deanna, 189
  Falkenberg, Jinx, 270
  Fields, Benny, 100
  Fitzgerald, Geraldine, 301
  Flynn, Errol, 151
  George, Gladys, 100
  Herbert, Hugh, 158
  Horton, Edward Everett, 87
  Hunt, Marsha, 158

  Hussey, Ruth, 178
  Hutton, Betty, 220
  Hutton, Robert, 279
  Kay, Danny, 188
  Lamar, Hedy, 113
  Laughton, Charles, 229
  Laurel and Hardy, 175
  Leslie, Joan, 279
  MacMurray, Fred, 186, 199
  Moore, Victor, 183
  O'Brien, Margaret, 158
  Olivier, Laurence, 186
  Peck, Gregory, 277
  Raines, Ellen, 301
  Russell, Rosalind, 273
  Sanders, George, 87
  Sturbi, Jose, 158
  Tierney, Gene, 115
  Turner, Lana, 87
  Wilson, Marie, 158
adoption
  agencies overcrowded with
    children, 226
  applications
  Child and Family Agency (To-
    ledo), 50, 52
  Family and Children's Bureau
    (Columbus), 43, 44, 46
  Hancock County Children's
    Home (Findlay), 159-60,
    161
  and Crittendon home, 50
  of Elaine and Johnny, 3,
    310-1

physical longings, 220
reunion ahead, 178-9, 183, 200
strengthening spiritual unity, 55-6, 167-8
See also love
Long, Ralph, 138
love
beauty of Reva, 203, 226, 283
and feelings of closeness while writing to, 264
into eternity, 54
joy of holding your hand, 109
longing for fullfillment of, 104
longing for Reva, 161-2
and moment we met, 131, 229
pledges of love, 138-9, 229-30
purity of, 168
reassurances of, 148-9, 167-8
Richard and Reva in loving embrace, **251**
Richard's regard for Reva, 181, 203, 226
ring as symbol of, 224
thankfulness for, 277
See also loneliness and separation; spiritual unity
Lowell, Capt., 78
Luce, Henry, xviii
Lutz, Lt., 69, 70

M

McClure (from Alabama), 71
McConkie, Col., 216, 221, 224, 227, 267, 270
McCorkie, Col., 276, 280
McDonald, Floyd, 300, 303
McDowell, Mrs., 170

MacFarland, Rev., 220
McGraph ("Mac"), 140, 144, 154, 156
McKinley, 195
McShane, Col., 211, 232
mail delivery
Army Post Office addresses, 323
Christmas mail delivery, 74
importance to soldiers, viii, xii
and local post office, 139
and postage rates, 34, 90-1
slow and interrupted delivery, viii, 30-1, 43, 146, 255, 268-9, 272-3
sudden influx of, 279
V-mail, 323
while in transit, 67
See also censorship of letters
Malacca Strait, 293-4
Malaneux, Miss (nurse), 235
maps
Burma (Myanmar, 1942-5), **xxiv**
Calcutta (1945), **118**
CBI theater (1942), **ii**
Findlay, Ohio, **117**
Margaret (Floyd's wife), 136, 142, 145, 152, 172, 173, 193
Margie, 40
Marilyn (Reva's niece)
birthday party, 39
and Bonnie's daughter, 181
gifts for Easter, 139
teasing Reva, 76
visiting Reva's school, 137-8
Mars Task Force, 18-9
Mary Ellen
church participation, 139-40
husband Warren on the Western front, 116, 173